OCCUPATION AND INSURGENCY

Occupation and Insurgency

A Selective Examination of
The Hague and Geneva Conventions
on the Eastern Front, 1939–1945

Colin D. Heaton

Edited by Steve Greer

Algora Publishing
New York

Library of Congress Cataloging-in-Publication Data —

Heaton, Colin D.
    Occupation and insurgency: a selective examination of the Hague and Geneva
Conventions on the Eastern Front, 1939-1945 / Colin D. Heaton; edited by Steve Greer.
        p. cm.
    Includes bibliographical references and index.
    ISBN 978-0-87586-609-3 (trade paper: alk. paper) — ISBN 978-0-87586-610-9
(hard cover: alk. paper) — ISBN 978-0-87586-611-6 (ebook: alk. paper) 1. World War,
1939-1945—Campaigns—Eastern Front. 2. World War, 1939-1945—Atrocities—Germany.
3. Soviet Union—History—German occupation, 1939-1944. 4. Counterinsurgency—
Germany—History—20th century. 5. Germany—History, Military—20th century. 6.
Geneva Convention (1929) I. Greer, Steve. II. Title.
    D804.G4H35 2008
    940.53'370947—dc22
                            2008008639

Front Cover: Mother and Children Walk Past Rubble of Home, 1940.
Image: © CORBIS

Back Cover: Author Colin D. Heaton, photo courtesy Anne Lewis Photography.

Printed in the United States

This book is dedicated to Dr. Russell Frank Weigley, Professor Emeritus, Temple University, who passed away on March 3, 2004. His body may be gone, but his kindness, wisdom and intellect will live forever in his works and through those he loved and assisted. As my first mentor I shall miss him very much.

Colin D. Heaton

About the Book

Occupation and Insurgency is a wonderfully researched book about Nazi domestic policy in the Eastern European lands Germany conquered from 1941 to 1944, a topic relatively neglected until now by military historians and Holocaust experts. Heaton's argument shows how counterproductive the Nazi's brutal treatment of the Slavic population was. By giving racial policy in occupied territories higher priority than the fight against Stalin, millions of potential supporters and soldiers were turned into efficient guerilla fighters who disrupted Wehrmacht supply and communications.

Vlasov's Army, a Wehrmacht unit comprising Russian volunteers led by Russian Lt. General Andrei A. Vlasov, demonstrated how willingly and effectively many Russians would fight against Stalin if given the opportunity. Unfortunately for both the Slavs and most German commanders in the East, Berlin did not appreciate the value of this demonstration.

Consequently, German leaders in the Eastern territories were forced to pursue the contradictory policies of subjugating local populations and fighting Stalin's Soviet Army. Germany dedicated enormous amounts of personnel, supplies and planning resources to suppressing these partisans, tangible assets that would have made a significant impact on the battle against Soviet troops. Had Germany treated conquered Slavs as potential allies against the murderous rule of Stalin, Germany might have won the war. In retrospect, the modern world can be thankful that this illogical and counter-productive policy contributed to Hitler's defeat.

Contemporary military strategists and commanders can draw many rich lessons from German tactics in Russia from 1941 to 1944. UN forces face the challenge of garnering support, or at least minimizing hostility, among local populations in occupied territories every day in Afghanistan, the Balkans, Africa and possibly Iraq. Germany's treatment of the Slavic people in Eastern Europe during World War II provides an eloquent example of how soldiers on foreign soil can turn even potentially helpful locals into the bitterest of enemies by treating them as inferior human beings. History often repeats the lesson that people defending their homes and families from foreign aggressors are motivated to fight with a degree of intensity and for lengths of time inconceivable to soldiers far from home carrying out orders with which they may or may not agree. Underestimating the importance of local public opinion in occupied territories is a costly mistake in terms of time, energy, supplies and human lives.

Bryan Mark Rigg
Author, *Hitler's Jewish Soldiers: The Untold Story of Nazi Racial Laws and Men of Jewish Descent in the German Military*, and *Rescued from the Reich*.

The war as we knew it, or as I knew it was one of victory and defeat, conflict and terror. Commanders in the field were always victims of higher authority, unable to comprehend the realities faced by the troops on the scene, hence the occasional failure experienced by all armies.

This book is astonishing in giving an objective opinion regarding German operations in the Soviet Union, with no visible prejudice or agenda attached.

Despite the legacy of our operations in total, I have never doubted the basic integrity of my soldiers of the Waffen SS. Yes, it is true that propaganda played a major role in our actions and opinions. However, it would be inaccurate to assume that most of us did not apply a moral and ethical program to fighting our enemies. Tragedies happened, of that there is no doubt. Heaton clearly outlines these abominations, attributed to both Germans and Soviets, using international law as the measuring stick.

I hope that important lessons are learned from this work so that warfare, despite its brutal nature, is never again an abomination.

Otto Kumm, SS Brigadier General
Recipient Knight's Cross with Oak Leaves and Swords

The Nazi Ambassador Walter Hewel told a tale about Joachim von Ribbentrop that Adolf Hitler loved to hear time and time again. As a gift for von Ribbentrop's fiftieth birthday in 1943, the senior officials at the Foreign Ministry decided to present their chief with an impressive mahogany dispatch box inlaid with semi-precious stones. The box was supposed to contain parchment copies of all treaties and international agreements negotiated under Ribbentrop since he had taken office in 1938.

After this setup, Hewel delivered the punch line, "The trouble was that we had a devil of a time rustling up any treaties that hadn't been violated or denounced by Germany." The anecdote never failed to make Hitler double up with laughter.

The significance of this exchange is not lost upon Colin Heaton. In *Occupation and Insurgency* he shows that the German strategic objectives were not going to be held hostage to the alleged counterproductive precepts of international law. Hitler routinely flaunted the fact that he would sign anything in good faith one day, and unhesitatingly break it soon after in the name, and on behalf of, the future of the German people. Treaties and laws were mere scraps of paper that were observed as long as they legitimized Hitler's interests. Accordingly, The Hague and Geneva Conventions then in effect were carefully scrutinized by the Germans and selectively utilized when in harmony with Nazi ends and means.

The German legal advisors, as demonstrated in the following pages, were master manipulators of the law. They were adept at interpreting treaty provisions and laws which facilitated German purposes. Loopholes and caveats were their specialties. For instance, the Germans were quick to point out that Stalin never ratified either The Hague or Geneva Conventions, thus making German adherence to the same unnecessary in matters concerning the Soviet Union.

Good lawyers have the ability to craft definitions, create distinctions, find escape clauses, selectively enforce provisions, keyhole, pigeonhole and cleverly dilute existing law to the benefit of their client. They try their case before a judge and duly sworn jury, and await the verdict and react to the outcome accordingly. If they win they celebrate; if they lose, sometimes they appeal.

As described in *Occupation and Insurgency*, the good lawyers of the High Command practiced all of the above, but in a more deadly fashion. The pens became swords; the courtrooms became battlefields, streets and villages. The soldiers assumed the roles of judges and juries, as well as ultimately, executioners. There were no appeals. The Germans conveniently created a legal fiction which distorted accepted judicial principles and pretended to justify heinous acts of barbarism in the name of the law.

Colin Heaton has succeeded in analyzing this perversion of international law. He convincingly and succinctly demonstrates the initial shrewdness exercised by the German High Command in legal matters surrounding the occupation of the Eastern territories. He also points out and correctly concludes that this legal manipulation and ingenuity served no legitimate purpose other than to undermine the German war effort. It emboldened the civilian populations of the occupied regions to resist, and it was this stiff resistance which successfully diverted German resources and manpower from other major fronts and duties.

In the German quest to subdue and manipulate the rules which provided the foundation for the international legal system, the High Command became blind to the victims of their so-called legally justifiable actions. The German mastery of this illegitimate rationalization and subsequent implementation, as Prof. Heaton documents, cost them the war.

Given the current international "war on terror", the involvement of United States forces on many fronts, their problems with indigenous personnel, and the ever changing political climate which governs these actions, this book may provide a guideline for both sides: those choosing to remove terror, and those wishing to implement it. In the end, it will be the rule of law which decides who was moral and ethical.

Albert H. Wunsch III, Esq.

TABLE OF CONTENTS

ABSTRACT

The purpose of this book, which was researched in part at the University of Strathclyde in Glasgow, Scotland, is to evaluate the military and political failure of the German government under Adolf Hitler and its attempts to introduce an effective and competent counterinsurgency doctrine following the invasion of the Soviet Union on 22 June 1941. In addition, the legality of German military and political actions are examined according to the existing international accords that were in effect during the war: primarily The Hague Convention of 1907 and Geneva Convention of 1929, with Geneva revised in 1949.

Based on the relevant sources and interviews with surviving participants, it seems clear that the German violations of international law, as well as their convoluted and ever-conflicting policies regarding the handling of noncombatants, proved to be their greatest detriment. Analyzing the historiography, it becomes clear that German military necessity was subordinated to the overall political agendas of forced labor and exploitation. These policies were often at direct odds with each other, as well as with other policies the military considered necessary to win the war. Had logic dictated the actions of German forces, millions of disaffected Soviet citizens would have rallied to their liberators' cause, and Germany could have had victory in the Soviet Union.

The contrasts between legitimate military operations and illegal acts committed by troops in the field provide the background for Germany's loss of perceived legitimacy amongst the conquered peoples; for the resulting hindrances faced by the military in general; and for the difficulty in formulating a universal and workable counterinsurgency doctrine suited to both military and political needs in the long term.

By openly violating international law in the USSR, Germany and its leadership created a hopeless situation founded on a set of impossibly conflicting agendas. In effect, this book argues that the war against the Soviets was technically lost on the human level as soon as it began.

Examining the actions of the German military, paramilitary, and political bodies, as well as their interpretation and execution of orders — including their complete abrogation of moral, ethical, and legal responsibilities — during the war in the USSR, Germany's failure to achieve overall success against resistance factions and the general populace disaffected with Stalinism becomes clear.

The failure of the Germans to fully appreciate and implement the requirements for winning the "hearts and minds" of the population goes to the root of the problem. Their failure to make the most of people's natural desire to be free from oppression and exploitation was their doom.

Acknowledgements

The following persons contributed to the success of this book, either through firsthand experience and interviews, or through academic and research guidance, editorial assistance or friendship and support over the decades: Prof. Conan Fischer, Dr. Richard Finlay, Dr. Bryan Mark Rigg, Albert Wunsch III, Esq., Leonidas Damianov Ivanovich Maximciuc, Otto Kumm, Hans-Dietrich Hossfelder, Adolf Galland, Dietrich A. Hrabak, Gunther Rall, Hans Baur, Karl Wolff, Gregor Koronov, Leon Degrelle, Mario Antonucci, Hans Hauser, Dr. Russell F. Weigley, Johannes Steinhoff, Michael and Ursula Steinhoff Bird, Jon Guttman, Milo Stavic, Jo Aspinwall, Allison Armour. Special thanks to Anne Marie Lewis, my partner in many ways who proofread and edited the manuscript for publication. Thanks to Steve Greer for a fine proofread and recommendations.

Special thanks to Cy Stapleton of The House of Gutenberg for providing photographs from his personal collection. Also, great appreciation to Dr. Benjamin Shepherd for allowing me to read through his dissertation prior to its publication.

INTRODUCTION

This book focuses upon German racial policy as instituted with the establishment of the Nuremberg Laws of 1935 and for the duration of the Third Reich under Adolf Hitler until 1945. It shows how this policy and collective mindset amongst the German officer corps and the supreme leadership hindered the development of an effective, timely, and unilateral counterinsurgency policy for the German armed forces in the Soviet Union, as well as their violations of applicable international laws which governed the conduct of the war in the east.

The reader will become quite familiar with the terms "counterinsurgency" and "insurgent." Counterinsurgency is, simply put, the efforts by conventional military or paramilitary forces to counter the activities of "irregulars" (civilians operating in a paramilitary or terrorist role), whether they be "partisans," "terrorists" or "guerrillas" (*see* Colin D. Heaton, *German Anti-Partisan Warfare in Europe, 1939-1945* for these legal distinctions) and to establish an environment of perceived stability according to existing civil or military law.[1]

The ruthless nature of the National Socialist racial policies and propaganda contributed heavily to the military's perception of the conquered Soviet peoples; their ingrained belief in the *Rassenfeind* (racial enemy) and German superiority were both factors which contributed to a false sense of security, thereby providing the military with a flawed self-perception and sense of invincibility.

The failure of the German military to address the core issues sparking insurgency actions against their forces, during both the initial invasion and the occupation that followed, were primarily due to the ever-conflicting policies of segregation, forced labor, extermination, and the socially-accepted *Untermenschen* mentality which permeated the ranks of the *Wehrmacht* from top to bottom.

Whilst discussing certain portions of the German military and paramilitary actions and their contributions to the Holocaust in areas of immediate concern to this book (only in relation to counterinsurgency), this book does not focus upon the Holocaust in particular, but rather will provide new insights into the failure of the NSDAP [2] and *Wehrmacht* on a macro-scale to comprehend the problem of civilian unrest due to German policies, and adequately alter its overall operational methodology regarding the handling of the populations in resistance.

These failures in providing overt legitimacy for their actions and stabilizing the regions provided the necessary impetus for the continued and escalating resistance, forcing the Germans to re-evaluate their methods on a micro-scale in the field. This approach apparently met with some success, as opposed to the overall Armed Forces High Command macro-scale approach to reducing the threats through alternative yet conflicting actions.

This book utilizes specific primary and secondary sources in the research, as well as examining German conduct towards these military and civilian populations under the existing international laws of the respective Hague and Geneva Conventions, which were both applicable. Most of the historians quoted in this book are cited for the relevance of their specific areas of research.

One major historian cited is Alexander Dallin, whose works on the German occupation of the USSR (in particular the Ukraine) constitute one of the most authoritative collections within the literature. However, while Dallin discusses specific examples during the occupation, such as *Odessa, 1941–1944: A Case Study of Soviet Territory under Foreign Rule*, he does not delve deeply into the legal aspects of German actions and thus is not cited as thoroughly as many others.[3] Another author briefly noted is Daniel Jonah Goldhagen. Judging from small excerpts of his research, Goldhagen again does not approach the international legal aspect, which is the primary focus of this research. Goldhagen is more focused upon moral and social aspects of German anti-Semitic policy as opposed to the salient military and legal considerations.

This book also incorporates oral testimony from various subjects who were interviewed over the last twenty years, and who were themselves active during the war in the counterinsurgency as well as conventional military roles, thus providing individual perspectives from both Allied and Axis participants. This book also frequently cites the thesis of Dr. Benjamin Shepherd, which traverses similar terrain regarding German actions against insurgents.[4] Where this work differs is in its extensive focus upon the existing international laws and its comparative analysis of German abrogation of those laws, as well as in the use of oral testimony as a supportive element to supplement the published sources.

The use of interviews in writing and researching history has proven itself important in the fact that the testimony of participants, when supported by primary source evidence, and the mutually corroborating testimony from other sources, often provides previously unknown details. This method assists in either corroborating or challenging previously-held beliefs, which may have a great impact upon historical understanding. It is important to remember that the interview itself is only as viable as the source, since memories fade and the interviewed subjects will often not provide self-incriminating evidence regarding their actions. Thus the very select nature of the interviews included within this book.

Examples of modern historians using interviews as oral history quite successfully are Stephen Ambrose,[5] Bryan Mark Rigg,[6] James Bradley and Ron Powers,[7] Dennis Showalter and Peter Pechel,[8] just to name a few. These historians have elevated the interview with living participants to a viable and critical level, thus creating a visual framework through which historians may envision these particular times through the eyes and testimonies of others.

Many of the interviews conducted were supported by the post-war interrogations of many of the subjects by the Allies, and detailed comparisons were made between those existing service records as well as the official German reports. Copies of the interviews used in this book in their entirety are located at the University of Strathclyde Department of History, Glasgow, Scotland and The Center for the Study of Force and Diplomacy, Department of History, Temple University in Philadelphia, Pennsylvania. Those interviews which have been previously published in an abridged form are so cited.

CHAPTER 1. GENESIS OF FAILURE

> I swear by Almighty God this sacred oath: I will render unconditional obe-
> dience to Adolf Hitler, the Fuehrer of the German Reich and people, Su-
> preme Commander of the Wehrmacht; as a brave soldier I will at all times
> be ready to sacrifice my life for this oath.[9]

This chapter will examine selected works regarding the racial policies of National Socialist Germany over the last four decades, the impact upon the military in general, and the development of counterinsurgency doctrine in particular, as well as the contrasts between opinions and conclusions within the existing literature.

The importance of the National Socialist influence upon the war and the conduct of the military is evident. Given the political turmoil in the post World War I years, it was considered that joining the NSDAP seemed to many people the only viable option against the threat of Communism (ac-cording to *Waffen SS* Brigadier General Otto Kumm), hence the great success of the *Nazi* propaganda machine in its recruitment and evolution.[10]

The post-war historical literature through the 1980s has been divided into the respective "functionalist" and "intentionalist" camps. Intentionalist and functionalist historians debated whether the actions of National Social-ist Germany were indeed a cause and effect of Adolf Hitler's direct influence and planning upon Germany and the NSDAP, or whether his presence was secondary to the ultimate course taken by Germany prior to and during the war.[11] Hitler's own words present the clearest picture of his focus and intent:

"Germany will either be a world power or there will be no Germany."[12] His personal beliefs were also expressed regarding the Russians: "By instinct, the Russian does not incline towards a higher state of society."[13]

The functionalists supported the argument that the events in question, both socially and politically, could have possibly evolved without the influence or direct participation of Adolf Hitler due to the dysfunction and dynamics of a Germany already in anarchic motion, and the rising Nazi regime and its eventual unchecked bureaucratic maze. Jonathan Steinberg states that "racialism so extreme ultimately makes civil administration impossible," which supports this book's consensus that Hitler presided over a disjointed bureaucracy.[14] Ian Kershaw states that: "Hitler's way of operating was scarcely conducive to ordered government."[15]

In addition, there was also the functionalist argument that Hitler's presence, even after the events of World War II were placed into motion, was not a necessary component in either starting or continuing the war, or even the resulting genocide policy, due to the various state and military organs created to oversee such events. This line of thought is challenged by Conan Fischer and supported by this author:

> Foremost among the variables was the figure of Hitler himself, without whom the development of Nazism as it existed would have been inconceivable. His ability to contribute to ideology, policy, and propaganda, and to function as the organizational linchpin of a turbulent movement, his ability to book charisma in the strict sense of the word, made him indispensable.[16]

The intentionalist argument stated not only that Hitler was indeed the primary character and catalyst in the rise of National Socialism, but that he was also the primary force behind the political and military machines. He was an autocrat with absolute authority who, if not in complete control of every facet of his massive bureaucracy, was at the very least the driving force in most (if not all) areas of German military, political, economic, and social life.[17] The following statement tends to support this argument regarding Hitler's forceful structuring and complete control of every facet of German life, either direct or indirect. This is especially true of the impact of Nazism upon the young: "Emigration was impossible. The Third Reich became their world. By the start of World War II they [young soldiers] were old enough to kill and be killed, yet still too young for their opinions to be consulted. War formed their memories and shaped their lives."[18]

This book takes the position that Hitler was in fact in complete control of German propaganda, education, military and political might, and was responsible for the subsequent disastrous course, despite his often conspicuous absence from specific matters of state and military concerns.[19] This includes his inconsistent "hands on, hands off" approach to directing events and overseeing the prosecution of his personal agenda by his willing subordinates. Hitler used those around him to fulfill his wishes, and mastered the use of propaganda, thereby ensuring that they catered to the same long-range concepts he himself embodied. As stated by Otto Kumm:

> We SS men didn't become soldiers simply for career reasons, but out of necessity. Germany was surrounded by enemies, and the Reich had to be protected from outside forces if it was to be built up from the inside....I have to say I liked being a soldier, no doubt about that, but I didn't see it as a career, more as a mission.[20]

This conviction and attitude is directly applicable to the development of German counterinsurgency doctrine. Its genesis, evolution, and ultimate failure were the result of many variables. While evaluating the various ingredients that eventually created a policy born from the roots of genocide, a picture of a severely corrupt and dysfunctional upper command echelon, completely out of touch with their subordinate field units emerges. As stated by Benjamin Shepherd: "That the forces which drove the German anti-partisan effort were so complex was due in no small measure to the chaotic institutional set-up of the Third Reich itself."[21]

In fact, the polemic contributing to the failure of German counterinsurgency may be laid at the feet of Hitler himself, his racial policies and edicts, thus formulating a mindset which proved counterproductive to his soldiers and blurred all logical and rational thought.

As stated in *Mein Kampf*, the non-German races were the greatest threat, which could either be interpreted as separate (but equal) to Bolshevism due to the perceived danger they presented, or each could be considered completely separate but supportive of the other. Either way, Judaism and Communism become equal partners to be destroyed, in Hitler's opinion.[22] These paradigms were the driving force in Hitler's foreign (as well as domestic policy), laying the groundwork for world war and mass murder.

The publication of *Mein Kampf* was the genesis of Hitler's "Jewish–Bolshevik" conspiracy program, a policy that would propel Germany and the world through six years of senseless slaughter. As stated by Hitler himself: "Bolshevism is Christianity's illegitimate child. Both are inventions of the Jew."[23] As stated by William Carr: "Hitler's foreign policy is only properly intelligible as an expression of his racist philosophy."[24]

During the post war period in question there was also a middle ground of "moderates" who probed both arguments and provided their opinions on the relevance of Hitler and the National Socialist German Workers Party on the chain of events. Historians such as Christopher Browning, Saul Friedlaender, Ulrich Herbert, Peter Longerich, and Mark Roseman, who supported the concept that Hitler may not have always known "what he wanted and [was] often not in full control, but who had concluded that in the end it was his finger on the button."[25] Hans Bucheim argued that "the *Fuehrer* combines in his own person the entire supreme authority of the Reich; all public authority both in the State and in the Movement stems from that of the *Fuehrer*."[26] Eberhard Jaeckel differed slightly and took the direct intentionalist viewpoint:

> For the sake of power, not principle, because he had none, Hitler employed terror; for the sake of power, he created the war machinery; this in turn led to war, lest his power might be reduced, and he continued the war "since peace would have been fatal to his retention of authority."[27] "There was and there is no National Socialism without Hitler. The two are identical... Everything else is simply a misunderstanding"[28]...Hitler was the dominant, decisive and ultimately determinant figure of National Socialism. This opinion can already be found in Bullock's explicit rejection of the view that described Hitler "as the pawn of sinister interests who held real power in Germany."[29]

Shepherd also supports this argument:

> These goals which, though radical and extreme in a general sense, were vague in detail and left much leeway in how they might be achieved. This "charismatic leadership" system, if system is the right word, meant that different elites were given free rein to build up massive and inevitably overlapping power bases, and this led in turn to fragmented decision-making in policy area after policy area.[30]

Richard Rhodes states that Hitler's ideals were basically transferred to his subordinates, many of whom harbored their own ruthless concepts, such as Heinrich Himmler, who willingly followed his leader and master: "For him I could do anything. Believe me, if Hitler were to say I should shoot my mother, I would do it and be proud of his confidence."[31]

Both perceptions; intentionalist and functionalist, while critical in the long-running historical debate (*Historikerstreit*) have been proven to be a futile endeavor, since both methods of analyzing Hitler's Germany are applicable in many areas.

With regard to analysis of the arguments within the literature, this book concludes that Hitler's mishandling of the counterinsurgency war and the slow, *ad-hoc* evolution that was the Holocaust is evidence supporting the functionalist paradigm from the military standpoint. His control over the political machinery promoting genocide and the war in general supports the intentionalist position, hence neither argument may overpower the other on this topic.

It is the contention of this book that the influence of Adolf Hitler and his personal involvement with the military conduct of the war was not the primary component. It was the driving force behind the Holocaust. His political will, despite his sporadic abstinence from personal involvement or interdiction between the various feuding departments (the current term "turf wars" seems appropriate) allowed for an integrated and cogent operational micro-scale counterinsurgency doctrine based upon "racial" concepts to evolve later in the war.

Methodology and political considerations were the primary instruments prohibiting tacticians and strategists from creating an early wartime counterinsurgency plan. Their inaction and flawed attempts continued to inhibit the progress of those leaders in the field, whether operationally or administratively, who were actively engaged in the development of counterinsurgency policy as the situations arose. In this sense damage control was the order of the day.

The handling of these situations often depended upon the immediate needs of the military or administrative power in charge at any particular time and place, regardless of any standing directives or obvious military necessity. These perceived needs often conflicted with other policies, such as appropriation of agriculture or slave labor. These actions often took place absent of any communication with adjacent commanders, higher authority, let alone approval from above.[32] The leaders in the field were forced to make decisions immediately without the luxury of direct contact with higher authority, thus forcing them into action. There "was no time to await orders and detailed formal directives of upper echelons ...[T]hings had to be largely improvised."[33]

This latitude and freedom of action should have been a blessing to commanders. However, operating under general guidelines without specific instructions, or with orders that kept changing assisted in the confusion. One example is the order issued by Army General Gerd von Schenckendorff in 1942: "The divisional commanders are absolute masters in their jurisdictions; in other words, they are to work independently. They are responsible, however, for carrying out my orders."[34] Additionally, as stated by Jonathan Steinberg, the confusion over who was a full, half, or partial Jew, Slav, part Aryan, etc., for whom the Nuremberg Laws did not apply, only increased the burdens placed upon the killers.[35]

For a dictator such as Hitler, who knew the exact figures for war production and troop movements to the finest detail, as well as the timetables for trains and the exact figures of agricultural expropriation, it is inconceivable that he was not the direct power behind the killing machine,[36] just as he was crucial in military policy.[37]

Likewise, Hitler's ability to delegate authority, and then remove himself personally from events (which eventually transpired in many areas within the government), provided a continuous pattern of confusion and inconsistency within the military and police. This confusion would plague the developers of unconventional warfare programs, explain the ad-hoc progression of the Holocaust, thus seriously hindering efforts to establish a rational and workable universal doctrine until the war had effectively been lost.

German racial laws are critical in the analysis, since they were the benchmark by which the initial pattern for exclusion and genocide of selected persons were established. It was these laws from which the original counterinsurgency doctrine was applied. Laws were even passed preventing German soldiers from having sex with those listed as social "undesirables".[38]

As the war in the USSR was launched and progressed, the resistance (or even the perception of resistance) was an excuse to kill. Prior to the war the Jews were chosen as the scapegoats, forced into second-class citizen status, and finally removed from all regions of German professional life. This was easily accomplished since Jews (and Gypsies (*Roma*)) were considered a *racial* rather than a *religious* enemy.[39] Since they were relatively easy to identify within society, in theory their removal would become less of a problem than eliminating a strictly "religious" enemy, such as Catholics and Jehovah's Witnesses, who were also targeted.[40]

Since Jews were considered a "race" as opposed to a "religion," there could be no conversion in order to become acceptable. According to William Manchester: "Every ethnic, racial and national group had its place in the Nazi scheme of things."[41] "None were safe; women, children, Jews, other religious, racial and political stereotypes, homosexuals, and the handicapped were at grave risk under Germany's new laws."[42] Steven Beller addressed the issue within the debate regarding the Jews in particular:

> Both "intentionalists" and "functionalists" are driven by the question of how many human beings, or more importantly how a whole society of human beings, could do such a thing. If there is a divide between the two approaches it seems to be one between an intentionalist stress on the existence of evil in the world, specifically Hitler's evil and that of his cronies, and a functionalist reliance on the evil consequences of modernity and fate.[43]

Germany was to be cleansed of undesirables and "purged of contaminants." Even the kidnapping of suitable children from their parents to provide future Aryan stock was not beyond the mind of men such as Heinrich Himmler.[44] As stated by Josef Goebbels at the Nazi rally in Nuremberg in 1938:

> Our starting point is not the individual, and we do not subscribe to the view that one should feed the hungry, give drink to the thirsty or clothe the naked, those are not our objectives. Our objectives are entirely different. They can be put most crisply in the sentence: we must have a healthy society in order to prevail in the world.[45]

The theory supporting the regime's approach to eventual genocide was "select one enemy that everyone can recognize: he is the guilty one.... And this enemy is the Jew."[46] Hitler himself made his will quite clear regarding the fate of those he deemed "undesirable": "Above all, I charge the leadership of the nation, as well as its followers, to a rigorous adherence to our racial laws and to a merciless resistance against the poisoner of all peoples; international Jewry."[47]

Jews were blamed for everything, from the post First World War capitulation and following economic collapse, the threat from Communism, venereal disease and prostitution, and the eventual resistance to German occupation. His propaganda laid the psychological groundwork for a mass acceptance of future events.[48] They were referred to as "spongers," "parasites," "poisonous mushrooms," "rats," "leeches," "bacilli," and so forth.[49] Julius Streicher published much of this rhetoric in his propaganda newspaper, *Die Stuermer*.[50] These events could have never transpired without the consent and

outright support of Adolf Hitler, as evidenced by Hitler's genocide speech to
Wehrmacht officers on 26 May 1944, as cited by Mommsen:

> By removing the Jews, I eliminated the possibility of any kind of revolution-
> ary nucleus or germ cell being formed. Of course, you could say to me; "Yes,
> could you not have solved the problem in a simpler way, or not simpler, for
> everything else would have been more complicated, but in a more human
> way."[51]

This perspective would carry over into the partisan/guerrilla war, where
race became the primary factor in how German commanders viewed irregulars. The insurgents themselves were de-legitimized and branded as "criminals" and "bandits" by Himmler, according to his "criminal doctrine" established on 14 December 1937. This action removed any pretext of protection
under international law, legitimizing even the most ruthless actions by the
military and police against them.[52] As the evidence shows, Himmler's plan of
reducing the insurgents' legitimacy (based upon Hitler's Jewish-Bolshevik
conspiracy theory)[53] for acceptable military consumption almost worked to
perfection, as stated by Hans Mommsen:

> When the subjugation and ill treatment of human beings drives them to the
> edge of existence, reducing them to naked and hopeless desperation, then
> the last quasi moral mechanisms governing human relations collapse in ru-
> ins. To the liquidators, but also to those who merely happened to come into
> contact with the business of murder, the victims had ceased to be human
> beings; they were classed lower than the most common criminals, whose
> individual identity was still recognized.[54]

The concept that Jews were in fact behind the partisan effort resonated
through the rank and file as an absolute truth. This situation is clearly seen
in the high level anti-partisan meeting held by General Gerd von Schenckendorff with Army, *SS*, *SD* and *Einsatzgruppen* leaders and officers from 24–26
September 1941. His statement, "where there is a Jew there's a partisan, and
where there's a partisan there's a Jew," was the primary message.[55]

The Final Solution was not created as a matter of "destruction for destruction's sake" or the implementation of an irrational utopian concept, but
rather a "means to a racially conceived end."[56] The counterinsurgency war
would simply become the militarily acceptable extension of this policy, aid-
ed by the world's most potent conventional military machine evolving from
small unit actions against selected individuals to large organized offensives.
This policy eventually culminated in the industrialized wholesale mass murder of millions, and all of these components had their specific roles.[57]

The end result of the Nuremberg Laws of 1935 was that, of the estimated ten percent of the doctors and dentists who were Jews, sixteen percent of lawyers, seventeen percent being bankers, and an even higher percentage of professors, all of whom had been the economic and intellectual backbone of German society were thrust out into a hostile environment.[58] As the net around the Jews and other undesirables later increased in size as German territory expanded through conquest, so did the rules against the *Untermenschen* (sub-humans) tighten, until finally becoming a strangle hold far beyond Germany's pre-war borders.

The established prejudice towards Jews and others would become the primary components in both the German effort to reduce resistance and their failure to develop proper counterinsurgency doctrine. These people were targeted and labeled "sub-human," and were not taken seriously by the upper echelons in Berlin until 1942. In addition, the conflicting rhetoric emanating from Berlin would also sidetrack the doctrine development effort. Officers and soldiers would become confused as the policy constantly changed during the war. Even Hitler's own writings on the subject of the Jews, Soviets, and the West had conflicting opinions, as stated by Richard Breitman:

> Hitler had explained in *Mein Kampf* that a country must fight for its very existence or it was doomed. The fighting capacity of a race depended upon its purity hence the need to rid it of impurities. The repercussions of this ideology carried over into foreign policy: "To wage war with Russia against the West would be criminal, especially as the aim of the Soviets is the triumph of international Judaism"...Hitler would probably be glad if he could now suppress all copies.[59]

German laws were re-written to suit the NSDAP agenda, as stated by Richard Breitman: "The desire to rely on existing laws and procedures also overlooked the Nazi regime's perversion of Germany's legal system; the deportation and killing of German Jews was not in fact illegal in Nazi Germany."[60]

The laws also justified the stealing of personal property and wealth, forcing hard working families to sacrifice homes, businesses and bank accounts, as detailed in Richard Z. Chesnoff's work.[61] The "social Darwinism" approach to the NSDAP racial policy was based upon Adolf Hitler's personal beliefs. His distortion and inclusion were influenced by well-known interpretations of previous "scientific" researchers during 1800-1900s.[62] However, Hitler also seemed unsteady and uneven in the applications of his own concepts. As stated by Mark Roseman:

> And if he [Hitler] did not always take the extremist position, he did not
> consistently play the moderate either: it was Hitler who sabotaged Interior
> Ministry attempts to exclude half and quarter Jews from the Protection
> of German Blood and Honor Act, preventing "interracial" marriages; the
> Reich Citizenship Act (in lieu of the Civil Service Act) of 7 April 1933, and
> the all important Nuremberg Laws of 1935.[63]

The fact that anti-Semitism was perhaps not as widespread as Hitler
would have hoped (counter to Goldhagen's thesis, which states Germans
by end large were all anti-Semitic) was cemented in the intense energies de-
voted to the propaganda campaign, both at home and abroad.[64] The people's
racial attitudes had to be forged in order for them to accept what would
eventually occur, and the military was no exception.[65] One of the most powerful propaganda mediums available to the *Nazis* was film, and the Party's
complete control of it.[66]

The Propaganda Ministry under Dr. Josef Goebbels was not only responsible for censorship and control of the press, but also for the production and
distribution of all films, including feature length films, foreign films, and
documentaries. The documentary became a powerful tool specifically directed towards the young minds of Germany. Films such as *The Eternal Jew*,
The Jew Suess of 1940 and *The Bone Mill* established "historical proof" of the Jews'
"crimes" against the European peoples. This propaganda method established
beyond doubt the *NSDAP* attitudes towards Jews in particular.[67] The barrage of anti-Semitic propaganda also had unexpected negative effects, especially upon foreigners to whom it was presented. His was stated by an officer
later involved in the conversion of former Soviet defectors, Captain Wilfried
Strik-Strikfeldt:

> Nazi propaganda was too crude to have any effect. An example is one of the
> many anti-Semitic Nazi propaganda films, *The Bone Mill*, designed to expose
> the horror of the Stakhanovite system. The film was too incredible to be
> taken seriously by Russians, and was sharply criticized by the prisoners.
> There were inaccuracies due to the ignorance of the German producers, a
> totally false presentation of condition of life in Russia; and the Nazi gospel
> of anti-Semitism left most Russians quite cold.[68]

During the war the *Nachrichten des OKW* (*Oberkommando der Wehrmacht*,
or Armed Forces High Command News) was delivered by trucks, carrying
newsreels and information which was often several weeks old, and "many
units went for weeks without seeing a *Wochenshau* (weekly news show)."[69]
These films were considered necessary for both morale and propaganda
value.

Hitler's reluctance to involve himself in anything not directly related to a situation commanding his immediate attention would be both a godsend and a curse to the men later attempting to create counterinsurgency doctrine. This situation existed until other forces came into play and controlled their actions, such as *Reichsfuehrer* and head of the SS Heinrich Himmler.[70] Hitler was also disinterested in personally supervising those domains for which he had appointed his personal representatives, often with obviously conflicting results. As stated by Ian Kershaw, he was "...uninterested in trivial matters of administration beneath his level of concern."[71]

Christopher Browning states: "He [Hitler] gave no specific orders to the likes of Hermann Goering, Hans Frank,[72] and the eastern *Gauleiter* but simply allowed it to be known what he wanted or approved."[73] Hans Mommsen stated: "Hitler had a habit of postponing or evading decisions on issues of fundamental importance, apart from certain aspects of foreign policy, for example, which he accorded temporary or permanent priority."[74] Hitler's apathy towards direct involvement at almost every level was perhaps the only factor that allowed the counterinsurgency developers to succeed. These facts are evidenced by some of the interviews conducted for this book; participants who experienced these dynamics and the conflicts of interest that occurred during the war.

THE DEBATE IN THE LITERATURE THROUGH THE 1960s AND 1980s

The post-war West German Republic followed the ideals of the Marshall Plan superbly, initiating a free democratic form of government, free market capitalism, and a complete program of *de-Nazification*. As stated by Alan S. Rosenbaum:

> Unfortunately yet understandably, the generation of German historians who dominated the profession during the 1970s and 1980s and who had themselves been adolescents in the Third Reich could not bear to study the Nazi atrocities with the same detachment and same ability to look into the abyss of genocide as their younger colleagues today.[75]

The post-war democratic paradigm became influential in the literature that followed the war. Many German historians worked to produce volumes which alluded to the German Army as being a distinct and separate entity from the *NSDAP*; not connected to the *Nazi* Party and therefore not involved *en-masse* in war crimes. They preferred to attribute such actions to the *SS*,

SD, Gestapo, Einsatzgruppen and other factions within the political and military system. This position is not supported by historians such as Jeremy Noakes and Geoffrey Pridham.[76] This "myth" as stated by Ben Shepherd was perpetuated through the actions of several organizations and individuals:

> This helped perpetuate the myth of a German Army, which had remained separate, decent and aloof from the crimes of the Nazi regime. Historiographically, the myth was personified by the US Army-sponsored "military studies" of the war in the east, to which former German generals contributed; by specialist studies of German occupation written by former military and civilian officials; and by the memoirs of high ranking officers.[77]

This data reflects the method of historical writing until the 1990s, as the "history from above" approach had always been the accepted standard. It would later evolve into a more unilateral examination, culminating in the history "from below" perspective, providing the accounts and experiences of those who were not of the upper echelons of military power, but the recipients and executioners of orders.

Much of this approach came about from the utilization of collated archives and records, as well as *Feldpostbriefe* for individual units at the division level. These reports reflected orders received, orders given and after action reports.[78] This is especially true of the counterinsurgency war, as "matters are not helped by the vagueness of the German Army files at this stage, which make it next to impossible to quantify exactly who was being killed."[79] The victims may not be always be evident, but the key figures involved in war crimes have been unearthed.

However, this area of research becomes problematic, as the division level is the lowest tactical level from which archival information may be retrieved. Regiments, battalions and companies sent their reports to higher authority, usually to the division intelligence section for analysis. Following this the division intelligence officer would review all materials, then forward the information to the division adjutant, and then the unit *Kriegstagebuch* (war diary) entries were made, as demonstrated by Truman O. Anderson.[80] While not always intact or even consistently accurate given that censorship, military security or even the complete withholding of potentially damaging information was possible, they do provide at least another perspective when available.[81]

Omer Bartov used these reports effectively while investigating opera-tions for various German units serving in the USSR.[82] Bartov provided evi-dence that proved NSDAP ideology was not merely mentioned, but infused into the rank and file, complete with the racist component and the justifica-tion for atrocities.[83] It must also be remembered that the German military swore their oath to Hitler, not to Germany, and SS officers were encouraged to renounce their previous Christian faiths, or *gottlaeubig* (a euphemism for atheism), and even if they complied this information was still retained in their personnel records.[84]

Many of the *Einsatzkommando* leaders and officers were highly educated men, graduates of German and other European Universities, with several holding doctorates. This education level had greater percentage than other military branches, thus heightening the horror of their actions.[85] Another determining factor in the placement of these men was their language profi-ciency, located in their personnel service records. It is clear that those men with the necessary eastern language skills were placed in higher command positions.[86]

Most of the indoctrination and propaganda focused upon the Germans blaming their misfortune and discomfort upon their *Rassenfeind* (racial en-emy), the final step towards moral justification.[87] Zygmunt Bauman exam-ined the reasons for the actions of the soldiers, and argued: "Nazism was cruel because Nazis were cruel; and the Nazis were cruel because cruel people tended to become Nazis."[88] As stated in *German Anti-Partisan Warfare in Europe, 1939–1945*:

> The German was also psychologically unprepared for what awaited him. He was subjected to many varieties of friendly propaganda, although all forms continued to purport his racial superiority. One day he may hear that all of the sub-humans must be relocated further east, especially Jews. Later he would hear that they must be eradicated, eliminated from the potential-ly poisoning the pure German blood supply, that they were "deemed to be a biological threat to the German people." He would also be told that not all Russians were Communists, and that the German crusade was established to free the Russians from Bolshevism, while at the same time condemning all Russians for supporting the Bolsheviks, while the Jews supported and assisted the powers in Moscow. Still later, the German soldier would hear other alterations as to the true policy of his country toward the eastern peoples.[89]

German propaganda was unquestionably the foremost factor in forging racial opinion, such as the statement that Russian women were actually

"Jews whose Jewish origin cannot be seen."[90] Bartov cites the opinion of Field Marshal Walther von Reichenau on the subject of race and prejudice:

> Regarding the conduct of the troops toward the Bolshevik system many unclear ideas remain. The essential goal of the campaign against the Jewish-Bolshevik system is the complete destruction of its power instruments and the eradication of the Asiatic influence on the European cultural sphere. Thereby, the troops have two tasks, which go beyond the conventional unilateral soldierly tradition. In the east the soldier is not only a fighter according to the rules of warfare, but also a carrier of an inexorable racial conception and the avenger of all the bestialities which have been committed against Germans and related races. Therefore, the soldier must have complete understanding for the necessity of the harsh, but just atonement of Jewish sub-humanity. This has the further goal of nipping in the bud rebellions in the rear of the Wehrmacht which, as experience shows, are always plotted by Jews.[91]

Bartov also concluded that the young political officers charged with indoctrination had also been young and impressionable during the early years of the Reich, coming from social and economic groups closely identified with supporting National Socialism.[92] This is also stated by Breitman:

> Even the harshest and most severe order had to be carried out without hesitation Himmler required every SS man to fulfill his duty to the utmost and devote himself to the German people and fatherland unto death. The task of the SS was to protect Adolf Hitler's state and to destroy anyone identifiable as an enemy or anyone who sabotaged the war effort.[93]

In many cases these political officers would accompany units on ethnic cleansing operations, sizing up the morale and dedication of the senior NCOs and officers, estimating the political soundness of the troops, and make reports that would usually end up in the headquarters of the SD.[94] Despite the efforts of the political officers and Propaganda Ministry it would later become commonplace for many Germans to question the "*Fuehrer* jargon" regarding the ineffectiveness and "sub-human" quality of their enemies after their experiences in the east.[95] Many officers and commanders found their men non-compliant with the more grisly needs of the program. A prime example of a commander who used the partisan war as a means to the *Nazi* political end was a Captain Brandt of the 350th *Infantry Regiment:*

> That the officers have to do the shooting whilst the men watch is simply unacceptable. The mass of the men are too weak; this is a sign that the true meaning of "partisan warfare" is something they have never learned, or at least have been badly taught.[96]

Mark Mazower and Michael Geyer also provided invaluable information regarding the average German soldiers' mindset.[97] The average German's mistrust of the local populations and the chronic fear of attack, ambush, exhaustion, reduced and ineffective manpower, coverage of massive expanses of inhospitable terrain, and *NSDAP* ideology and racist concepts culminated in the eventual atrocities.[98]

Likewise, Theo Schulte also concluded that the conduct of mid-level officers and units operating in the rear areas reacted to potential threats due to a combination of ideology, pressure from superiors, and punishment for operational ineffectiveness, and the unusual hardships and nature of the war in the USSR.[99] However, Schulte differed in his approach. While identifying the ideological and racist components and actions of the rank and file, he also examined the rare instances where an older, more gentle and traditional application towards handling the populations was evident, which is discussed further in this book.[100]

A prime example is the comment by a Lieutenant Meyer of the *221st Security Division*: "Belorussians regard us as liberators from Bolshevism; the Poles regard us as liberators from Russia and Bolshevism."[101] SS Brigadier General Otto Kumm stated how well the populations generally responded to kindness:

> The amazing part of the effort to convert the masses to our ideology hinged upon how well they were treated. On the one hand, we could reduce a village and think that we had solved the problem in that area, only to realize that the problem had just increased in severity. However, when we assisted in the rebuilding of towns, churches, or even allowed the local civil administration to maintain control over their people without a strong military presence, we yielded greater results. This fact was self-evident to those of us in the field. We could not convince our superiors in Berlin to agree to such a method. This was where we had failed.[102]

The High Command also back-tracked upon its own doctrine of complete destruction during April 1942, when *OKH* (*Oberkommando des Heeres*, or High Command of the Army) issued the directive as recorded in the Intelligence Section (*Ia*) of the *221st Security Division*: "It must be made clear to every German soldier that any civilian whom he mistreats might join the partisans and be facing him with a gun the next day."[103]

This conflicting position between upper level military commands and the political elements operating separately supports the statements by Kershaw and Mommsen. The inconsistencies only assisted in the troops' confusion, such as orders issued during *Operation Dreieck* in July 1942 in the Gomel region by the *221st Security Division*. The orders stated that "ruthless measures ...be carried out vigorously; avoid unnecessary harshness, particularly the unnecessary burning of houses."[104] This example alone leaves much to interpretation.

The degree of ruthlessness demonstrated by each respective unit, its officers and soldiers is not readily appreciable, given the fragmenting of the primary sources. However, the degree of compliance exhibited throughout the units receiving these directives is at best speculative. What is not speculative is the impact. Whether negatively or positively these units had a major impact upon the populations.[105] Supporting Kumm's evaluation on treatment and the dividends is Peter G. Tsouras:

> Russian civilians living in the area where the reconnaissance was made, who had been treated well by the Germans billeted in their villages at an earlier date, were of great assistance. Local guides led the patrol around enemy and partisan strongholds, and provided shelter in farm houses.[106]

Truman O. Anderson's research on German reprisals in the USSR produced an opinion that such actions were determined by varying influences; not always attributing these acts to ideology or racial attitudes, nor even the exposure to the war by the troops.[107] Both Schulte and Anderson agreed that *NSDAP* ideology was the critical component, even if they attributed other factors as having an equal if not greater importance upon events at various times.

The great difference between the German and Western Allied approaches to these same conditions were vast. German commanders had little to fear from their superiors when committing murder in the east, especially when "justified" with an "accurate" after action report. Christopher Browning makes the argument that "the broad support for German racial imperialism in the east was one foundation upon which the future consensus for mass murder would be built."[108] Courts-martial of soldiers for such activities were quite rare unless they were solitary acts without superior authorization.

The history from below approach is marked by the emergence of the following works by Martin Broszat, Detlev Peukert, Ian Kershaw, Lutz Niethammer and Christopher Browning, just to name a few.[109] This method of research became important as a measure of how the "average German" was analyzed during the course of the war, thereby avoiding the chronic elitist approach of focusing only upon the upper echelon ranks and personalities. This approach is critical when assessing counterinsurgency doctrine and effectiveness from the persons who were involved. Their actions in response to either real or perceived threats further perpetuated the carnage. They succeeded in simultaneously blaming their victims for the insurgency and their own responses to irregular activity.

The ruthless nature of the war understandably presented a similar method in handling insurgents and civilians. A prime example is from Richard Overy regarding the attitude and appointment of the former *Reichsgauleiter* for East Prussia, Erich Koch, who was reassigned to the Ukraine. "I am known as a brutal dog...Our job is to suck from the Ukraine all the goods we can get hold of...I am expecting from you the utmost severity towards the native populations."[110]

This program of economic exploitation was the prime force behind the war itself, an endless supply of slave labor and the massive potential of the eastern grain reserves.[111] Non-cooperation, even the failure to surrender "just one cow might spell the destruction of an entire village."[112] The report from the *221st Security Division* in 1943 was not unique: "The agricultural population is not meeting its quotas. This however is hardly surprising in the view of bandit activity."[113] These programs were the primary factors that promoted the massive insurgency movements against German occupation, which were undoubtedly by Hitler's design, as stated by Norman Rich:

> Hitler had set forth a very clear and very specific program for expansion into Eastern Europe at the expense of Russia; but few of Hitler's contemporaries, especially foreigners had bothered to read this ponderous volume carefully, if at all, and fewer still could believe that the extreme views set down by Hitler, the frustrated political adventurer, would continue to be taken seriously by Hitler, the responsible statesman.[114]

Supporting this line of thought is Sigrid Wegner-Korfes, who argued that the Germans failed to understand the Soviet population, their love of the land and their inherent patriotism, if not to Stalin, then to their mother country, thus ensuring the forthcoming resistance.[115]

The beginnings of the *Historikerstreit* began to focus upon the Army leadership and soldiers as being uninvolved with crimes in general. However, this myth was rapidly challenged as time progressed, with historians such as Manfred Messerschmidt,[116] Klaus-Juergen Mueller[117] and Christian Streit[118] (among others) attacking this myth by establishing direct links to *NSDAP* ideology and its direct embodiment within all aspects of the military, including the *Wehrmacht Heer*.[119]

In fact, the Army was involved at least to the point that "*Einsatzgruppe C* did not seem to think that eliminating Jews was its principal task," as Army units were conducting these missions as well.[120] Likewise, *Einsatzkommando 8* of *Einsatzgruppe B*, operating with *Army Group Center* recorded all of its deeds and the supporting Army units, even recording the pretexts used to justify the murders.[121] The involvement and support provided by the Army to the *Einsatzgruppen* is also reflected by French L. MacLean's listing of *Einsatzgruppen* officers approved for Army combat awards by commanding Army generals, hence the integration of both forces to achieve a common goal.[122]

Streit actually focused upon "anti-Bolshevism" as the major catalyst for the illegal activity, a common bond amongst most of the German officers and soldiers since the Communist Revolution of 1918–19. This event brought together many hands into the prosecution of the espoused racist doctrine by men who, in normal life, would possibly have had no other interest in the *NSDAP* or anti-Semitism, as anti-Bolshevism was cause enough.[123] This was particularly true of the counterinsurgency war.

Historians addressed the issue of the role of the senior officer corps in the crimes attributed to the German military, in particular the analysis of the various orders issued, such as the *Kommissarbefehl* (Commissar Order) issued by Hitler via Field Marshal Wilhelm Keitel through his High Command on 17 May 1941. The order was again disseminated throughout the military on 6 June 1941, just prior to *Operation Barbarossa*, which was obviously premeditated and ultimately accepted as legitimate doctrine by the majority of the senior command structure, and thus implemented by the rank and file.[124]

Germany's war against the Soviet Union was a "total war" from the first day of *Barbarossa* on 22 June, 1941.[125] The rigid German military structure and discipline required an expectation of immediate obedience to orders. These soldiers did not exist in a democratic society in either their civilian or military lives.[126] This order later included Jews, prisoners of war, and finally the bulk of the Soviet population in general and was enthusiastically carried out.[127]

There were dissenters who objected to these orders, such as Army General Gerd von Schenckendorff, who forbade the shooting of POWs and destruction of villages in many cases,[128] and Field Marshals Walther von Brauchitsch (although wavering in his morality), Gerd von Rundstedt,[129] Fedor von Bock[130] and Wilhelm *Ritter*[131] von Leeb.[132] In regard to von Schenckendorff's varying orders (which Christian Gerlach believes were issued to ease his conscience),[133] one order in particular is quite interesting:

> Anybody, including women, of whom it is proven that they either belong
> to a bandit group, have actively aided the bandits or carried out reconnais-
> sance for them, is to be dealt with as ordered [shot]. Children fall into this
> category only when they are old enough to understand the implications of
> their actions. Such understanding is beyond children of ten; these are to be
> punished but not shot.[134]

There were other luminaries who also disagreed with the policy (in
varying degrees), and challenged Himmler's authority. Army Generals
Hasso *Graf* [135] von Manteuffel, Franz Halder,[136] Wilhelm *Ritter* von Thoma
and Ludwig Cruewell,[137] SS Major General Wilhelm Bittrich, and even the
notorious SS Lieutenant General Erich von dem Bach-Zelewski.[138] Manteuffel
openly stated that he "would arrest any SS, SD or *Geheimstaatspolizei* (*Gestapo*)
official who attempted to recruit his men for any duties without his express
permission."[139] Manteuffel also refused to allow his junior commanders to
detach their troops for SD or SS use, which created friction with Himmler in
Berlin, as stated by SS Lieutenant General Karl Wolff:

> I do not remember exactly how this information came to be known by the
> Reichsfuehrer, although I can tell you that I had never seen him so upset
> about anything personally. Once Manteuffel's statement had been con-
> firmed, I was ordered to draft a letter to the general, asking him to clarify
> his position on this matter. Within two weeks Manteuffel had responded,
> and his blunt method of dealing with our office only made the problem
> worse. Himmler finally had a meeting with Hitler, and most of us on the
> staff were present except Goering. Himmler wanted to know what should
> be done about Manteuffel and his disregard for the field orders. Hitler sim-
> ply said: "I would not concern myself with Baron Manteuffel. He seems
> to have his house in order." I don't believe that Himmler thought this a
> satisfactory answer, and he never forgave Manteuffel for threatening his
> field commanders.[140]

Wilhelm Bittrich was at direct odds with the comments made by
Himmler regarding the racial cleansing operations to be conducted during
a meeting with *Waffen* SS leaders in Russia in 1941. Bittrich openly opposed
Himmler to at least fifteen other high-ranking NSDAP representatives,
which included colonels and generals of the SS, SD and *Gestapo*. Men such
as Karl Wolff, Heinrich Mueller,[141] Erich Koch, Felix Steiner, Josef "Sepp"
Dietrich, F.W. Krueger, Herbert Gille, Paul Hausser, and Theodor Eicke
heard his comments. Following the speech, Bittrich remarked: "The things
Heinrich says are sheer nonsense! Things will go badly if we don't change
our ways," calling the *Reichsfuehrer* "a fool" without anyone reporting him to
Himmler.[142]

Bittrich's opposition was based upon the pragmatic belief that the populations would be far less receptive to German occupation if not handled properly, although he is not known to have ever disobeyed a direct order. Bach-Zelewski, despite his being the first overall commander of anti-partisan units in Russia, and one of the original leading figures in the *Einsatzgruppen* and counterinsurgency planning later in the war also had reservations. According to Karl Wolff, who knew Bach-Zelewski well:

> He believed that Hitler was Germany's only hope to alter the misfortunes of the past. However, given that, he openly disagreed with Himmler on policy. Along with Bittrich they routinely had their men removed from areas that might be considered suspicious regarding partisan activity, such as peaceful villages.[143]

The correlation between Bolshevism and Judaism was an abstract and erroneous application of logic within the Third Reich. This position was fostered by Hitler and his chief lieutenants and filtered down from the High Command through the ranks, as stated by Helmut Krausnick and Hans-Heinrich Wilhelm.[144] Their works illustrate the connection between radical racist political policy and military operations. Both concepts were driven by the political machine supporting the concept of the *Volksgemeinschaft*, both in formal military and *Einsatzgruppen* operations.[145] Krausnick also explained in greater detail in his work *Hitler's Einsatzgruppen* how some Army officers, while perhaps not at all interested in National Socialist dogma were motivated by their own racial prejudice.[146]

Peter Jahn demonstrated this reality by examining the long-standing racial enmity within German society pre-dating Hitler and the *NSDAP's* actions and perceptions, which simply made the converting of the masses a much simpler task.[147] Jahn also explains how the experiences of First World War officers and men, known as the *Frontkaempfgeneration* (front line generation) as well as *Freikorps* veterans serving on the Eastern Front developed their prejudices after witnessing the "primitive conditions" of the Russian people in comparison to their own nation.[148]

Also of interest is the number of *Einsatzkommando* leaders and senior officers who were veterans of the First World War. In that conflict, fifty-three were decorated for valor, with twelve receiving the Iron Cross in both classes and seven the 2nd Class, with the remainder suffering wounds in action and decorated accordingly.[149] It is also interesting to note that twenty-nine percent of the concentration camp officers were medical doctors, while twenty-five percent were lawyers or legal assistants, with twenty-seven percent of the *Einsatzgruppen* officials being former policemen.[150]

During World War II Hitler and Himmler maintained a keen interest in the careers and activities of the *Einsatzkommando* leadership, thus fostering fierce competition within the killing units and their leadership in order to energize their efforts. Two former *Einsatzkommando* officers earned the Knight's Cross for their efforts; SS-Major General Bruno Streckenbach on 27 August 1944, as commander of the 19th SS *Volunteer Division "Lettisches"* (Latvian) *Nr. 2*, and SS-Lieutenant General Friedrich Suhr on 11 December 1944, while commanding SD troops fighting partisans in France.[151]

Seventy-nine *Waffen SS* men were awarded the Oak Leaves, with one being an *Einsatzgruppen* leader (Streckenbach) on 21 January 1945. This seems interesting when compared to the twenty concentration camp officers who were awarded at least one grade of the Knight's Cross, either before or after their tour of camp duty, including Theodor Eicke (with Oak Leaves), the first commandant of Dachau and commander of the 3rd *Waffen SS Panzer Regiment* (later *Division*) *"Totenkopf."*[152] It is also interesting that one of the rarest and most prized awards was the Anti-Partisan Badge, available in bronze, silver and gold, yet only six active *Einsatzgruppen* officers (no enlisted men) received the award in any grade, despite the thousands of men assigned to the various anti-partisan units. Most of these awards went to Army and *Waffen SS* men.[153]

Martin Broszat also pointed out how these officers' attitudes were supported by their personal wartime experiences from 1914–18.[154] These men relied upon their primary group experiences from the First World War and the post-war upheaval, which was "corrected" in their opinion by the rise of the *NSDAP*.[155] In fact, as stated by Shepherd, most of the early opposition to what had occurred in Poland against Communists and Jews in 1939 disappeared following the victories of 1940 and beyond.[156] As long as the political system worked, the military system could take care of itself, and both followed a strict paradigm regarding their objectives in total.[157]

Judaism and Bolshevism were intertwined as a single threat to be extinguished, and this paradigm extended into the prosecution of counterinsurgency (or "anti-partisan," "guerrilla") doctrine. Soon "Jewish-Bolshevism" became the slogan to justify systematic murder and perceived as justified by the majority of the German military command structure.[158] This reality was further fuelled by the early military perception that the Soviet citizenry in general supported the "Jewish–Bolshevik" structure, as well as the partisan war, and thus perceived as a security threat to be eradicated. This perspective was shared by the vast majority within the military, Army and SS alike.[159] This rhetoric would be adjusted as the war progressed, as analyzed in the following chapters.

This argument regarding security is supported by Richard M. Fattig, who used the history of the Franco-Prussian War as the backdrop for the attitudes displayed towards irregulars during the First World War.[160] Other examples include Christopher Browning and Rolf-Dieter Mueller regarding perceptions from the First World War. Both examined the economic applications of counterinsurgency and pacification, including deportations.[161] Mueller goes even further to discuss the German plans for the use of forced labor, as does Ulrich Herbert, which became a prime motivation for resistance among the locals under occupation.[162]

Michael Geyer argues that the reason the German officer corps went along with the NSDAP program in general was due to its loss of status during the interwar years. By following a politically driven machine that again placed the military at the top of the social hierarchy at the expense of others, they once again achieved the status they had coveted and lost.[163] It would be these same officers faced with the mounting problem of insurgency, who would have to break with traditional methods and adopt policies that worked best, often in violation of standing orders, international law and acceptable policy. This application would also prove to be difficult in the fact that, as stated by Omer Bartov in *Hitler's Army*:

> While the generals had little scruples about issuing orders to shoot men and uproot whole populations, they feared that executing women and children might cause disciplinary problems among the troops, and normally preferred the SS and SD to carry out such unsavory tasks.[164]

Justification for such actions was provided by the recent history of the *Freikorps*, the right-wing radical movement pre-dating the National Socialists. The *Freikorps* was perceived as the primary instrument in thwarting the Bolshevik threat in 1918-19.[165] In addition, the firm belief in the destiny of the Germans to push into the USSR, in a *"deutschen Kulturmission"* as described by Klaus Latzel, was deemed a legitimate reason for executing such policies.[166] Part of the program included the liquidation of "Jewish-Bolshevik political intelligentsia" which would also come to color German thinking regarding active counterinsurgency operations.[167] This was especially important when

Jews were to become the scapegoats for every irregular act committed in the field.[168]

Daniel J. Goldhagen's *Hitler's Willing Executioners* stirred an even greater debate by his assertion that the Holocaust was simply the end result of centuries of underlying (if not open) anti-Semitic feelings within Germany. Part of Goldhagen's thesis is supported by the fact that many German and European Gentiles knew what was occurring and did nothing to intervene; simply turning a blind eye to the events, whether they were actively in participation or not.[169]

Goldhagen could have taken his argument even further by extrapolating the killings under the guise of counterinsurgency doctrine, and analyzed the actual soldiers and commanders who participated in the acts, either during justified military operations or simple round-ups and murders.

In rebuttal to Goldhagen's arguments on that topic, Hans-Ulrich Wehler and Dieter Pohl challenged his assertions, focusing upon the Hitler "dynamic" as the real catalyst for the anti-Semitic hatred and the resulting genocide.[170] This position (in rebuttal to Goldhagen) is supported by Meir Michaelis, who asserts that "anti-Semitism on such a scale was truly unique to Hitler, and not part of a European norm."[171] This author asserts that, if Goldhagen were accurate in his assessment, a similar policy of exclusion and genocide would have occurred prior to Hitler and his brown shirts.

Also in challenging Goldhagen, if the Germans were so completely supportive of this policy *en-masse*, why did Heinrich Himmler issue top secret orders regarding the locations and activities of the death and concentration camps? This veil of secrecy also extended to the *Einsatzgruppen* operations, where German soldiers not assigned to these tasks were kept away from the actions to maintain the secrecy.

However, Goldhagen failed to detail the racially motivated atrocities of other forces, most notably the Hungarian (such as *Operation Csobo* in July 1943), Romanian, and Italian allies fighting alongside German troops, which is addressed by Anderson and recorded in German military records.[172] Christopher Browning also touches upon the Goldhagen theme: "These policies were very much in tune with widely held views and hopes in much of German society concerning the construction of a German empire in Eastern Europe."[173] Yet Browning does not go so far as to attribute blanket anti-Semitism and mass murder as the will of the entire German nation, only attributing those acts and events to certain units and individuals.[174] This opinion is supported by the very secret nature of the killing centers and *Einsatzgruppen* operations on Himmler's direct orders.

The debate raged through the 1980s when works emerged outlining the long-term premeditation of the regular officer corps regarding the economic exploitation and killing of the populations under their occupation. These officers executed orders as much from military necessity as racial prejudice.[175] However, there were opposing views, such as that of Alfred Streim, who decided that the majority of Soviet POWs died as a result of neglect, forced labor, disease and meager rations as opposed to an official policy of eradication.[176]

Ernst Nolte argued that the brutality of *Nazi* Germany was deemed as appropriate in order to counter the perceived greater danger of Josef Stalin's Soviet system.[177] Joachim Hoffman joined Nolte in this perception, as Hoffman used the Partisan War Directive issued by Stalin in July 1941 as a method for the end to justify the means, especially when the fate of Germans in the hands of irregulars was revealed.[178] Another supporter of the justification process was Jorge Friedrich, who also debated that German ruthlessness was necessary as a method of response to the barbarity exhibited by the Soviets, and the persecutions were simply a method of population control to establish German authority and halt anti-German actions.[179]

However, Juergen Foerster came to a different conclusion in his works on the topic.[180] Foerster decided that field officers, often in the position of interpreting orders did so to their own advantage and willingly carried out the most extreme orders, often superseding their own authority in committing atrocities. These men believed that the best method or "preventive maintenance" was the liberal and constant use of terror.[181]

Foerster also argued that there were several factors which promoted the ruthless response of the German military to the perceived threat confronting them. Limited manpower on a broad front, the hardships of the war, weather and terrain, time constraints placed upon senior commanders to attack and conquer objectives, and the rise of more organized and ruthless irregular forces all contributed.[182] Foerster also stated that these factors did not justify the mass murder of millions. They simply helped fortify an already existing belief in the racial inferiority and bestial nature of their enemy.[183] Richard Overy supports this thesis. In *Russia's War* he cites a letter written by a German NCO dated July 1942, justifying the killings:

> Recently a comrade of ours was murdered in the night. He was stabbed in the back. That can only have been a Jew, who stands behind these crimes. The revenge taken for that act brought indeed a nice success. The population itself hates the Jews as never before. It realizes now, that he is guilty of everything.[184]

These factors definitely contributed to the failure of the Germans to see beyond their own prejudice regarding an effective response to the insurgencies they faced. These actions only became intertwined with the overall genocide, albeit perhaps through more direct and militarily acceptable methods.[185]

Examples in the literature regarding individual German perceptions provide insight into the mainstream thought processes on this subject. In *Hitler's Army*, Omer Bartov cites one German in France who remarks that "the French had skidded to a new low...Yes; this society has lost not only its vitality but also its morality."[186] This attitude towards the French provides insight into how the Germans would perceive the Russians, as also stated by Bartov, citing the same German: "They're all no better than a bunch of scoundrels."[187] This attitude was also reflected against the Americans and British, who were considered "mongrel races" and infested with "Jews and Negroes."[188]

On a different note, Hitler also believed that the British government would take no action against his treatment of Jews and Communists, that "they would never unite as a collective body to effectively hinder his ambitions."[189] Even those Germans whose interviews were used in this book, in many cases, provided their own feelings on race in the east, such as *Waffen SS* Sergeant Major (brevet 1st Lieutenant) Hans Hossfelder:

> It was one thing to enter Russia and combat the Red Army, kill partisans and the like. We had been indoctrinated to believe that they were a subhuman culture, slightly above the status of animals, and this was not too hard for many of us to believe...Men had done so much killing, it almost seemed to be just a part of the job. I do not say that it is right now, or even that it was right back then. It was only right according to the times we found ourselves in, given the particulars of the circumstance. It was very sad.[190]

Klaus-Jochen Arnold also provided fuel for the debate in a detailed study of the occupation of Kiev in 1941. He supports the contention that German forces supporting illegal acts did in fact contain Army contingents, and points out that there was little in the way of provocation needed to exact "retribution" against suspected irregulars and their popular support system.[191] These were obviously racially based missions to roundup the

Jews and other undesirables as part of the greater plan under the pretext of military legitimacy.

THE HISTORICAL DEBATE ON ATROCITIES AS OF TODAY

Despite the strict guidelines of the racial policy and its lethal outcome, there were variations and deviations, many of which were sanctioned by Hitler personally. Bryan Mark Rigg's stellar publication, *Hitler's Jewish Soldiers* outlines how Hitler personally authorized special dispensations for individuals in the military of Jewish descent, and he examines the *Mischlinge* policy in great detail.[192] The fact that Hitler offered reprieves and issued the controversial *Deutschbluetigkeitserklaerung* (German Blood Certificates) proved his personal involvement and direction of the Holocaust beyond any doubt. Hitler's indecisiveness on this and other issues would both assist and hinder those men creating the doctrine necessary for combating the irregulars in the east. The gray area regarding "Jewishness" would also become an issue later during the recruiting efforts.

Hans Mommsen supports this author's theory (at least with regard to the counter-insurgency mindset) that *Nazi* Germany was "a well oiled machine which simply gained momentum as it moved along...The inner contradictions of the system-a magnified reflection of the contradictions in the National Socialist program necessarily led to its internal and external disintegration, while preventing early destruction from within."[193]

Tens of thousands of Germans who qualified as *Mischlinge* served in the German military, including several luminaries of high rank, such as *Kriegsmarine* Admiral Bernhard Rogge.[194] Perhaps the most famous of these was *Luftwaffe* Field Marshal Erhard Milch.[195] Milch served in the capacity of Air Minister before the war was an early financial supporter of the *Nazi* Party, thus Hitler's favor was assured. This flexible application of the Nuremberg Laws to suit a preordained agenda demonstrates the often confusing and ever-changing nature of racial policy and perceptions. The ultimate reality of this ever-shifting and hypocritical process would culminate in the lowering of the racial standards as the war progressed.

In the 1990s the emergence of the *Wehrmachtausstellung*, a traveling museum created in 1995 containing photographs, letters, and documents detailing the role of the Army on his subject has sparked severe controversy over the actual actions of "ordinary soldiers" during the war.[196] One of the most vivid contributions was Hannes Heer's research into German Army counterinsurgency operations in Belorussia during 1941-43.[197] This article used extensive records from the Soviet tribunals of Germans in captivity, and the conclusion was that German military counterinsurgency actively overrode tactical necessity in order to promulgate an extermination mentality.[198] The *Wehrmachtausstellung* had brought to the forefront what many people did not want to accept; average soldiers committing crimes by any definition, regardless of the justification at the time and circumstance, thus stripping away the veneer of Army exculpation.

The *Wehrmacht* was locked into the greatest struggle in history; it was a war of race as much as politics and economics, which is arguably the basis for all warfare. As stated by Richard Overy: "The bloodiest chapter in the history of German conquest was the subject of race."[199] This is evidenced by the work of Mark Roseman, who stipulates that the Wannsee Protocol of 20 January 1942 simply addressed already long-standing concerns, decisions eventually drawing all of Germany's armed forces into the program.[200]

While not providing an entire picture of every soldier and unit, the *Wehrmacht-ausstellung* exhibition does provide an insight into the collective experience and culpability of the military in general, and the Army in particular. One example of a regular soldier "borrowed" for an anti-partisan sweep by an SS unit with his superior's blessing is chronicled in Guy Sajer's *Forgotten Soldier.*[201]

Part of the problem regarding some of the missing supporting information was the fact that thousands of pages of documentation regarding counterinsurgency operations, and even outright war crimes, were destroyed under the admitted direction of SS Lieutenant General Karl Wolff. This was especially true if they contained *Sonderkommando* and *Einsatzgruppen* missions, many of which must have been supported by Army troops.[202] However, despite Wolff's efforts thousands of documents survived and are now archived.

Historians have been addressing these issues over the last two decades. The active participation of all segments of the German military in the commission of atrocities, or even the justified execution of those irregulars deemed as legitimate under the Geneva and Hague Conventions is no longer debatable, as revealed by Christopher Browning,[203] Christian Gerlach,[204] and

Rolf-Dieter Mueller.[205] Gerlach examined wide-ranging extermination and economic exploitation policies, where the regular armed forces were active in both security support and actual misconduct, providing a study from top to bottom within the ranks of specific units.[206]

The debate has shown that, regardless from where the research originated, either from the top or bottom the end result is clear. *Nazi* Germany's program of racial discrimination in peacetime evolved into a program of mass murder throughout Europe during wartime. The insurgency war became only a small segment of this fact, yet it became perhaps the most capably defended program with regard to the extermination of those who were deemed a threat, real or imaginary according to the individual commanders tried and exonerated after the war.

Finally, the debate between the two fields of thought simply proved that, despite the position taken on any topic regarding the Third Reich, both intentionalist and functionalist arguments had their merits. What the current literature has embarked upon is less an explanation as to *why* and *how* Hitler, Germany, and the NSDAP committed their crimes, but rather how many average Germans (including soldiers) were willing participants in these acts. This book focuses upon certain acts, which may or may not be defined as war crimes. This study includes the "racial war" as it was fought within the context of how these actions, policies, and conflicts either assisted or impeded the adoption of counterinsurgency doctrine, and whether specific actions constituted violations of the laws of war.

The next chapter discusses the international laws in effect during the war; the actual burdens, responsibilities and roles of the military and insurgents, as well as the various specifications with examples of both legitimate and perceived violations. The laws are explained while detailing how loosely both the Geneva and The Hague Conventions were interpreted in order to suit the various German and even Soviet agendas.

CHAPTER 2. *WEHRMACHT* ACTIONS AND THE LAWS OF LAND WARFARE

> We teach the SS man that many things may be forgiven upon this earth, but one thing never — disloyalty.[207]

This chapter evaluates, explains, and defines the illegal and legal actions of the *Wehrmacht*, inclusive of all branches of the German Armed Forces during the war in the USSR in their handling of insurgents and civilians. While the policies of *Nazi* Germany towards the conquered peoples are important in total, those facts not relevant to this book, such as the laws of war at sea and in the air which are not included.

Regardless of how well the general population was perceived and treated in the occupied territories in general, it would be both the suspected insurgents and their supporters who would feel the wrath of both German political and military authority. The nature of the retribution and the subsequent handling of the populations was by end large illegal, despite many clear examples provided of individual and collaborative efforts on the part of specific units, soldiers, and commanders to adhere to an acceptable moral and legal method of conduct.

In fact, Himmler was not altogether certain of the regular armed forces in supporting the coming events, and he needed to "test *Wehrmacht* tolerance and contrive *Wehrmacht* complicity," thus ensuring across the board legitimacy for his actions.[208] Certain circumstances arose which gave many of the SS, SD and Army commanders (some high ranking, such as Admiral Wilhelm

Canaris of the *Abwehr*) cause for concern regarding each others' actions, as cited by Rhodes.[209] Ironically, even *Waffen SS* Colonel General Josef "Sepp" Dietrich, not always the most agreeable with either his Army or SS counterparts, was even relieved that Reinhard Heydrich, the master puppeteer of mass murder had died as a result of his wounds in Prague, asking "is the swine dead at last?"[210]

There were many instances of German military leaders showing compassion and extending humanitarian aid, including decent treatment toward the populations in their attempt to adhere to the laws of war. However, this was predominantly true only if these populations were not perceived as an enemy militarily, racially, or politically, despite the standing orders and racial platform of the NSDAP. Distinguishing between partisans, guerrillas and civilians became difficult, until finally the distinctions mattered very little. In many cases, the particular actions of the irregulars determined the treatment the population would receive in general. However, George Ginsburgs presents the obvious argument that:

> It is quite definitively established that the chief, and perhaps the only real reason why the traditional laws of warfare were not at all adhered to in the conduct of military hostilities on the Russian Front lies in the conscious and premeditated decision of the Fuehrer and his entourage to wage a "total" war of annihilation and extermination, wholly unhampered by even the most elementary considerations of international law and morality.[211]

Reports of partisans attacking while wearing German uniforms, as well as committing crimes against the Russian people while so disguised were common (although illegal). Such events hardened the already severe German position towards both insurgents as well as the innocent.[212] As stated by the commander of the *707th Infantry Division*, General von Bechtolsheim: "This criminality has been consciously grown and nurtured here for a quarter century. All are guilty, young and old, men and women and not just any individual sector of society. So the battle must be carried out with the utmost ruthlessness!"[213]

When treated well the populations generally responded in kind, and when not treated well, German forces found themselves engaged in lengthy and protracted counterinsurgency operations, which nearly always resulted in the mass murder or deportation of noncombatants.[214]

In examining the international laws applicable to this book, the legal approach to killing civilians according to the German military must be addressed. On 13 May 1941 the *Conduct for Courts Martial (Kriegsgerichtbarkeitser-lass)* was issued, followed by the *Guidelines for the Conduct of the Troops in Russia (Richtlinien fuer das Verhalten der Truppen im Russland)* on 19 May 1941, which outlined the expectations of German soldiers, which were galvanized by the Commissar Order (*Kommissarbefehl*) of 6 June 1941.[215]

These three directives were issued by then Army Commander-in-Chief Field Marshal Walther von Brauchitsch, in order to clarify the expected conduct of the military as a preventive measure against potential damage to discipline and morale.[216] The criminality of the expected actions was thus understood by the High Command; hence the need to clarify to the soldiers what conduct was allowed and expected in this "new war."[217]

This is not to say that German soldiers, even those of the SS and SD did not suffer penalties by killing Jews or others without complete authorization. The case of SS *Untersturmfuehrer* (2nd Lieutenant) Max Taeubner is a case in point. Taeubner was not part of a detailed *kommando*, but killed Jews along with many of his men and Ukrainian assistants without orders. He was court-martialed, not for the unauthorized killings, but for taking photos of the process and having them developed in a German photography shop back home, and then sharing them with friends and family. It was ironically this breach of security which caused his downfall.[218]

These orders unleashed the military and their collaborators against the civilian populations, thus allowing for full discretion to be used against suspected insurgents, as well as those clearly targeted for extermination, such as Jews and political commissars, in clear violation of international law. These actions were primarily within the purview of The Hague Convention of 1907.[219] Hague was quite clear in that "the taking of collective sanctions against localities, from which opposition stemmed, including hostage taking, was illegal in all cases."[220] The following situations are prime examples of these particular violations during two specifically chosen anti-partisan missions: *Operations Zugspitze* and *Nachbarhilfe* respectively:

> Though it was not possible to locate and destroy the bandits, the regiment was able to comb the area thoroughly, an area which previously had not been entered by German forces. In the course of the operation it became clear that a number of villages had been thoroughly infested by the bandits. With the division's permission, seven villages were destroyed. 141 accomplices of the bandits were shot by the GFP [German Field Police] and about 400 people were taken [as hostages] to the reception camp in Unetscha.[221]

> The population of the forest villages, or of the villages at the edges of the forest is working without exception with the bandits. It is immaterial whether this cooperation is voluntary or coerced; it alone is sufficient reason to deal the partisans a decisive blow by evacuating the population and burning down the villages in these areas.[222]

> By burning the area indicated in red...the partisans' basis of supply and shelter is removed...as far as these areas are concerned, it has been made clear to the troops that every individual encountered is to be regarded as a bandit. This removes any source of confusion or consideration regarding the civilian population.[223]

These actions were just a few that precipitated a full re-evaluation of The Hague and Geneva Conventions after the war. Following the war, the Allied Tribunal at Nuremberg drew up a list of specific situations in which reprisals could be "legally conducted" and incorporated into the law:

> It had not been possible to apprehend the actual perpetrators of an attack.

> The population as a whole had been party to the offence thus supporting the action.

> Those selected for reprisal had been active in the commission of the act(s).

> Those selected had been taken from the actual location of the event in question.

> Proper judicial proceedings had been carried out according to acceptable laws.

> The reprisal was the method of last resort after all other methods and investigations had failed.[224]

German forces had varying methods by which to handle their problems. There was some concern that undisciplined retaliation would create chaos, thus regulations needed to be employed. The directive of 3 August 1942 issued from *OKW* outlined the method by which retaliation could be meted out:

> Collective punishment measures, so far as they involve the shooting of inhabitants and the burning of villages, are without exception to be carried out only by order of an officer at the level of battalion commander or higher, and only then once it has been proven that the inhabitants, or particular individuals, have been supporting the partisans.[225]

Regardless of the positive efforts of the few officers and soldiers recorded in this chapter, "the Axis populations knew in their hearts that they had been led into campaigns of violence which the rest of the world deplored."[226] Given the nature of the racial war in the USSR, there were actual examples of soldiers simply being humane.

One example was the commander of the 444th *Security Division* operating with *Army Group South* wanting rations for Jews to be protected and dispensed accordingly to "prevent the anti-Semitic Ukrainian population from depriving them."[227] Also, a Colonel Groscurth of the 259th *Infantry Division* tried unsuccessfully to prevent the killing of children by the *SD*.[228] Another example of a humanitarian gesture is cited by James Lucas regarding the account of a 2nd *Waffen SS Panzer Division "Das Reich"* soldier named Anton Fehlau, on 5 March 1943 in Kharkov:

> Our battery had to send a heavy truck to the Town Commandant who told us to drive to a German field bakery. There the vehicle was filled to the brim with freshly baked loaves. These we were to deliver to a given point in Kharkov. En route we decided on a short break, took one of the loaves and began to eat it. All the houses round about were shuttered and seemed to be empty, but when an old man came out of one, approached us and made begging gestures for something to eat. Without thinking, I flung him a loaf and then all of the doors opened and people rushed out, falsely believing that we were distributing bread. We started the truck and drove off in a hurry, but when we reached our destination in Kharkov we learned that the whole truck load had in fact been intended for the Russian civilian population.[229]

Lucas provided another example, citing Ewald Ehm, also of *"Das Reich,"* regarding his former company commander, SS Captain Heinz Macher of the *"Deutschland Regiment"* and a large group of children:

> They collected quickly whenever it was mealtime and stood silently with their huge eyes staring at the food. Nobody had the heart to drive them away and Macher decided on a course of action. He told me to go to the kitchen and tell the cook to make a thick soup out of what was still left in the field kitchen and the men had eaten. That way we fed the children. I might add that many of our comrades were already feeding the children from their own rations.[230]

One method of actively using the populations while also achieving their loyalty was to employ locals to perform specific non-military tasks, such as tradesmen and craftsmen. By paying them a wage this was conducive with international law under Geneva 1929, and not considered slave labor. Lucas also cites another example regarding the treatment of a Soviet POW by Horst Herpolosheimer of *No. 11 Company, "Der Fuehrer" Regiment* of *"Das Reich"*:

> My platoon was in a position on the railway embankment at Bereka. The morning of 16 February [1943] had been a quiet one. There had not been much in the way of shelling or enemy action of any sort when suddenly thirty Red Army men came in to surrender. They were absolutely terrified. One of my comrades acted as interpreter and through him I asked whether there was a cobbler among the group. A middle-aged man, trembling from head to foot, admitted that he could repair boots. I calmed him down, gave

him cigarettes and later that evening took him to our "B" echelon. Not long afterwards I was wounded twice and spent a long time in hospital. What with convalescent leave and a number of other things it was not until a year later that I met that Russian again and, this time in southern France... He saw me, fell on his knees and kissed my hand in gratitude. I told him to get up and asked an interpreter what he was saying. The interpreter told me that my Russian said he had never been so well treated in all his life. He worked well, received the same rations as a German soldier, was paid for his work and could buy a bottle of wine every day. Whenever we met he continued to thank me. In all my war service I never saw such a contented and happy man as my Russian soldier.[231]

Shepherd provides a further example in his citation of a "Lieutenant Meyer" of the *221ˢᵗ Security Division* operating in Yelnya-Dorogobuzh regions:

> The population willingly declared itself to the German troops, supplying valuable information about the movements and intentions of the partisans. It supported the *Wehrmacht* in every way and in places provided militias for the active combating of the partisans.[232]

These interactions between German soldiers, former enemy soldiers, and civilians demonstrated the positive effects that resulted from humane and decent treatment. However, as Truman Anderson stated regarding the civilian approach to the Germans: "A pragmatic day-to-day calculus of personal survival played a much more important role than did either pro-German or Soviet patriotism."[233]

Despite these specific acts, many German units and commanders were still not inclined to promote good will through humanitarian handling of the populations. The continuous liquidations and forced deportations eclipsed such humanitarian gestures, eroding German legitimacy and the good will initially experienced by many German soldiers.[234] As stated by Shepherd:

> Army files contain numerous examples of objection to harsh policy and attempts to ameliorate it, but those officers who were genuinely motivated by compassion would have been foolish to put their case in anything but pragmatic terms. This was the case even with those officers who, as time went by, were increasingly critical of policy.[235]

An opposite example is provided by Omer Bartov, citing a "Corporal K. Suffner," whose observations regarding the anti-Semitism of the Ukrainians is important in comprehending the great assistance offered to the Germans during their occupation: "Bolsheviks and Jews have murdered 12,000 Germans and Ukrainians in a beastly manner...the surviving Ukrainians arrested 2,000 Jews and exercised a frightful revenge. We swear that this plague will be eradicated root and branch."[236] A similar attitude was reflected in the actions of Colonel Hans Wiemann,[237] a World War I veteran and commander of *Landesschuetzen-Battalion 45*, who ordered a pacification operation in the Gomel region:

> Security and pacification measures are to exacted ruthlessly. Partisan suspects and any civilians who are possibly in contact with the partisans are to be dealt with using the utmost harshness. If the population does not voluntarily participate in the anti-partisan effort (through information and reconnaissance) then it is to be treated as suspect.[238]

Another example of counterproductive actions, which overshadowed the positive efforts of the minority of humanitarians, and completely illegal is provided by Burleigh and Wippermann, who chronicle the comments of a former Roman Catholic priest, SS Lieutenant Colonel Albert Hartl, former aid to SS Lieutenant General Reinhard Heydrich and the *RSSH* emissary to the Jesuit monastery in Krakow, prior to the invasion of Poland on 1 September 1939:[239]

> Among them there were those who were highly ambitious and who wanted to report to Berlin the highest possible number of shootings, and others who attempted as far as possible to sabotage the order to carry out the shootings...Among the latter was *Brigadefuehrer*[240] Schulz, who, as he told me, disapproved of the mass shootings, and therefore had himself transferred as soon as possible from the command of a task force, which I recall was stationed in the Lemberg area.[241]

Also cited by Burleigh and Wippermann (supporting Hartl's account) officers and men who did not want to participate on moral grounds were transferred at their own discretion, but other than risking terminal rank without future promotions, there was no evidence of any serious retribution taken against these men for their decisions.[242] Another entry in *The Racial State* sources the diary of a *Waffen SS* soldier named Felix Landau, who describes a clear violation of the Geneva Convention, Article 2:

> Twenty-three have to be shot, including the women I mentioned before. They are remarkable. They even refused to accept a glass of water from us. I was posted sentry and had to shoot anyone who escaped. We went along a country road for a kilometer, and then turned off right into a wood...we looked for a suitable spot for the shooting and burial....The condemned were given shovels in order to dig their own grave. Two of them were crying. The rest certainly had extraordinary courage. What could have been going on at that moment in their heads? I believe each of them had a small hope that somehow they would not be shot....Curiously, nothing disturbed me. No pity, nothing....Slowly the hole grew bigger; two wept incessantly. I let them go on digging, for then they would not think so much. In fact, they grew quieter while working.
>
> Their valuables, watches, and money were piled together. After they had all been lined up together in a clearing, the two women were taken to the edge of the grave to be shot. Two men had already been shot in the bushes

by our Criminal Police Commissar. I did not see this, as I had to watch over the rest. The women were seized and taken to the edge of the trench, where they turned around. Six of us had to shoot them, divided so that three of us aimed at the heart and three at the head. I took the heart. The bullet struck and brain mass burst through the air. Three to the skull are too much. They almost tear the head off. Almost all of them fell down silently together, although it did not work in two cases, where they screamed and whimpered for a long time. The revolver shots were no good....The penultimate group now had to throw those who had been shot into the mass grave, then they had to line up, and then fall of their own accord into the grave.[243]

Given these examples, a contradictory viewpoint supporting the illegal orders issued to soldiers is the testimony of Peter Peterson, a veteran of the elite *"Grossdeutschland" Panzer Division* as presented in *Voices from the Third Reich*:

I really wanted to join the SS. They were the elite and had the best looking uniforms. But then I had an upsetting experience. One of my friends, who was two years older than I was, came back in 1942 to visit his old school.... He told me that he had been at the front and had taken prisoners. He asked the battalion staff what he should do with them. The *Waffen SS* general in command of the sector said, "shoot them." My friend protested that the prisoners were not partisans, but regular soldiers, and that he could not legitimately shoot them. He was ordered back to the battalion, where he received a terrible bawling out. He would be sent to take command of a firing squad where he would be shooting partisans, German deserters, and who knows what else. He told me that he had not had the courage to refuse to obey this order, since he would have been shot. Then he returned to the front. Later, when we heard that he had been killed, we had a memorial ceremony. He had fallen on the field of honor.[244]

The example established by commanders in the field always set the pattern for the conduct of the troops, so illegal orders issued from above would always be taken as justification for barbarity from the soldiers below. Prime examples are the actions of Army Field Marshals Ferdinand Schoerner, Walter Model, *Luftwaffe* Field Marshal Albert Kesselring, and Army Major General Karl Wilhelm von Schlieben, all of whom issued orders not to take prisoners or to execute persons in captivity.[245] One example of Schoerner being in control of such an event is described by Breitman:

An architect among them received the order to prepare to excavate the pits. Soviet prisoners of war guarded by German soldiers followed the architect's directions, digging about five pits, ten meters long by ten meters wide and about three meters deep. A ramp at one end of each pit made it possible to march the victims in....The total capacity was set for about twenty-eight thousand bodies.[246]

There were exceptions to these orders, as stated by Mommsen:

At best, army officers adopted a defensive attitude: they restricted themselves to their own fields of competence, attempting to prevent a collapse of discipline within the ranks or, at least personally, avoided becoming directly implicated in criminal measures. Virtually all those involved in the mass murder of Jews clung to the pretext offered them by Himmler and others that their work was a grim necessity arising from a unique situation. Such mechanisms played a central part in the realization of the regime's criminal policies. These were invariably carried out under the pretext of tackling exceptional situations, which in fact had been created by the dynamics of the system.[247]

As stated by Overy: "Efforts by regular soldiers to prevent brutalities were swept aside by Himmler's army of officials and policemen. Atrocities were permitted in the name of the 'higher law of racial survival.'"[248] This fact is supported by the memoirs of Field Marshal Wilhelm Keitel, who wrote that Hitler "allowed for courts-martial against soldiers who committed excesses against civilians," and these were to be left to the discretion of the unit commanders, as opposed to a general policy.[249] Interesting is the fact that in the 'German Manual of Military Law', or the *Heeresdienstvorschrift (HVD)*, paragraph 47 states:

> The order must be confined to the pursuit of some military objective. Outside the sphere a military order has no purpose and therefore is not of a binding nature. Pursuit of a military objective is only justified if it serves some higher national purpose and if the military organization as a whole forms an integral part of a wider State organization. If a military command runs counter to the general State system, it has neither purpose nor justification and anyone issuing such a command is guilty of dereliction of duty as a loyal citizen of the State.[250]

This manual clearly states that any actions not applicable to military operations in the name of the state were thereby illegal; hence the killing of civilians should have been so classified due to their lack of military importance. By creating the illusion that civilians were a detriment and threat, this military directive fell into abject irrelevance.

Liberal interpretation of this law was definitely one of the crutches upon which many commanders tainted their reports regarding the actual numbers of "combatants killed," as opposed to the simple murder of innocent civilians. Thereby killing was legitimized as a necessity for "state preservation;" therefore orders were carefully worded and the rules changed to accommodate the killers. According to Reitlinger:

> An even more important factor was that, provided it was not accompanied by sadism or indiscipline, murder of Jews had been expressly stated to be both necessary and non-criminal. This fact carried with it a danger for anyone seriously trying to evade a criminal order; refusal to obey could easily be made to appear as refusal to obey an official order...Naturally open re-

fusal to obey an order cannot be written off as completely impossible, but it was attended by considerable unnecessary risk.[251]

Jonathan Steinberg also states:

> Courts and codes of law continued to exist, if diluted. In the Soviet Union there was an administrative vacuum.[252] Legal restrictions on killing civilians were being stripped away. SS units could take executive measures against civilians without interference. Soldiers could commit crimes without threat of prosecution, and certain categories of people could be killed even if resisting passively.[253]

Many times the reports were delivered to the intelligence sections unaltered, such as the report from the *203rd SD*, which clearly stated "that many people killed in the cleansing operations are not actually partisans."[254] Death to all who qualified was the ultimate reality, as stated by Mommsen:

> The constantly escalating spiral of brutality, which immunized the regime's killers in their murderous handiwork and dulled the senses of those who witnessed it was an essential precondition for systematic mass murder to become concrete reality. The fate of Soviet prisoners of war in German hands, less than a third were to survive captivity, played at least as important a role in this."[255]

Partisans fell under no protective guidelines as far as Germany was concerned, and according to Geneva 1929 and Hague 1907, they were correct if caught in the act, and this was supported by the highest echelons of the German command as stated by Albert Kesselring: "The partisan war was a complete violation of international law and contradicted every principle of clean soldierly fighting."[256] In contrast, the Soviet perspective regarding irregulars (without differentiating between *partisans* and *guerrillas*) was quite different, seeing irregulars as civilians continuing the legitimate struggle against an invading enemy, as cited by Ginsburgs:

> There is full agreement among Soviet jurists that partisans are protected by international law and The Hague and Geneva Conventions relative to regular combatants, and that the summary execution or maltreatment of captured guerrillas is a crime under international laws of warfare.[257]

Even the Soviets stipulated that irregulars had the responsibility of carrying arms openly and abiding by the laws of warfare themselves, in citing Article I of The Hague 1907,[258] although many times their actions defied not only law but logic, as stated by former Soviet Captain Gregor Koronov:

> Well, we knew that somehow we had to create some partisan activity, resorting to conscription in many cases, and the political commissars went around the villages, trying to recruit even the old and very young. When this did not work due to the flood of refugees coming to the east, our commissar, Fedor "something," asked for volunteers to attack a village of "collaborators'. We went in, shot the people, killing over thirty, and then took

a couple of German prisoners and placed them in the street, shot them, and laid them out as if they had been part of the massacre. Later another time our unit had some disciplinary problems, and the men to be punished were given civilian clothes and ordered to carry grenades into the German lines... [T]his sort of activity provoked the Germans into reacting, and their predictable brutality would surpass ours, and the desired result would produce several partisan groups wanting revenge. Unfortunately for our commander the truth was later learned about his activities against the civilians. One of the men who joined our unit had escaped the massacre, and he identified several people, and he spread the word to others. He killed our CO and then deserted to the enemy. This was a very nasty business.[259]

One of the arguments was that even conventional units used "guerrilla tactics" that were acceptable under international law according to Article I, The Hague 1907,[260] as well as the fact that irregulars often worked with or were attached to regular military units.[261] The Soviets even argued the point that the restrictions placed upon irregulars under Hague and Geneva hindering their "legal" effectiveness "were outdated,"[262] while defending the irregulars' right to execute Germans,[263] as well as reclassifying all German POWs as "common criminals" and stripping away their legal protection under international law.[264] Their defense was that Germans guilty of "war crimes" lost their protection under the law, just as the Germans argued that the irregulars similarly lost their protective status.

Even the most humane German officers held little sympathy for those irregulars captured in open combat, and whose participation was irrefutable. The standing order of the day is provided:

> Every Partisan found is to be shot. If the local inhabitants are hostile to German forces, treat them with the utmost brutality. If friendly, harness them in the struggle against the Partisans. Destroy anything that could be of the slightest use to the partisans. Foul all water supplies.[265]

According to Norman Rich: "To confront successfully and eventually eliminate this danger was the crux of the German political leadership, to which all other considerations had to be subordinated."[266] Soldiers for the most part did follow their orders, legal or not. As stated by Mommsen: "One effect of years of Nazi propaganda was that for the average German there was no psychological alternative to loyalty to Hitler short of placing oneself outside the bounds of the nation."[267] Other issues were also at play in the inability to conduct a universally accepted campaign of understanding and tolerance among all German units, commanders, and soldiers, as illustrated by the following:

> Reports constantly come in that properties are being vandalized or pillaged outright by members of units stationed in the area. These actions are highly un-comradely, for they can cause a dearth of sufficiently equipped accommodation for the troops who have been sent to the rear to recover from particularly harsh frontline combat. They also contravene orders and indeed are acts of plunder. I shall ensure that reports are submitted on any similar cases in future.[268]

Of the major belligerents during World War II, all but two of the major powers ratified the Geneva Convention of 1929, these nations being Japan and the USSR.[269] Germany did sign and ratify the document under the Weimar Republic, thus placing itself responsible for its actions during the war. Hitler had removed Germany from the League of Nations (as did Japan) and openly violated the Treaty of Versailles, yet he never repudiated the laws of warfare. Even *if* the Geneva Convention of 1929 had *not* applied to Germany, The Hague II and III Conferences of 18 May-29 July 1899 and 1907 respectively still provided international laws and mandates governing the actions of Germany's (and all nations') soldiers and government during times of conflict.[270]

The Hague Conferences were first established at the request of Tsar Nicholas II Romanov of Russia for "the purpose of regulating arms, maintaining peace, and ameliorating the conditions of warfare, essentially establishing the first rules of engagement."[271] The Second Conference of 1907 (referred to hereafter as the "Convention") established the laws of land, sea, and air warfare, outlawing specific weapons, such as poison gas and expanding ammunition (dum-dum rounds) and aerial bombardment, for which balloons were the primary delivery system of the day.[272]

Perhaps the greatest outcome of The Hague 1907 was the ratification of the establishment of basic human rights drafted in 1899, focusing upon the protection of civilians following the events arising during the Second Boer War of 1899-1902. This important distinction regarding human rights separated The Hague from the earlier Geneva Conventions until 1929, when the language was included regarding civilians in wartime, defining their protective status. The original Hague Convention also differed from Geneva, in that Hague was meant to be an arbitration forum to prevent war and subsequent collateral damage, while Geneva was designed to provide guidelines once war had ensued. The Hague also established rules of engagement between belligerents prior to their adoption into Geneva 1929. Both of these conven-

tions precipitated the creation of the Permanent Court of International Justice in 1921.[273]

Had Hitler openly denounced either convention, given the change in the
government in January 1933, it is certain that the German government itself
could not have been held *legally* responsible for its actions according Geneva,
although morally the end would have probably been the same given the acts
committed. The individuals *within* the government and military would have
been liable for their personal actions, and therefore subject to prosecution
for their personal crimes under either of the two conventions during an international post-war tribunal.[274] The laws as stated were clear: "No party to
the Geneva Conventions can absolve itself or another party of liability for
grave breaches of the Geneva Conventions (Article 52)."[275]

On this note the actions of the German military as detailed in this chapter provided the victorious Allies with the legal ammunition to prosecute the
high-ranking administrators, commanders, and individual soldiers accused
of committing war crimes during the war on all fronts, as witnessed by the
subsequent Nuremberg Trials and subsequent prosecutions decades after
the war.[276]

International laws have dictated the conduct of war and of soldiers who
participate since the First Geneva Convention of 22 August 1864, at the sug-
gestion of Swiss national Henri Dunant.[277] Limits were placed upon how far
military leaders and governments could go in the prosecution of war. As
stated by Michael Walzer, these parameters regarding belligerence and conduct assist in determining the vital difference between *jus ad bellum* (justice of
war) and *jus ad bello* (justice in war): "A legitimate act of war is one that does
not violate the rights of the people against whom it is directed."[278]

These laws were initially drafted with the primary purpose of limiting
unnecessary suffering among combatants, but most important was the intention of protecting civilian populations against the actions of soldiers. The
primary forums discussed here are the Geneva Conventions of 1864–1929, The
Hague Convention of 1899–1900, and the Brussels Conference of 1889–90.[279]

I. THE GENEVA CONVENTIONS

Following the First World War the issue of insurgents was barely addressed by the Geneva Conventions, with Article 2 failing to stipulate clearly

the immunity of civilians from reprisals, although POWs were clearly protected.[280] Article 2 of Geneva 1929 did provide civilians the same status as POWs regarding the wounded and ill.[281] However, the German military (and Soviets) had made it clear that POWs would not be considered as "protected" in all cases. German policy as of 25 November 1939 stated that "association with POWs is forbidden...The POW is a member of a nation which forced us into a world war and therefore he is an enemy of the nation."[282]

The evidence of Hitler's personal attitude towards POWs is found in the post-war interrogation of Colonel General Edmund Glaise von Horstenau by the US 7th Army Counterintelligence Corps. According to Horstenau, Hitler was going to denounce the Geneva Convention of 1929 regarding the humane treatment of prisoners had the war lasted another three months.[283] Hitler had even stated that: "Germans in Allied hands would have to expect the same fate."[284] Horstenau stated that everyone on the General Staff and the upper echelons of the government were opposed to this plan, with the sole exception of Josef Goebbels, whose stepson Harald was ironically a POW in Canada. Even the ruthless Party Secretary Martin Ludwig Bormann was opposed to Hitler's plan.[285]

The German forces operating in the Soviet Union during anti-partisan operations disregarded these laws on a regular basis, albeit in many cases their actions, while ruthless, were not always illegal given the provisions contained within the various conventions, sections and articles. Less important than the existence of resistance is the evidence of German reprisals and the conduct of their operations against irregulars. These acts included slave labor, offensive operations, destruction of property, direct contact methodology and interpretation, and the complete disregard of the existing protocols:

> The systematic murders of the local populations that had begun in the late summer, such as the 33,711 Jews, partisans, commissars, POWs and others killed in reprisal for the bombing of the Continental Hotel, headquarters for the 6th Army at Babi Yar, near Kiev in the Ukraine on 29-30 September 1941 (eventually over 100,000 bodies would fill the great ravine) were a portent to what the population in general could expect.[286]

Given the nature of the German forced labor policy this section becomes relevant for several reasons. First, it was the labor policy, brutal occupation methods, appropriation of personal property, land, livestock, and the destruction of homes in violation of international law that provided the greatest impetus for resistance throughout the Soviet Union. Second, the decrees, such as the *Nacht und Nebel* ("Night and Fog") Decree issued by Keitel in 1941, with the full support of Adolf Hitler would lay the groundwork for subsequent violations of international law.[287]

The most significant and visible factor regarding the exponential rise of resistance and the immediate loss of perceived legitimacy by Germany were the *Sonderkommando* and *Einsatzgruppen* operations.[288] Following these illegal actions there were a myriad of regular Army commanders who supported the continuance of violent occupation and brutal suppression. Perhaps no *Wehrmacht Heer* (Armed Forces 'Army') senior commander was as ruthless as Field Marshal Ferdinand Schoerner, who openly supported *Einsatzgruppen* operations and ordered the murders of Soviet civilians and POWs.[289]

The *Nacht und Nebel* Decree ordered for increased pressure to be placed upon civilians and allowed "for the seizure of personal property and the execution without trial of persons suspected of compromising German security in the occupied zones."[290] Hostage taking of civilians purported to support the resistance was also exercised, especially in the active counterinsurgency campaigns against partisans, in blatant violation of Geneva Protocol I, Article 75, Section 2c.[291] The *Nacht und Nebel* Decree also allowed for the systematic murders of "all male Jews from ages seventeen to forty-five, but soon the age limitation meant nothing."[292] Keitel and his subordinates openly violated Protocol I, Article 86, Section 2, which states:

> A superior who has information to the effect that a subordinate was committing or was going to commit a breach of the Geneva Conventions must take all feasible measures to prevent or repress the breach. If the superior fails to act, he or she can face penal discipline.[293]

The following citations of the Geneva Conventions attempt to clarify the rules under which both German and irregular operated, although the confusion becomes compounded when the definitions of "combatant" and "non-combatant" become subject to individual interpretation. The German commanders in the field generally made that decision based upon the evidence before them in lieu of standing orders, as illustrated in the following examples:

> It was clear from the agricultural stockpiles in Guta that the village was being used as a bandits' strongpoint. Of the thirteen men present, the eight able bodied men were therefore arrested.[294] A bottle of (gun) powder was found in a house in Sinowjewka. Ammunition detonated when the house was burned down by order of the regiment. A sawn-off shotgun and rifle

were found in the ruins, which despite a thorough search beforehand had not been found. The owner of the house admitted that her husband was with the partisans and had left the ammunition behind after his last visit. The woman was shot, and her children handed over to the headman.[295]

The ambiguity of these distinctions included the "legal status" of irregulars dependent upon their actions, as stated by Overy: "Partisans sometimes walked a thin line between military hero and gangster."[296] The confusion amongst soldiers is stated by Italian Captain Mario Antonucci:

> In fighting regular soldiers there are many advantages, such as easily identifying your opponent, understanding that there are accepted rules of warfare, and the knowledge that you could possibly out maneuver a conventional force. With partisans this was not the case, you never knew where you stood, and the accepted rules of war did not apply. The fact that the Germans performed the way they did made life very difficult for us.[297]

German perceptions were of the partisans as being not only beneath contempt, but also fair game and not protected under the law. This was especially true after Stalin invoked the Partisan War Order in 1941, to which Hitler stated: "It gives us the opportunity to exterminate anyone who is hostile to us. Naturally the vast area must be pacified as quickly as possible; this will happen best through shooting anyone who even looks askance at us."[298] *Waffen* SS Senior Colonel Leon Degrelle provides another perspective from a combat leader:[299]

> The one thing my men and I knew was that however large and present the threat presented by the Soviet Army, the partisans were the worst enemy to fight. Since they did not wear uniforms, unless they were in German clothing sometimes, and they blended in well with the local population, which created a problem in choosing who was and who was not a partisan. Unless you caught one with a weapon, or were actively engaged against them, it was impossible. Later during the war they were absorbed into the Red Army infantry and tank units, and sometimes they were given uniforms. I would say the most disturbing aspect of fighting the partisans was that unlike the Soviet military, the partisans adhered to no set doctrine, used no set order of battle that we could study, and basically struck where it was the most opportune. In this method they excelled, yet they could not engage in a prolonged firefight. If we caught and cornered them they were dead, and they knew it. That was why they fought like fanatics.[300]

The actions of the *Nacht und Nebel* Decree violated dozens of the Geneva Convention protocols. One example was the "relocation" of civilians, whose homes may have been destroyed, with many people being executed for failing to follow the movement orders.[301]

Geneva Conventions I-III and the subsequent 1925 Protocols (ratified in 1929) were in effect, and the following Articles violated by German forces during the war are cited: Protocol I, Article 3 (on killing civilians); Articles

22 (protection for POWs), Article 23 (on soldiers in enemy uniform);[302] Article 37 (on killing the wounded); Article 48 (on distinguishing between military and civilian land and dwellings); Article 51 (protection of civilians in occupied territories); Article 126 (access to POWs and treatment); Article 143 (access to civilians who are protected); Article 54, Section 2 (on livestock and land); Article 85, Section 3 (on indiscriminate attacks upon civilians); Article 85, Sections 4 (on the right to fair trials) and 5a (on racial discrimination or outrages upon personal dignity); Protocol I (on the use of poison gas); Article 11, Section 3 (on individual burials; mass graves not allowed); Article 77, Section 1 (protection of children); Article 51, Section 7 (on protection of civilians against attacks). Geneva Convention I was in effect with specific modifications in Geneva II-III, Article 13, Sections 1-2, which stated that combatants were defined as:

> Members of the armed forces of a party to an international conflict, members of militias or volunteer corps including members of organized resistance movements as long as they have a well-defined chain of command, are clearly distinguishable from the civilian population, carry their arms openly, and obey the laws of war.[303]

With the capture of suspected irregulars the Geneva Convention still applied to children. Even those captured as participants in warfare may not be harmed or executed if younger than eighteen years of age, and must be removed from hostile areas to a safe region, and must not be forced into the military, as outlined by Protocol I, Article 77, Sections 2 and 5; Protocol II, Article 4, Sections 3c and 3d.[304] If and when captured, children must also be segregated from adults unless with their families for their safety (Protocol I, Article 77, Section 4). In addition, mothers with infants and pregnant women had similar protection under Protocol I, Article 76, Sections 2-3; foreigners (neutrals) must be repatriated from the hostile environment as soon as possible.[305] The sick and wounded were also given special protection stemming from the Geneva Convention of 22 August 1864, inaugurated by Henri Dunant and ratified at every subsequent Convention.[306]

Where the German counterinsurgents focused was upon Protocol I, Article 50, Sections 1-3, which stipulated that civilians are only classified as such if they "are not members of the armed forces, militias or volunteer corps, organized resistance movements, and residents of an occupied territory who spontaneously takes up arms," and are guaranteed safety under Protocol I, Article 51 in total.[307] This argument is supported by the previous citation of Article 13, Sections 1-2, which separates and distinguishes the non-combatant from the recognized combatant, and Protocol I, Article 44, Section 2, which preserves the status of those captured as "protected" even if identified as a noncombatant (such as a partisan) that violate the laws of war, as long as that person has not committed a major crime, such as killing a soldier.[308]

However, the application of these rights is dependent upon the insurgent as well, since it is generally accepted that the treatment of the civilian population is dependent upon the conduct of that population. According to Walzer: "Soldiers must feel safe from civilians if civilians are ever to feel safe from soldiers."[309] Given the nature of the German occupation, Soviet civilian reprisals against their own people as well as the Germans, and the nature of the war in general, the reality of the situation is stated by Overy: "Neither German soldiers, nor the thousands of Soviet citizens who worked for their new masters, were safe."[310]

Partisans and guerrillas, while being different politically were totally indistinguishable from each other ideologically where the Germans were concerned. All were considered a threat and termed as "illegal" persons and "bandits" thus ostensibly removing their protected status. Even the existing conventions failed to apply any distinction between the two groups, which has only recently been included within the historiography. According to *German Anti-Partisan Warfare in Europe, 1939-1945*:

> The difference between a *partisan* and *guerrilla* may be stated as thus: "guerrillas" are a force that offer resistance to *either* a foreign *or* domestic nation state or pretender to statehood, or an incumbent national regime that operates contrary to the ideology and wishes of the irregular force in general, hence the initiation of a "guerrilla" campaign to overthrow that government.[311] Partisans fight as a paramilitary force to expel a foreign invader, supporting a threatened or denounced government and the represented military, hoping to gather external alliances and support deemed necessary for long-term survival.[312]

These are the accepted basic distinctions between the two paramilitary groups according to this author; simple ideology. Both use the same methods, and both may lay claim to the title of "nationalist" although the political realities determine which group legitimately claims that sobriquet. International law to this day does not make a clear distinction between the two groups, and the Germans were no exception. It is strange to this author that we have landed on the moon, cured diseases and split the atom, yet the human experience has failed to properly protect and define these groups under a single acceptable and unambiguous legal referendum.

Upon capture, civilian paramilitaries in either of these categories lost their protection if captured during open conflict by the Germans. The law applied unless they carried their weapons openly, wore rank or identifiable insignia, and could be classified as soldiers from a recognized uniformed military organization, all of which would have mattered little anyway. By not wearing uniforms or being easily recognized from noncombatants their fate was clear. In clear language, Protocol I, Article 44, Section 3 states:

> Guerrillas who follow the rules spelled out in the Geneva Conventions are considered to have combatant status and have some [not all] of the same rights as regular members of the armed forces. In international conflicts, guerrillas must distinguish themselves from the civilian population if they are preparing or engaged in an attack. At a minimum guerrillas must carry their arms openly...a guerrilla must have a well-defined chain of command.[313]

Civilians and the subdued military could have been disarmed for security purposes under Protocol I, Article 63, Section 3, but they "may bear light individual weapons in order to maintain order and self-defense," which was allowed at the discretion of the military power (in this case Germany), as stated in Protocol I, Article 65, Section 3.[314] However, these persons must be clearly identified and carry identification cards under Protocol I, Article 66 as ratified in Geneva IV of 1949.[315] This was often done by German commanders using foreign auxiliaries.

Under the German occupation, passes were issued to the foreign auxiliaries stating their authorization to carry weapons, as employees of the Third Reich. A division commander in the Army at the rank of brigadier general or above was required to sign such "free passes" and maintain a copy in the division file. Higher authority was also to be informed as a security measure. *SS, SD* and *Gestapo* officers at the rank of mere major could issue the same passes.

While some German commanders were exempted from prosecution after the war for executing civilians as irregulars, others were not. Civilians were also subject to local penal laws, and the German authorities in occupation *were* the law. The definition of "civilian" would become perhaps the most difficult task of commanders and the post-war prosecutors. Com-pounding the confusion was the misguided interpretation of Geneva 1929, which posed a problem for military leaders and commanders, as well as prosecutors, as stated by Strikfeldt:

> Unfortunately there is an order that the provisions of the Geneva Conventions do not apply to Soviet citizens or Soviet prisoners of war, ostensibly because the Soviet Union has not adhered to the convention. A pity. If law and decency have been trampled on for years it is all the more desirable for us to show that we respect and uphold them. Our task as soldiers is to beat the enemy. But we must do so while observing the accepted rules of warfare. This was the first time I heard that there were different rules for the conduct of war in the west and east.[316]

The differences between the east and west can also be seen in the comparative analysis regarding the treatment of legitimate military POWs; those captured in the west had an exponentially higher survival rate than those captured in the USSR.[317]

Where the Germans failed in their application of international law regarding the USSR was the fact that, since Germany *was* a signatory to Geneva 1929, the armed forces were expected to adhere to the rules *even if their enemy did not*. One belligerent not adhering to the laws as a signatory never excuses the other nation from not acting in accordance with the law, "demonstrating that the majority of nations will not, and should not tolerate violations as witnessed during the war."[318]

The forced conscriptions of POWs into military service or forced labor was in direct violation of Article 130, while the concentration camps and torture violated many areas of the conventions, but specifically Article 3.[319] In addition, the occupying power was responsible for the open posting of crimes warranting the death penalty available for full viewing, in the applicable languages, and applying the law to everyone equally, even its own soldiers as stated in Article 100.[320] The forced labor policy was in direct violation of Protocol II, Article 4, Section 2f, which stipulates to the "illegality of slavery" and Article 52 on civilians and POWs forced into dangerous labor.[321] The use of human beings in forced work without adequate compensation or access to legal and civil recourse is defined by Geneva *as* slavery.

The German use of slave labor also violated the 'Temporary Slavery Commission by the Council of the League of Nations as of 12 June 1924," as well as the "League of Nations Convention to Suppress the Slave Trade and Slavery of 26 September 1926."[322] Although this convention was a ratification of the General Act of the Brussels Conference of 1889-90 dealing with the African slave trade, the scope was expanded to include slavery in all of its forms.[323]

This international position resulted in the subsequent Convention of Saint-Germaine-en-Laye of 1919. As defined by the conventions: "Slavery is the status or condition of a person over whom any or all of the powers to the right of ownership are exercised."[324]

II. THE HAGUE CONVENTIONS

With regard to the German prosecution of the war in Europe, and in particular the anti-partisan war in the USSR, The Hague Conventions ratified on 4 September 1900 have been considered the secondary (or fall back) international legal forum for the conduct of war in support of the Geneva Conventions. Stalin never ratified either convention, a fact which Germany would use as a primary weapon of justification, although he never outright declined to conform to Hague, even stating he would.[325]

According to Jonathan Steinberg, it was the German interpretation of the existing laws, since the Soviet Union had been dissolved under German occupation, and therefore The Hague Conventions did not apply.[326] George Ginsburgs addressed the issue of non-Soviet compliance with The Hague Conventions of 1899 and 1907, although the USSR did adhere to The Hague of 18 October 1907 for the adaptation into Geneva 1929 regarding maritime warfare; also adhering to the Geneva Conference of 17 June 1935 on gas and bacteriological warfare, while failing to adhere to Geneva of 27 June 1929 regarding the treatment of the sick and wounded.[327] Ginsburgs also stipulates that the failure of Stalin to ratify The Hague in total is "not conclusive, and therefore did not exempt Germany from fulfilling its obligations."[328] While more vague and less detailed in its Articles, several stand out and were rewritten and incorporated into Geneva 1929.

Such factors in Section I "On Belligerents," Chapter I "On the Qualifications of Belligerents," in Article I included that superiors be responsible for subordinates and their actions, wearing identifiable uniforms and emblems, openly carry arms, to conduct operations in accordance with the laws and customs of war. Militias and volunteer corps were considered legitimate if adhering to the applicable rules. Ginsburgs related the invocation of the Soviets that their adoption of guerrilla warfare was "an inherent right separate from the normal conventions as a people's right to survive."[329]

Chapter I, Article 2 also states that resistance personnel may be considered as legal belligerents if they "respect the laws and customs of war."[330]

Article 3 states that "the armed forces of the belligerent parties may consist of [both] combatants and non-combatants. In case of capture by the enemy both have a right to be treated as prisoners of war,"[331] although the irregulars must adhere to the strict guidelines regarding open distinction between themselves and civilians.

Chapter II, Articles 4-20 concern the handling of POWs, their welfare and retention of personal property, while Article 6 stipulates the limits of POWs engaging in labor, and that "their tasks shall not be excessive, and shall have nothing to do with military operations," and also provides that they must be compensated for their work.[332] Article 13 provides protective status to those "who follow the army without directly belonging to it, such as newspaper correspondents and reporters," etc. These persons have entitlement to POW status providing they have the appropriate documentation.[333] Article 18 stipulates that POWs "shall enjoy every latitude in the exercise of their religion, including attending at their own church services," which provides for the freedom of religion, while Article 20 requires POWs to be repatriated upon conclusion of hostilities.[334] This law the Soviets openly violated following the war until repatriation of remaining POWs in December 1955. It must be stated that Stalin's desire to not accept all the provisions of Hague or Geneva was due to the fact that POW camps were to be visited and inspected by neutral observers, such as the International Red Cross. Stalin the megalomaniac, who desperately needed slave laborers, and even enslaved and murdered his own people was not about to subject himself and his gulags to such scrutiny.

Perhaps one of the most important sections of The Hague Convention is Section II, "On Hostilities," Chapter I, Articles 22-28. These Articles limit the amount of deadly force which may be implemented, as well as placing limits upon weapons (Article 23); killing or causing further injury to captured, sick or wounded soldiers (Article 23), and expressly prohibited the declaration of "no quarter" by either party.[335]

With regard to the *Nacht und Nebel* Decree (as previously mentioned under Geneva), this illegal order also falls under The Hague regarding confiscation of property under Article 23 (see also Section III Article 42), while civilian towns fall under Article 24. Article 26 states that "the Commander of an attacking force, before commencing bombardment, except in the case of an assault, should do all he can to warn the authorities," a practice abandoned in the USSR and other locations.[336]

The German application of lethal response to captured military and paramilitary members also fell under The Hague, Section II, Chapter II "On Spies" and Articles 29-31 provide an interesting companion to Geneva. The accusation of espionage and the protection of rear area security was the prime defense for the actions of German commanders, yet the rule reads: "An individual can only be considered a spy if, acting clandestinely, or on false pretences, he obtains, or seeks to obtain information in the zone of operations of a belligerent, with the intention of communicating it to the hostile party."[337] The rules also state under Article 30 that those accused of espionage must be given the benefit of trial and the ability of self-defense.[338]

Another area of contention for both lawyers and historians is the determination of "capitulation" and "occupation" with regard to the legal status of irregulars. Since a paramilitary force belonging to a government which has legally capitulated (for example France surrendering) may not subsequently bear arms again without violating both the Geneva and Hague Conventions (which the French Resistance did violate). Paramilitary forces, which claim the right to bear arms and the protections under Geneva must also adhere to the laws of war. By carrying arms following the surrender of their national government they fall under the civilian or military legal system of the occupying nation. Henceforth, any acts attributed to irregulars against non-military targets under these conditions may be legally labeled "terrorism." [339]

This clause under The Hague, Section III, Article 42 clearly states that "territory is considered occupied when it is actually placed under the authority of the hostile army," while Article 44 states that "any compulsion of the population of occupied territory to take part in military operations against its own country is prohibited," which means no paramilitaries may operate against an enemy force in its own country once that hostile force has invoked its own code of laws and established a replacement government in those regions.[340]

Likewise, the population under occupation is protected by all of the accords of both conventions as long as they remain passive and do not engage in active paramilitary operations, unless they are following the guidelines of Geneva 1929, Protocol I, Article 44, Section 3; Article 50, sections 1-3, and The Hague Convention, Section I, Chapter I, Articles 2-3 respectively.[341] Another major component of Hague stipulates in Section III, Article 50 that reprisals may not be "inflicted upon the population on account of the acts of individuals for which it cannot be regarded as collectively responsible."[342]

Within the German military there were senior commanders who knew that violations of the Laws of Warfare were being committed and argued against such practices, such as Lieutenant General Lemelsen, commander of *XLVII Panzer Corps*:

> I have observed that senseless shootings of both POWs and civilians have taken place. A Russian soldier who has been taken prisoner while wearing a uniform, and after he had put up a brave fight, has the right to decent treatment.[343]

The directive from *Army Group North* exemplifies the handling of the rising partisan problem on 31 January 1942:

The recent revival of partisan activity in the rear areas...demands that action be taken...with the greatest ruthlessness. Partisans should be destroyed wherever they appear, as should their hiding places, if they are not needed by our troops for accommodation.[344]

In contrast to this Draconian measure is the directive issued by the *Panzer Division "Grossdeutschland"* regarding the handling of prisoners and civilians:

> All commissars-politruks who fall into the hands of our troops are to be transferred immediately to the divisional intelligence section. Shooting by the troops after taking them prisoner is expressly forbidden.[345]

These opinions were not restricted to the highest ranks, as stated by Hans Hossfelder, who provided an interesting perspective on the war from a ground soldier's viewpoint:

> Many people have often wondered if we actually had standing orders to shoot women and children., and I know that there have been many denials regarding this by former SS members. However, it was unfortunately true. I can state that these types of orders were not as commonplace in my unit as others, obviously. When we speak about the partisans, it must be understood that these were of course criminals even under the Geneva and Hague Conventions, since they forfeited their noncombatant status upon taking up arms against us. Our handling of these people was considered within our right, although there were many excesses and outright war crimes committed against innocent people. This cannot be completely overlooked.[346]

Hossfelder's candid remarks about the conduct of the war from his experience cannot be considered unique among German veterans. The reality of the ruthless policy as executed by field commanders becomes more comprehensible (although not always justifiable) when one evaluates the method of the Soviet resistance from 1941–44. At that time most partisan units were absorbed into the Red Army and their leaders given the customary ranks. This action alone guaranteed their protection under Geneva and Hague, a least in theory.

Civilians operating as insurgents and bearing arms without the benefit of distinctive clothing, such as uniforms, were not protected under Geneva or Hague completely, as stipulated in The Hague Convention, Section I, Chapter 1, Article 1 and Geneva I and II, Protocol I, Article 44, section 3; Articles 66 (in total) and Article 50, Sections 1-3, and Geneva II, Article 13, sections 1-2.[347]

The soldiers involved with combating partisans were clearly reliant upon their superiors for guidance and leadership in this area, and this failure of commanders to personally take control of such actions against suspected or captured irregulars also fell under international law. A clear example of violations as previously outlined is cited in *The Einsatzgruppen Reports*:

Einsatzgruppe C:
Location: Rovno.

III. ACTIONS

On 5 July 1941 Jews were executed as reprisal for the bestial murder of the Ukrainian Nationalist leader Dr. Kirnychny in Rudki. The Ukrainian population on their part set the synagogue and Jewish houses on fire. 150 Ukrainians were found murdered in Stryj. In the course of the search it was possible to arrest 12 Communists who were responsible for the murder of the Ukrainians. It concerns 11 Jews and 1 Ukrainian who were shot with the participation of the entire population of Stryj. End message.[348]

These actions violated several rules of war. Analyzing the acts as described, one can clearly see that this message describes in detail how the laws were openly violated. The first and last sentences admitted that a reprisal killing took place, without regard for any appearance of a trial, thus violating Geneva 1929 Articles 2-3; Article 44, Section 2; Article 50, Sections 1-2; Article 51 in total (*see* Section 7 in particular); Protocol I of 1925 and ratified 1929; Article 75, Section 2c; Article 85, Sections 3-4; Article 86, Section 2; The Hague, Section II, Article 30 (on trials); The Hague, Section III, Article 50 (on reprisals).

The second sentence states that the following rules were violated: Geneva Protocol I, Article 48 in total; The Hague, Section II, Article 23; Section III, Articles 24 and 42 respectively.[349] Although the message came from *Einsatzgruppe C*, responsibility for the actions still falls under the German command authority, since they were the force in occupation and therefore the "legal" authority. Allowing such actions by one group of locals against another, even when the military remained uninvolved still violated all of the above Articles from Geneva and Hague, and qualified all participants and senior leadership for prosecution.

Given the violent nature of the counterinsurgency war in the Soviet Union, and the methods by which the Germans attempted to handle the growing problem, the amount of evidence provides the intent and direction of German policy. The following example is the order issued from Hitler through Keitel on 16 December 1942:

> The enemy has thrown into bandit warfare fanatic, Communist trained fighters who will not stop at any act of violence. The stake here is more than to be or not to be. This fight has nothing to with a soldier's chivalry nor with the decisions of the Geneva Conventions. If this fight against the bands, in the east as well as in the Balkans is not carried out with the most brutal means, the force at our disposal may in the future not last out to master this plague. The troops are therefore authorized and ordered in this struggle to take any measures without restriction, even against women and children if these are necessary for success. (Humanitarian) considerations of any kind are a crime against the German nation...[350]

IV. Aftermath

The post-war trials handed down both death and lengthy prison sentences to those convicted of war crimes, with several judgments ruled in absentia, such as in the case of Martin Bormann, SS Lieutenant Colonel Adolf Eichmann and SS Captain Dr. Josef Mengele. In addition, Bach-Zelewski agreed to testify against his more ruthless former comrades at Nuremberg, regarding their activities to be "excessive" in handling the civilian problem. Zelewski was convicted of war crimes while serving in Poland, yet the tribunal acquitted him of crimes against partisans while on duty in the USSR, as these actions were "deemed appropriate under the circumstances" under the existing Geneva Conventions of 1929.[351]

For those Germans captured by the Red Army, Soviet defense attorneys appointed to the cases of generals and senior officers argued that their clients were not guilty simply because they had followed orders: "In effect, numerous Germans known to be guilty of war crimes had by then fallen into Soviet hands, and many would be publicly executed, guilty or not, yet the Kremlin chose instead to set up a show trial in which exclusively Russian citizens were convicted."[352] The Soviets were less interested in "real justice" than in purging more of their own people after the war. Part of this was because of the unique nature of Soviet law; it did not apply to foreigners, including the Germans, yet collaborators or former POWs were within Stalin's reach.[353] POWs were considered traitors. This was not to be the case in the Western Allied tribunals, with exception to collaborators who were tried in fair courts. Several were tried in absentia, with the most famous non-German being Leon Degrelle, who escaped to Spain in May 1945. Degrelle, who lived in Spain until his death on 1 April 1994 was not charged with war crimes, but with treason by Belgium in three separate trials

Another German luminary whose actions were important and provide a similar interpretation of Geneva 1929 is *Luftwaffe* Colonel General Kurt Student, a former World War I aviator and the "Father of the Paratroops." He was on trial after the war for the killings of civilians on Crete in May 1941.[354]

During *Operation Mercury*, German paratroops landed in the olive groves near the village of Kandomari near the Tavronitus River, which was actually a dry gulch. Many Germans were injured after landing in the olive trees and were immediately set upon by the local villagers, who attacked them with kitchen and farm tools before they could disengage from their parachute harnesses. The investigating officer, *Luftwaffe* 2nd Lieutenant Karl-Lothar Schulz, upon discovering the massacre contacted his superior, Colonel Bruno Braeuer, who in turn informed his superior, Major General Ludwig Heilmann. Kurt Student was immediately informed at his base in Salonika, Greece via radio.[355] Student replied almost immediately and issued specific orders as to the conduct of the troops and the pursuant investigation, stating precisely how the procedure was to occur: "All operations are to carried out with great speed, leaving aside all formalities and certainly disposing of special courts... These are not for beasts and murderers."[356]

The order was carried out and the villagers of Kandomari paid the ultimate price for their actions. Firing squads eliminated the civilians found with German equipment and bloody weapons following a sweep of the homes and farms, with the event captured on film by *Kriegsberichter* (War Correspondent) Franz-Peter Wexler on 2 June 1941.[357] Following these events Student issued the clearly illegal directive that "ten Cretans will be shot for every soldier killed by civilians."[358] At Student's trial, his attorney argued that his client's actions were properly in line with the literal translation of Geneva 1929, Article 2. Student was convicted, although this line of defense saw his conviction overturned on appeal. Bruno Braeuer would not be so lucky. He was tried and executed in Crete in 1947 for the same offense, and his grave is located at the German cemetery at Maleme.

Another more recent event was the trial of former *Waffen SS* Captain Erich Priebke, who had been living under his own name in Argentina and discovered in 1994.[359] Priebke was eventually arrested for the murders of 335 civilians suspected of partisan activity in the Ardeatine Caves near Rome in 1944. Italian partisans had been attacking German troops, killing several, and wreaking havoc as US Army Major General Mark W. Clark's 5th Army approached Rome. Priebke's defense was based upon the order issued by *Luftwaffe* Field Marshal Albert Kesselring, Commander-in-Chief of the Italian Front (known as the *Gustav Line*), ordering all partisans killed upon capture.[360] Priebke was ironically acquitted in the Italian court to where he had been extradited. However, he also faced trial in Germany for the same offense, where he drew a fifteen-year sentence. That judgment that was later reduced to five years confinement in July 1997.[361]

The fates of most the *Einsatzgruppen* leaders were similar to that of the other major war criminals, as listed by French L. MacLean.[362] Seven senior leaders; Paul Blobel, Dr. Wilhelm Fuchs, Dr. Erich Isselhorst, August von Meyszner, Erich Naumann, Otto Ohlendorf, and Dr. Eberhard Schiengarth were sentenced to death, while "seventy-one received lesser sentences ranging from less than five years incarceration to life imprisonment."[363]

The post-war trials also brought out much of the truth behind the orders which were issued, how they were complied with, and what was actually on the minds of the officers involved regarding their "partisan war" if their post-war testimony can be believed. The testimony of General Hans Roettiger, former Chief of Staff to the 4th *Army* and *Army Group Center* in an affidavit submitted to the criminal court stated:

> I have now come to realize that the order from the highest authorities for the harshest conduct of partisan war can only have been intended to make possible a ruthless liquidation of Jews and other undesirable elements

by using for this purpose the military struggle of the Army against the partisans.[364]

General Heusinger, the former Chief of Operations Section for the General Staff stated:

> It had always been my personal opinion that the treatment of the civilian population and the methods of anti-partisan warfare in operational areas presented the highest political and military leaders with a welcomed opportunity of carrying out their plans, namely the systematic extermination of Slavism and Jewry.[365]

IV. CONSIDERATIONS

The laws of war, as stipulated by Geneva and Hague were in effect during the Second World War and applicable to all parties in some form, whether these nations were signatories or not. German leaders understood the basics of the laws, as proven by the dissent displayed by the select few mentioned in this book. This is demonstrated by the open challenges to the laws by senior military and political officials in their subsequent defenses at their trials.

The actions of Germany during the war in the USSR were, for the most part illegal, and this fact cannot be legitimately challenged. What may be challenged is how legitimate *were* the various individual interpretations of the existing protocols in handling the irregulars, given the sometimes conflicting language contained in Geneva and Hague. This matter of "unclear" legality was mentioned by Kesselring, who referenced Articles 1 and 2 of The Hague Convention of 1907 regarding civilian irregular activity in the attempt to justify his own actions.[366] It was due to these very circumstances that the laws were redefined in the post-war Geneva Convention of 1949. The purpose was to extend greater protection to irregulars and civilians, reduce ambiguity and hold those who violated the laws accountable.[367]

The end analysis supports the contention that, regardless of the understanding individuals may have had regarding the language of the law, the German leadership and military were required to follow to the letter those laws which were clear, and provide the "benefit of the doubt" where their was such ambiguity.

If Germany had followed these actions, the resulting insurgency problems would have been less severe. However, had German actions been in accordance with the very spirit of these two international conventions, this would have ironically violated the very tenants of Hitler's concept of National Socialism and his desire for complete European domination.

The following chapter details the illegal orders issued, the primary persons and units involved, and the ambiguity of the laws as interpreted. Also included is the propaganda effort by the Germans in converting the populations as the war demanded amendments to the strict racial policy.

Chapter 3. Illegal Orders, Directives, and Propaganda

This chapter details the existence and application of German racial and economic policies, the effect upon the USSR, and the insurgents who fought their invaders. Included are the various propaganda campaigns directed at both the insurgents and the general Soviet population. Also analyzed are the irrational racial policies proper, ever-changing to suit the needs of a German military bled white of manpower and suffering from labor shortages.

Economic exploitation, the use of forced slave labor, and the effects of occupation would color and hinder the German military's perspective in developing a universally appropriate counterinsurgency doctrine. Propaganda is one of the most useful tools in any arsenal, either political or military, and the Germans were masters at its employment and it was considered as useful as bullets and guns.

Interestingly, given what is historically accepted regarding *Nazi* policies of enslavement and exploitation, the following hypocritical comment from Hitler is relevant: "Bolshevism practices a lie of the same nature [referring to Christianity], when it claims to bring liberty to men, whereas in reality it seeks only to enslave them."[368] In addition, Germany's economic interests in Russia extended beyond the bountiful Ukrainian breadbasket. Of equal concern was the petroleum of the Caucasus:

> I think there's still petroleum in thousands of places. As for coal, we know we're reducing the natural reserves, and that in so doing we are creating

---

65

gaps in the sub-soil. But as for petroleum, it may be that the lakes from which we are drawing are constantly renewed from invisible reservoirs.[369]

David Welch argues in his basic point that "propaganda *is* and *was* more effective when supporting or exhorting existing beliefs and values, as opposed to creating new and different concepts, which are alien to the masses."[370] The same is true in either creating support against enemies or bolstering the morale and convictions of one's own population. Germany painted the war in the east a "crusade, a war of ideologies, in which all decent conventions were ignored,"[371] as well as operating with the philosophy that "the idea of treating war as anything other than the harshest means of settling questions of very existence is ridiculous."[372] Their political paradigm proved that point; the military and police hammered the point home.

OKW Directive No. 33 issued on 23 July 1941 by the Chief of the General Staff (*Chef der Generalstabs*), Field Marshal Walther von Brauchitsch, provided German forces with the authority to kill at will and use terror as a primary tool in handling the populations.[373] However, it was also stipulated that these measures were to be a "direct response" to insurgency action on occasion, as opposed to a primary method of operation, which was at best ambiguous.[374]

Adding further to the confusion with even more conflicting information, *OKW* issued the Hostage Decree on 16 September 1941 (which was instituted all across Europe), stating that fifty to a hundred civilians was a "fair exchange" for every German killed by the partisans. As stated in the previous chapter this act was illegal under international law.[375] Another *OKW* directive was later issued on 24 March 1942, concerning propaganda suggestions from subordinate units in the handling of the locals, which in turn challenged the authority of the *Einsatzgruppen, Sonderkommando* and Reich Labor officials. This directive stated:

> The troops are to be reminded at frequent and regular intervals that firm but fair and correct treatment of the population is the best weapon for maintaining security and keeping the partisans down. They are also to be reminded that mindless and violent requisitioning, particularly against persons protected by German pass (local militia men, informers) can effectively destroy all efforts at pacification. Any officer or man who transgresses this order can expect the harshest punishment.[376]

The authority of the special death squads emanated from *Reichsfuehrer-SS* Heinrich Himmler, who directed his subordinate Reinhard Heydrich to issue orders for the use of locals recruited to assist in carrying out their tasks due to limited German manpower.[377]

For Hitler, the war against Stalin was personal, and despite whenever other fronts were active or threatened he always had his primary focus upon the Soviet Union. Hitler issued dozens of personal decrees regarding the partisan war. Many were contradictory with his own established policies and existing OKH and OKW decrees, as well as being juxtaposed to the efforts of his various departments and provincial governors.

The first decree regarding the partisan war and population handling due to the positive propaganda recruitment platform was Directive No. 43, issued on 18 August 1942, followed by the OKW directive of 11 November 1942. Both suggested "just treatment" be used and subsequently authorized the active recruitment of civilians against the partisans.[378] This was in direct response to the plethora of Communist propaganda issued the previous autumn that had to be countered.[379] However, these concepts were cultivated not for the humanitarian benefit of the Soviets themselves, but to further Germany's sprawling agenda through conquest, occupation and enervation. In Hitler's own words:

> If popularity and force unite, and if thus combined they are able to last over a certain period of time, then an authority can arise on an even more solid basis, an authority of tradition. If finally popularity, force, and tradition combine, then an authority may be regarded as unshakeable.[380]

However, even given all these directives, the 18 August Directive still mandated that officers had the authority to shoot prisoners and suspected persons.[381] Another directive issued to the *183rd Security Regiment* on 4 July 1943 stated: "Evacuation, reprisals and destruction of villages only with the division's [meaning the commander's] authorization."[382]

This directive was followed by an order issued on 3 December 1942, regarding the difference in the handling of partisans who deserted with their weapons prior to a counter-insurgency operation, in which case these people were to be treated as POWs. Those surrendering either during or after an engagement were to be shot.[383] The Germans understood the value of pre-emptive propaganda:

> An enemy with only the prospect of death staring him in the face will fight to the end bitterly and tenaciously, thereby inflicting greater loss upon us... Amongst the partisans are a large number of amoral fellow travelers, and the best means of weakening and undermining partisan morale is to target

this particular group with an unrestricted propaganda effort enticing it to desert.[384]

The confusion was to only increase. As stated by Gerald Reitlinger:

> It seems to be assumed that the nature of orders was clear and unequivocal, that they were all 'official orders' which any German must unquestioningly obey wherever and however he might be subject to the authority of the State, *Wehrmacht*, the Party and, last but not least, the *Fuehrer*. In fact, however, the nature of the orders issued under the Third Reich was by no means so clear and unambiguous. The legitimacy of orders issued and accordingly the duty to obey were based upon two entirely different/concepts.[385]

Hitler's personal will regarding mass murder was followed by his chief lieutenants, especially Heinrich Himmler, Reinhard Heydrich, Hermann Goering, and Josef Goebbels, who felt that the proper attitude was needed amongst the military, and especially within the *Waffen SS* and Army. Likewise, many officials attempted to comply with the conflicting directives. Some officers like Erich Koch, Ferdinand Schoerner, and Walter Model (and others) used the most ruthless measures.

Other officers, such as Wilhelm Bittrich, Otto Kumm and Leon Degrelle ordered leniency, such as Russian women being treated decently. Requisitioning was to be minimal, and village leaders were to be the direct civilian authority in handling situations. Families were to be allowed the minimum necessities for survival.

Above all else, in order to facilitate the labor drive, agricultural collections, and minimize defections to the partisans (*Bandenbekaempfung* or "galvanizing of the bandit war"), violence was to be avoided if possible.[386] However, German legitimacy was also damaged in this regard by the actions of their Hungarian allies, who committed acts that made even the hardened and racially-motivated SS and SD (more concerned with ideological problems than military concerns)[387] shudder, and which damaged what little progress had often been made:

> For example, as a general rule they [the Hungarians] beat up all road menders and foremen, arrest people with German passes and often beat up the inhabitants of entire villages. The [population's] willingness to work is suffering greatly as a result of all this.[388]

Many Germans were unmoved. Himmler felt that with the proper indoctrination his men would carry out their orders with less morale debilitation, since:

> They recognized that Nazi policies challenged traditional or conventional standards of morality. They wanted the weight of authority to override any qualms of conscience or simple distaste for unpleasant tasks."[389]

Himmler apparently knew that his men were not simply murderers waiting to be unleashed in all cases, as stated by Breitman:

> On December 12 [1941] he composed a secret order addressed to all higher SS and Police Leaders and their subordinates, as well as to SS officers in conquered territories in the east. He stressed that commanders and superior officers has a "holy duty" to ensure that their men did not suffer damage to their character or spirit from carrying out just death sentences on enemies of the German people.[390]

Historical records illustrate how the concept of removal and even liquidation of targeted populations accelerated as the war progressed. The initial *Einsatzgruppen* murders, which were unique in 1941, soon became business as usual throughout the USSR, with the increasing activity supported by similarly increasing propaganda through the use of *Propaganda Staffeln*.[391] The rules covered such topics as "justification" and "pacification" duties, as cited by Mommsen:

> By contrast the spurious justifications of the *Einsatzgruppen* for the murder of the Jewish population, ranging from housing shortages and the danger of unsanitary conditions through partisan warfare reflect their need to justify a crime that went beyond the casual connection of racial-biological anti-Semitism.[392]

Supporting this argument is Hannes Heer's belief that officers initiated the killing, under the pretext of resistance in order to carry out the extermination directives.[393]

Military effectiveness was interpreted as either evacuation or annihilation, sometimes both, such as the early and brutal example set by the 8th SS *Cavalry Brigade "Florian Geyer"* (later becoming a full division, by 1943, and commanded by SS Major General Herman Fegelein) during their operations in the Pripet Marshes in 1941, although this was not an *Einsatzgruppen* unit.[394] The belief in evacuating villages under threat of partisan conversion is stated by Captain Meyer of the *221st Security Division*:

> Evacuating villages in the bandit area has a detrimental effect upon the bandits. It prevents the bandits from filling their ranks with the inhabitants. The supply of food, which came primarily from the inhabitants of the evacuated villages, is no longer possible. When the bandits are prevented from harvesting and exploiting the best land, this affects their supply very badly. The bandits' mood is greatly impaired...[395]

The official record from the *221st Security Division*, which contains the statement written by SS Major Karl Haupt on 8 July 1941, supports this concept:

It has been firmly established that, wherever Jews live, the cleansing of the area encounters difficulties. For the Jews support the training of partisan groups and the destabilizing of the area by escaped Russian soldiers. The immediate and complete evacuation of all male Jews from the villages north of Bialowiecza has therefore been ordered.[396]

The structure of the *Einsatzgruppen* was different than other military formations, even though both units often worked together, with soldiers from both groups transferring to the other.[397] The *Einsatzgruppen* formations were even distinct from the *Waffen SS*, as the commanders of these various units carried higher rank than normal for formations of this size. The example is listed from smallest to largest.[398]

Einheit (unit/squad), numbering between eight to twelve men commanded by either a senior *SS/SD* sergeant or lieutenant. Squads were normally commanded by sergeants and staff sergeants.

Teilkommando (platoon), four platoons, each with thirty to forty men. Normal units were commanded by a lieutenant, but these were usually commanded by a *SS/SD* captain or major.

Einsatzkommando (company), made up of four *Einheite*, commanded by a *SS/SD* major through colonel, instead of a captain.

Einsatzgruppe (battalion), made up of four field and one headquarters company for administration purposes. This size unit would normally be commanded by a lieutenant colonel, although senior *SS/SD* colonels and generals commanded these.[399]

How Himmler expected these men who, before the war were more than likely normal, upstanding, moral members of their societies, to murder civilians and prisoners without suffering any debilitating effects, as well as maintain some semblance of perceived legitimacy and self-respect, is inexplicable.

Part of the program of justification was the continuous imposition of rules and laws further reducing Jews, insurgents, and others as illegitimate human beings without protection. This removed their status as non-combatants, and is found in the documents of *Feldkommandantur* (Field Commandant Command) *528 (V)*. This document describes the measures used to accuse Jews of anything and everything, and thereby establish the precedent for retaliation under the pretext of anti-partisan operations.[400] Part of this propaganda included the attempted alienation of the Soviet populations from the "Jews and Bolsheviks," thus uniting the various peoples under a common cause:

> The Jews and Bolsheviks are mercilessly leading millions of your broth-
> ers, fathers and sons to certain death, in order to save their own miserable
> skins. So long as life is treating him well, the Jew-Bolshevik is unmoved by
> the worst sufferings of the people.[401]

> Supervising 'Jewish councils, marking Jews out, banning ritual slaughter,
> putting Jews to work, criminal penalties (for Jews), confiscation of Jewish
> property, and "accommodation of Jews in special areas."[402]

Advertising to the military provided further justification that even unarmed people were dangerous:

> In parts these people are prisoners who have escaped from or been left be-
> hind by the POW columns marching through the locality; in part, they've
> been sent to the rear by front-line troops accompanied not by German per-
> sonnel but only by the general instruction "go west". Most were wander-
> ing around weaponless. However, this doesn't rule out the possibility that
> wandering individuals, particularly officers, join partisan groups that they
> stumble across.[403]

The fact remains that the German soldier was also a German citizen, and
his nation's policies, right or wrong were expected to be followed without
question. Combined with the exposure to the barrage of anti-Bolshevik and
anti-Semitic propaganda, the fear of the unknown enemy, as well as anti-
German Communist propaganda perhaps explains why so many soldiers
found themselves lured into the killing. The following is an extract from the
Mitteilungen fuer die Truppen (Memorandum for the Troops), which perpetuated the propaganda:[404]

> Anyone who has ever looked at the face of a red commissar knows what
> the Bolsheviks are like...We would insult the animals if we described these
> mostly Jewish men as beasts. They are the embodiment of the Satanic and
> insane hatred against the whole of noble humanity...The masses, whom
> they have sent to their deaths by making use of all means at their dispos-
> al, such as ice cold terror and insane incitement, would have brought to
> an end all meaningful life, had this eruption not been dammed at the last
> moment.[405]

One attempt at checking the potential for morale debilitation among the
Germans was the recruitment of foreigners to perform these tasks, which
was also part and parcel with the labor policy.[406] Another method was selective recruitment of the Germans themselves:

> The men of the various *Sonderkommandos* who carried out these ideological
> orders were not in fact chosen at random from the broad mass of the *Waffen
> SS*; they were a clearly definable circle, specially devoted to their singular
> and highly secret task.[407]

One of the men given this mission of recruitment of foreign killers was
SS Lieutenant General Arthur Seyss-Inquart and his associates. This ruthless

application of economic and agricultural exploitation, as well as his slave labor practices earned him a place on the gallows after the war.[408] As stated by Breitman:

> On 25 July [1940] Himmler had authorized the creation of auxiliary police forces from the reliable non-Communist elements among the Ukrainians, Estonians, Latvians, Lithuanians, and Belorussians...called *Schutzmannschaften* (defense forces). The creation of *Schutzmannschaften* and their future use as executioners reflected more than just a shortage of German policemen. Whereas Himmler, Daluege, Bach-Zelewski, and some other high officials had some concern for the morale of German police, they did not much care what happened psychologically to the non-Germans as long as there were enough of them to carry out their appointed tasks.[409]

Another officer involved in the early days of the foreign recruitment for the development of counterinsurgency doctrine was Captain Nicholas von Grote, a Lithuanian by birth and former soldier in the Imperial Army of Tsar Nicholas II of Russia. His education at various universities and fluency in English, French, German, Russian, and every Baltic language and dialect witnessed his recruitment into the *Abwehr* as a *Sonderfuehrer* (Special Leader)[410] under the direction of Colonel (later Brigadier General) Henning von Tresckow, who answered directly to General Reinhard Gehlen.[411]

The Reich Labor Service (*Reich Arbeitsdienst*) was established on 26 June 1935 by Dr. Robert Ley,[412] who was directly responsible for the bulk of the forced labor used by Germany, and in particular by Dr. Fritz Todt and his *Organization Todt* prior to and during the war.[413] An integral part of the labor program was Fritz Sauckel, *Gauleiter* of Thuringia and Plenipotentiary General, who had almost limitless power to harvest the peoples of Europe for slave labor.[414] Sauckel was ruthlessly enthusiastic in his duties and scoured all of Europe for slaves as increased wartime necessity demanded more laborers, thus heaping greater responsibility upon both political and military leaders to assist in this task.

These pressures included commanders focusing upon those deemed suitable for labor, and those more suited to military auxiliary work. This had the effect of hindering the *Einsatzgruppen's* sole task of focusing upon certain racial and political targets for elimination, thus weakening their already strained and over-stretched command and operational capabilities.[415] In addition, the simultaneous *Wehrmacht* operations also hindered the labor effort:

> The various military operations have brought no relief whatsoever, and German influence continues to disintegrate. Forced labor recruitment is having an extremely bad propaganda effect. It would be better to carry out

labor recruitment in unpacified areas, so as to show the peaceful areas that they may work under German protection.[416]

Ironically, the policy would initially exclude Jews in general from technical labor, only relocation or execution by directives, although many Jews were in fact pressed into manual slave labor where they died.[417] However, Jews were just one of many targets for the labor policy enforced by the *Arbeitseinsatz*:

> When asked, the unit responsible for agriculture in Bobriusk declared that there are still significant labor reserves in its rural areas, who can only be described as "surplus mouths". The *Fuehrer* has declared that recruiting labor from the eastern territories is vital to the war effort. All over German occupied Europe the last available resources of labor are being mobilized, by force when necessary, if they have not been mobilized already. Nowhere has this been more thoroughly realized than in the Reich itself, where our women are being put to heavy physical work in armaments factories and other concerns. It seems quite unacceptable, in view of the situation, that the Russian population be exempted. The Russians are used to being forced to work, and if other means fail then they should be forced using the harshest measures.[418]

Grote and Tresckow understood that part of their job was the analysis and incorporation of the ethnically suitable within the military. They also examined the labor policies and those groups targeted for exploitation.[419] As laborers were needed for the Reich, so were military auxiliary volunteers needed for the anti-partisan war, and therefore a more constructive propaganda effort was needed. This became exceedingly evident following the commonly understood intelligence reports regarding the population's views on the immediate future:

The successes of the Red Army and the rising partisan activity in the rear areas, skillfully exploited and exaggerated by enemy propaganda, have almost totally destroyed the population's belief in the victory of German arms.[420]

> In every village the population was in a good mood. Everywhere the bandits were welcomed and fed, and so far as I could see this was all done willingly and without any pressure from the bandits. The bandits had brought two accordions with them, which they brought out at every village they rested in for the villagers to dance to. The villagers didn't see at all intimidated when they chatted with the bandits. The bandits too seemed in a remarkably good mood; I was made to watch while they danced to harmonica music.[421]

Grote understood how to convince the peasantry, appealing to their desire for freedom from Stalin and exploiting their love for the land. In fact, it was through his office that the original February 1942 proclamation to "break up the Soviet collective farming system" was reintroduced under the program resembling sharecropping, thus providing something resembling hope to the people.[422]

In addition, the offer of protection to people threatened by the Communist political officers and partisans, if they did not halt their work for the Germans, would have been well received by those already predisposed to a pro-German orientation.[423] According to Shepherd, this German maneuver "left the [Soviet] partisan propaganda machine momentarily stunned."[424] However, Germany still planned on exploiting the farms for their own war effort.[425] This fact would create food shortages that pushed the populations into the partisan camps despite the best German overtures:[426]

> As far as agriculture is concerned, the security situation has deteriorated again. In the Bobriusk area just fourteen per cent of the *Wolloste* remain pacified, in the Gomel and Klinzt area just thirty-seven per cent. By night the entire region becomes the partisans' area of operations. From every forest fires burn and rockets climb into the air to light the way for the Red Air Force.

Of equal (if not greater) importance was the peoples' love of religion and freedom of worship, which Stalin had taken away.[427] Allowing the population to practice their Russian Orthodox religion (including Islam in the Caucasus and parts of the Crimea) proved to pay dividends, as Stalin had many reasons to fear his own people. The freedom of religion denied o Germans a home was one of the more invaluable propaganda tools available to the Germans.[428] Hitler recognized this fact very early: "It is doubtful whether anything can be done in Russia without the help of the Orthodox priest. It's the priest who has been able to reconcile the Russian to the fatal necessity of work-promising him more happiness in another world."[429] Stalin later corrected this by easing religious constraints himself as a counter to the German effort.

> For years the Russian Orthodox Christians were forced to live a subterranean existence. Churches and monasteries were closed down and their communities disbanded. Before the revolution there were 50,000 priests and 163 bishops in the Russian Church. By 1941 there were around one hundred priests and only seven bishops. Their lives were closely monitored by the regime. Thousands of practicing Christians received communion in secret masses, but the risks they ran were enormous...Stalin, the ex-seminarian...told the British ambassador that, in his way, "he believed in God." The word began to appear in *Pravda* with a capital letter.[430]

In response and in contradiction to this reality *Organization Todt* began using its massive slave labor force to rebuild damaged churches and erect new ones.[431] The Propaganda Ministry began supporting the clergy, and the results were remarkable:

> There was an Orthodox church in Borisov. The Bolsheviks had used it as a store. The *Wehrmacht* restored it to its proper use, and this is not as "an opium for the people," but because, thank God, to act like this has always been an army tradition. The church was decked out with flowers and greenery, the approaches spread with clean white sand. The locals came out in their best clothes. The field marshal [Fedor von Bock] and his officers attended the opening service. There were thousands crowded into the square in front of the church and into the streets leading off it. The service was one of thanks and prayer. The people could feel that the conquerors themselves bowed down to the Lord of All...Many brought children, aged between one and twelve, to be baptized. As most of the Orthodox clergy had been evacuated, if not murdered, in many areas there was a shortage of priests. But a number of Catholic priests from eastern Poland and White Russia [Belorussia] had followed on after the *Wehrmacht* on foot. They spoke Russian, and thanks to them baptisms, marriages and burial services were conducted without regard to race or denomination.[432]

This common sense approach to handling the populations was in itself ingenious, both from a political and military perspective, although it was overshadowed by the horrors that had preceded the program and continued unabated. In many cases the clergy were recruited as spies and saboteurs, or as agents to counter Soviet propaganda due to their hatred of Stalin.[433]

Many of these priests had maintained an active and integrated anti-Communist network throughout Eastern Europe ever since the revolution, and were thus invaluable to the German effort.[434] In general, German anti-Communist propaganda was considered "well received" by these organizations.[435]

One problem facing the Germans was the Soviet youth, who were by end large idealistic and patriotic "because they had never known anything before the Soviet Union, and also because they felt robbed of their prospects by the hardship and upheaval which the German invasion had brought in its wake."[436] One German opinion emanated from the administrative section of the *203rd Security Division* regarding the handling of the people:

> The Russian is as trusting as a child and wants to be treated as such. He is devoted and obedient and is used to poverty and privation. If however he feels his trust is being betrayed or sees that promises are not being fulfilled, he becomes treacherous and deceitful and rears up against his master.[437]

These actions were the genesis of a new branch created on 14 March 1942, the *Wehrmacht Propaganda IV (WPR IV)*, initially commanded by Army Colonel Hans Martin as a liaison between the Propaganda Ministry and *OKW*.[438] The success of this massive undertaking was reflected in the *SD* reports from

June-October 1942.[439] Under the direction of this particular office in conjunction with the Propaganda Ministry, the effort was launched. In July 1943 propaganda units distributed 178,000 newspapers and magazines, 60,050 brochures, 250,000 placards and 813,700 leaflets.[440]

Additionally, the establishment of Russian language radio broadcasts proved to be arguably the most effective in certain regions, although few Russians had access to wireless sets.[441] However, despite these efforts there were attacks "upon the propaganda tactics which had been determined by higher-level policy makers, slating the slogan 'the battle against Bolshevism' as totally inadequate for propaganda purposes."[442] "Spoken propaganda, which exerts a direct influence upon its recipient, proved particularly effective. When skillfully presented it strikes a chord among the population and banishes the people's initial reservations."[443]

By 1943 a large part of this effort was personally attended to by Gehlen (then a colonel), who wanted "better treatment for partisan deserters,"[444] culminating in the Basic Order Nr. 13a issued by *OKW*, which stated that deserters located outside of the combat zone "were to receive preferential treatment," making the effort to distinguish between threats and non-threats,[445] and "partisans surrendering in the course of combat would not be shot, but accorded the same treatment as prisoners of war."[446] Under international law at that time, they were accorded no such legal protection, and the SS was stacked with lawyers to point this fact out.

These directives sounded decent on the surface, yet one must also remember that POWs were not always guaranteed safety upon surrendering. Immediate death, slow starvation or cruel labor was most likely their fate.[447]

In another twist of irony, in keeping with his primary concern over agricultural expropriation and its being interrupted by irregular activity, Reich Marshal Hermann Goering issued his own directive on the partisan war 26 October 1942:

> 1. When combating partisans and clearing of partisan infested areas, all livestock to hand is to be removed to a safe area and the food reserves likewise cleared away to deprive the partisans of them.
>
> 2. The entire male and female workforce which may be liable for *Arbeitseinsatz* is to be forcibly recruited and taken to the plenipotentiary for *Arbeitseinsatz* to be used either in the rear or the homeland. Children are to be specially accommodated in camps in the rear.[448]

In addition to the previously mentioned officers, Russian born Lieutenant Emil Duerksen joined the office as director of Russian Language Propaganda, which was delivered by sea, air, artillery, radio, mobile loudspeakers, and even couriers.[449] So effective was this method in specific regions, such as Belorussia, it was copied by Ilya Ehrenberg for Soviet use against German troops under the direction of Soviet Marshal Fedor Ivanovich Tolbukhin, yet this effort met with little success.[450] Despite the forward momentum, there were still great gaps in the differences between theory and practical application of specific policies and agendas:

> The enormous moral credit, which the German *Wehrmacht* possessed at the time of the invasion has almost completely evaporated, and belief in German victory destroyed. This is due to our mistaken perceptions of the Russians, in particular our tendency to draw no distinction between Russians in general and Bolsheviks in particular.[451]

All of these Germans previously mentioned would prove pivotal in attempting to alter the stereotypical mindset of their superiors and subordinates. They would become primary members in the establishment of the foreign anti-partisan auxiliary forces soon to be placed under the command of Lieutenant General Andrei Vlasov. Vlasov's force of defectors would be the greatest success story of the German propaganda campaign during the war, although still not as successful as its creators would have wished.[452]

Duerksen was also responsible for working with exiled Russian Alexander Stepanovich Kazantsev, a devout follower of the self-appointed leader of the NTS (*Natsionalno Trudovoi Soyuz*), or National Labor Union leader Viktor Baidalakov.[453] This organization was based in Belgrade, Yugoslavia with departments in Budapest, Paris, and Bucharest and completely staffed by expatriate Russians since the early 1920s.[454] This became the nucleus for Field Marshal Gunther von Kluge's "experts" recruited for the front and support units.[455] The platform for recruitment was thus outlined. Deserters and converted POWs were to receive better than average treatment, as well as rations equal to the *Ostarbeiter* (Eastern Workers) to surpass even "their Red Army experience."[456]

Part of the "hearts and minds" campaign was the use of propaganda films showing happy laborers and "open letters" from the workers themselves.[457] One method of promoting the proper atmosphere was to make the working conditions better; better food, lighter work schedules and "more comfortable transportation during the winter months."[458] Other methods included the distribution of free alcohol to recruit more workers[459] and providing entertainment such as theaters and plays.[460] Part of the propaganda program was to instill pride and confidence among the Russians:

> The population needs particularly to be made to understand that it cannot stand idly by, but must make its contribution to the building of a new Europe...It must also be made to see that life in Germany is good to the Russian worker, and that the *Arbeitseinsatz* is only for a limited period.[461]

These events gathered some support from the locals: "Everywhere the population goes out of its way to support us,"[462] although such actions inevitably depleted the male populations in certain areas. His occurred either through "volunteerism" or forced recruitment (or being shot for non-compliance),[463] which sometimes created problems during harvest time. This support came at the realistic expectation that the locals would alter their allegiance whenever necessary to ensure their survival due to both German and partisan methods:[464]

> The farmers' attitude is that they'd gladly help us and have no reason to be pleased at the arrival of the Germans, but unfortunately "nothing doing". The Germans frighten them that much. Peasants are even threatened with the burning down of their villages if they supply the partisans.[465]

Much of this support came from the knowledge that Gehlen, along with several senior commanders had "advocated a degree of self governing for the occupied territories."[466] However, the continual forced labor and murders weakened even this major step in reducing counter-insurgency threats. So precarious was the situation the following intelligence summary was sent:

> The population's resistance (to *Arbeitseinsatz*) was so strong that the recruitment in July 1943 of those born in 1925/6 was a total failure in most areas of the division's jurisdiction. This was despite every conceivable propaganda effort by the division itself.[467]

Hitler had no intention of providing a comfortable or even secure environment for his conquered subjects. Every device of a seemingly "humanitarian nature" had an ultimate end: the service of *Nazi* Germany. Even Tresckow and Gehlen knew that no amount of religious or humanitarian assistance could halt the insurgency campaign as long as the death squads and plunder went unchecked.[468]

One example was the order issued from the 207th *Security Division*: "The fight is to be executed ruthlessly. It is a question of exterminating partisans, not taking them prisoner, unless this is necessary for gleaning information."[469] However, "Gehlen [while supporting humanitarian overtures]...

maintained that while he felt it necessary to woo the population more effectively, he fully acknowledged its racial inferiority."[470]

All of Germany's major companies needed workers, such as IG Farben, Porsche, Krupp, Bayer, BMW, Daimler-Benz, Junkers, Messerschmitt, Bloehm und Voss, and many others. These firms demanded that any and all potential labor needed to be exploited.[471] Those deemed unsuitable for work went straight to the death camps, while those selected for work were in fact "worked to death."[472] In fact, the slogan "Slavs are Slaves" appeared in all of Krupp's factories as a reminder to the Germans not to mingle with the subhuman elements, further reducing German perceived legitimacy in the eyes of the foreigners.[473]

As stated by Norman Rich: "The labor force recruited in this manner was hardly the most efficient or reliable, while the repercussions of such methods of recruitment were catastrophic for the German occupation governments."[474] In addition, as more civilians fled the Germans, more laborers had to be recruited within the *Banditengebieten* ("Bands' Regions" or "Bandits' Regions") as it was known, which increased the level and chances of direct confrontation.[475] Mommsen also stated the reality of the labor program:

> After all, work camps of all kinds, voluntary labor service, compulsory labor and ultimately the practice of working people to death were the civilian counterpart of military service, which sent millions to the slaughter.[476]

The rise of Hitler and the *Nazis* were the catalyst, while the war they created provided the necessary opportunity to create and execute their plans of destruction and murder. Often the political and military entities were at odds with each other as how to best implement specific orders, handle not only the killings, but also the mental and emotional welfare of their men. Orders were often conflicting and changing, especially when field reports to higher authority went unheeded or were ignored, thus creating confusion, if not ambivalence among the commanders and soldiers in the field.

Often Hitler did not believe his own intelligence reports, thus delaying actions in order to have additional and corroborating information supplied, especially if the information presented was not good news. One such event was the report delivered by Reinhard Gehlen to Hitler during his meeting in late November 1942. Gehlen gave Hitler projected figures on Soviet military and materiel replacements, as well as a report on the rising insurgency. Hitler did not believe the reports, given the high numbers of Soviet killed and captured to date, and he dismissed his intelligence officer in anger, an event witnessed by Hans Baur, Karl Wolff, and Adolf Galland, all of whom were present.[477]

Captain Wilfried Strik-Strikfeldt was on the ground floor of the counter-insurgency program's propaganda operations, and he related a similar event regarding Hitler and his inability to comprehend the truth:

> On 12 January 1945 the Red Army launched a general offensive from the Kurischer Hof to the Carpathians. I learned later that General Gehlen had not only provided accurate details of all enemy dispositions, but had also pinpointed the sectors of attack and foretold the probable objectives. He had produced a remarkable report, which Hitler proceeded to describe as "bluff" on the part if the Staff. I was told Gehlen presented the report personally to Hitler in the presence of [Colonel General Heinz] Guderian. Presumably Gehlen too would have been dismissed, if his predictions had not been so quickly and completely confirm.[478]

There were many operators in the field who knew that the best method of conversion was propaganda, such as a certain "Major Schmidt" of the *203rd Security Division*, who promoted the concept of giving the population hope, yet provided his own thoughts on the process:

> If we could offer some kind of goal to aim for then we could conduct a successful propaganda effort. It should nevertheless be remembered that the Russian has absolutely no love for the Germans, and he never will. He feels, maybe unconsciously, that he is inferior to the Germans, and this inferiority complex has been strengthened by Bolshevik influence.[479]

In addition to the complexity of utilizing propaganda as a useful tool, there was another viewpoint that was taken to heart and clearly stated by *Rear Army Area 582* regarding the use of captured and defecting Soviets: "No prisoner enters the *Wehrmacht's* service out of idealism. The reason he's prepared to is his terror of the POW camp and the prospect of a better life alongside German troops."[480] Hans Mommsen also related the problems and lack of communication between the various departments, and the inability of Hitler to clearly see the problems facing his military:

> Under wartime conditions the information gap between ministries in Berlin and the *Fuehrer's* headquarters assumed astonishing proportions. This was further aggravated by Hitler's increasing refusal to take on board any information which was unpleasant or contradicted his picture of events. He finally issued instructions that he was not to be burdened with news of this kind any longer.[481]

Richard Overy also details Hitler's approach to this problem:

> The easy victories persuaded Hitler that he had an inspirational grasp of strategy and operations. As the war went on he concentrated the war effort more and more in his own hands and trusted almost no one to give him

advice. The German war became a remarkable one man show in which intuition displaced rational evaluation, and megalomaniac conviction ousted common sense.[482] There was no central staff to run the war effort. There was no unity of command, no formal structure to oversee military operations that united army, navy and air force around the same table. The idea of a war committee flew in the face of everything Hitler understood by the term leader. Blindness to reality was thus compounded by a refusal to accept reality.[483]

The fact that Hitler intentionally kept his military and political forces divided and at odds with each other, in order to maintain complete control undermined Germany's war effort in general, and the counterinsurgency war in particular.[484] Often Hitler would issue orders to specific officers, but not all, and at the very last minute, and only when absolutely necessary, with such information being disseminated sparingly.[485] Hitler did not even believe that the various branches and agencies needed to be equally informed (if at all) in a timely fashion of his plans in detail for his will to be achieved. His method only added to the confusion in the field, again centralizing the command authority with himself at the expense of his subordinate leaders and departments:

> The relative efficiency of the National Socialist system was based precisely upon Hitler's principle of conferring limited powers for specific tasks, and allowing political co-ordination between institutions only where it was unavoidable. Any institutionalized communication between the lower levels of government was systematically prevented. Responsibilities were thus segmented.[486] Part of the problem was the chancellor's sometimes pathological belief that important decisions should be reached only within small groups of trusted advisors and then presented as accomplished facts to the relevant constitutional bodies, whether the cabinet, the *Reichstag* or *Reichsrat*.[487]

Likewise, in his personal handling of the war, Hitler maintained an atmosphere of competition amongst his various departments, often allowing the various directors and leaders to argue and compete amongst themselves over technical, military or political issues. One example was SS Colonel General and Governor General of Poland Hans Frank's request to Hitler for the procurement of Jewish labor. Hitler referred him to his arch nemesis Himmler, whom Hitler stated was "the competent authority to approach about the matter."[488]

In the end, Hitler's disregarding critical information, and his predictable responses to unpleasant information created an atmosphere of "don't ask, don't tell" within the military. This was especially true if situations arose which needed to be reported to him directly. Senior officers were more concerned with their own careers, rather than challenging incompetent authority, or even raising issues that could have been ill received. These facts forced them to eventually keep their information and opinions to themselves.

Those men opposed to the blatant inconsistency of the methods, or even the issuance of directives which countered military necessity, law and logic, went largely unheard. This created a vacuum where information and intelligence were carefully distributed throughout the military, even less among field leaders and their superiors, adding to the confusion and assisting in conflicting actions. Another factor was that the German military was an unforgiving autocracy, with little reservations about punishing their own to make a point. Even disobeying a simple order could mean a labor camp or execution in many cases. James Lucas cites the comments of an SS captain:

> The most dreadful thing was to leave one's comrades in the lurch. In war was the risk of being killed. Traitors and cowards were certain to die. The division had spent three weeks in battle but not one man thought of running away. In battle one has many chances of surviving, but no one escaped the execution squads. The SS evidence of their vigilance is frequently mentioned...and one SS man...recalled seeing bodies hanging from lampposts, each corpse bearing a placard proclaiming the dead man to have been a traitor or coward.[489]

Supporting this fact is the statement issued by General Pflugbeil regarding the conduct of German troops, especially those involved in the anti-partisan war:

> Every soldier must be made to understand clearly that any unauthorized retreat means certain death. He must also understand that the proper, decisive use of weapons and the right use of terrain ensure that success will be his. Every man needs to be fully aware that it is the worst possible disgrace for a soldier to allow ammunition, equipment or dead or wounded comrades to fall into enemy hands. A soldier may die in battle, but he will have died a hero's death like so many who have died for Germany before him. The coward, however, must die, as all traitors fully deserve. Let there be no doubt that cowards will be dealt with mercilessly in full accordance with military law.[490]

Most soldiers simply accepted the way things were and continued about their business, as stated by Mommsen:

> Ever more embroiled in the feverish and confused process of decision making, the traditional elites in the apparatus of government, in the army and economy, were forced either to join in the cumulative radicalization of the regime or to decline into political oblivion.[491] Only the personal drive of the men concerned determined how far they were able to interfere in local or regional affairs; significantly, party influence at the local level varied to a remarkable degree with the political forces involved.[492]

A prime example of a commander not conferring with Berlin due to these problems was Field Marshal Gerd von Schweppenburg, who was less rigid in his thinking than many of his peers. He decided to initiate counterinsurgency activity by training his soldiers in the field *before* they became casualties, operating without orders from Hitler and proving quite successful.[493] Schweppenburg was even successful in recruiting anti-Communist guerrillas who functioned within his own forces with great success, operating in the forward reconnaissance, rear area security and intelligence gathering roles, again without consulting his superiors.[494] He also managed to accomplish this without coercion, and therefore without violating international law.

Field Marshal Wilhelm List also followed Schweppenburg's lead of training and foreign recruitment while commanding the *12th Army*, which included *III Panzer Corp* in the region of Kharkov and the Caucasus-Samara regions between 25 March and 28 May 1942. The effort met with positive results, and also without his consulting Berlin.[495] He also managed to accomplish his tasks without breaking the laws of warfare. The only gray area was the law forbidding the forced induction of foreign nationals into military service. If they volunteered, there was no violation, with the exception of recruits being answerable to their respective national laws.

For the German soldiers (especially those in the counterinsurgency campaign) their war was one of confusion, terror, and basic survival. Morale was always a concern, with a prime example displayed in *The Goebbels Diaries*, in which he propaganda minister recounted a letter sent to him from Field Marshal Ferdinand Schoerner regarding German morale, and one of the greatest reasons was logistics:[496]

> The result was that the food was atrocious even if it had been prepared by an expert, which in most cases it had not, for most outposts lacked a proper cook. Normally the troops received about 15 grams of fat per day to be distributed among four pieces of bread.[497] This, as I have already reported, is barely enough for a single slice of bread. Of course, it's possible in theory to spread 15 grams over four slices, but the result is that you can hardly even see it.[498] Perhaps most ominously, the commander pointed out that the troops saw their food situation as no better than that which had presaged the collapse of morale on the Western Front in 1918.[499]

The in-fighting and confusion within the High Command and the various departments meant that "there was simply no forum in which the war effort could be viewed as a whole."[500] As stated by Hans Mommsen and cited by Omer Bartov:

> The picture drawn by the regime's propaganda of troops frantically fighting for the National Socialist cause, was false even concerning the elite formations of the *Waffen SS*...The mentality of the average *Landser* was characterized by soberness, rejection of the far from reality propaganda tirades, and by a firm will personally to survive. Certainly, under cover of the commissar order there were grave encroachments by the army against the defenseless civilian population handed over to it and against prisoners of war; the partisan war led to an unprecedented brutalization of the conduct of war by both sides. But the average soldier had little influence on this and could hardly find a way of avoiding the escalation of violence. [501]

The German military mentality regarding the value of human beings according to the National Socialist definition of race, as well as their own sense of invincibility, was based upon a program of intensive and repetitious propaganda and indoctrination. These factors would propel the ruthless nature of German policy, as well as establish the German mindset regarding the irregulars they encountered in the east:

> These lesser breeds, separated from Europe by no natural barriers, had been held at bay over the centuries only by the bravery of the Germans, whose racial qualities had enabled them so far to withstand a numerically superior foe.[502]

Propaganda not only the represented the opinions of the High Command and Hitler, it was also a tool, a weapon by which war was waged to create an atmosphere of justification for atrocities. Whether enforcing slave labor policies or killing civilians, the political machine was the driving force, pushing soldiers to do their worst by projecting the ills of society. The primary message was blaming the war and the soldiers' problems upon the irregulars, who were presented as "Jewish" and/or "Bolshevik" instigators. This approach assisted the collective killing effort, since "front-line soldiers who see such people as *franc tireurs* who commit murder and who deserve no mercy."[503]

German soldiers were subjected to many forms of propaganda, both friendly and enemy, and the German soldier was totally unprepared for what awaited him in Russia.[504] The conflicting opinions the German soldier was subjected to reflected the inconsistency of his own government's position on race. Propaganda constantly wavered and was reevaluated depending upon the conditions and necessities at the front.[505]

Even Hitler's own war against religion seemed hypocritical, given some of his many statements where he invoked his divine right, stating his destiny and objectives as a "holy calling, acting in the sense of the Almighty Creator, by warding off the Jews, I am fighting for the Lord's work."[506] "However, the success of the German propaganda campaign was demonstrated by the fact that few Germans are known to have been swayed by Soviet propaganda, believing in the superiority of their cause if not their leadership."[507] This success against enemy propaganda was a double edged sword. The German projection of invincibility was shattered following several setbacks, such as Moscow in 1941, Stalingrad, Kursk and North Africa in 1943, and the Allied invasion of Normandy in 1944. The Soviets absorbed these events which bolstered their resolve. The Germans committed the greatest error of all by believing their own propaganda.

German forces employed in rear areas did not confine themselves to the location, pursuit, and eradication of irregulars harassing German troops and cutting communications and supplies. Their operations also included enforcing the racial policies, collecting civilians for localized forced labor, transportation of forced labor back to work in German owned firms, and the extermination of those falling within the NSDAP paradigm as "marked for destruction."[508] The sheer failure to even consider adherence to international law, let alone common sense is stunning.

Often in the guise of "anti-partisan" operations entire villages were destroyed and multitudes murdered or sent to labor camps.[509] Even more frequent and initiated from the first day of the invasion on 22 June 1941 was the confiscation of land, livestock and crops, increasing the level of resistance exponentially and eliminating any possibility of convincing the locals of the benefits of living under German military and civilian local administrators. These were the factors that provided Soviet propaganda fodder for the masses and the impetus for resistance.

I. Economics and the Military: Labor and Force

Hitler and the High Command had long planned not only for the subjugation of Europe based upon economic and military necessity, but also forced labor for the *Arbeitseinsatz* (labor force for the Reich). This program was based upon the structure of racial quality according to their own doctrine.[510] As stated by Norman Rich: "race, far from being a mere propaganda slogan, was the very rock upon which the Nazi church was built."[511] It would be the subject of race that would define the Soviet war, as well as the partisan war, hence ultimately the genocide policy as agreed upon at Wannsee on 20 January 1942, which would actually create and increase the local resistance.[512]

The need for labor and the methods by which it was procured violated the basic tenants of international law, as discussed in the previous chapter. This policy of exploitation that fuelled the resistance movement forced Hitler and his military leaders to act with ever increasing brutality against any and all perceived resistance. The impact of Hitler's personal will upon these events was obvious, as stated by Hans Mommsen: "To argue that Hitler did not totally approve the policy of extermination in the east and did not incite his subordinates to execute it, directly or indirectly, is certainly absurd."[513] This argument would also have to apply to the slave labor program.

The German approach to slave labor, as well as genocide was illogical. Germany needed manpower in many areas; hence the foreign recruitment in the anti-partisan war. Yet, despite the growing personnel shortage, the *Nazi* regime murdered millions of potential laborers who could have supported the war economy, defying logic. Eberhard Jaeckel stated that:

> In 1942, during the advance on Stalingrad, at the height of the Russian campaign at a time, therefore when one would imagine that the entire labor force and every means of transportation would be needed for that one goal-at that very same time long trains filled with Western European Jews rolled across Europe, almost according to schedule, to the extermination camps in the east. There the victims were murdered together with their Eastern European fellow sufferers at the very moment when the German front needed every munitions worker and piece of rolling stock.[514]

One of the reasons Hitler and his subordinates felt some measure of comfort in their handling of their Jewish problem was the indifference they perceived from other nations, especially the United States, France and Great Britain.[515] On its face, Vichy France proved to be the most enthusiastic in assisting the *Nazis* during the Holocaust. Unfortunately this fact is not to be seen in French history textbooks. The conquered territories were to be administered from Berlin by appointed *Reichkommissars* and Governor Generals, men selected to be military rulers of specific regions, and these areas were to be divided accordingly:

> 1. *Reichkommissariats*-formerly occupied areas governed from Berlin by a regional *Reichkommissar* and supported by military garrisons (including indigenous personnel), which included the USSR (except the Crimea) and Baltic States.

2. Greater German Reich-nations occupied and absorbed into the Third Reich as proper parts of Germany such as France, Norway, Morocco, Algeria, Tunisia, Denmark, Holland.

3. Satellite States-primarily those nations allied to Germany through convenience such as Romania, Hungary, Finland and Bulgaria.

4. Annexed/Subjugated States-these include Austria, Yugoslavia, Croatia, Crete, Moravia, Bohemia, Sudetenland, Poland (including Danzig-West Prussia and Wartheland), Belgium (Wallonia/Flanders, Alsace Lorraine), Luxembourg, Crimea and Greece.

5. Independent Neutral States-Spain, Portugal Slovakia, Switzerland and Sweden.

6. States under Guidance-referring to states too far away or deemed unnecessary to directly or unable to effectively control, such as Great Britain, Italy, Libya, Cyprus and other islands under former British control.

7. Unassigned border States — Eastern Finland and Lapland. [516]

Long after the German invasion of the USSR, Hitler ordered the Forced Labor Act in 1942, primarily directed against the French and other Western Europeans in order to supply German industry with enough manpower.[517] This policy already existed in the east under the direction of Richard Walter Darre, Reich Minister for Food and Agriculture and Reich Peasant Leader (as of 12 January 1934). The policy was expanded as German policy required the confiscation of all goods, arable land, livestock, and forced labor.[518] The German attitude towards the Russian peasant was markedly different than the attitude toward their Western European neighbors, as stated by Strik-Strikfeldt, while working for Gehlen:[519]

> It happened that just before our arrival a German artillery officer had turned up to requisition horses. He produced no requisition order, and refused to give the farm manager a receipt. "Why should I?" he said. "There is a ruling that these *untermenschen* should not be treated like the French and the Belgians. Property means nothing to Russians."[520]

The problem of food and labor as visualized by Berlin was clearly stated by Hermann Goering:

> In all the occupied territories I see people living there stuffed full of food, while our own people are going hungry. For God's sake, you haven't been sent there to work for the well-being of the peoples entrusted to you, but to get hold of as much as you can so that the German people can live. I expect you to devote your energies to that. This continual concern for the aliens must come to an end once and for all....I could not care less when you say that the people under your administration are dying of hunger. Let them perish as long as no German starves.[521]

This sentiment echoes the activities of Prussian Gauleiter Erich Koch while in the Ukraine. It is clear that the German prosecution of the partisan war had three distinct aims: removing the Jews and other undesirables under the pretext of legitimate warfare; reducing the surplus population in an ef-fort to stretch food supplies, and reduce the existing and potential partisan threat through enervation.[522] The delusion that starving populations would be more manageable was stated in the diary of Josef Goebbels in February 1942: "The inhabitants of the occupied areas have their fill of material wor-ries. Hunger and cold are the order of the day. People who have been hard hit, generally speaking, don't make revolutions."[523]

Dr. Alfred Rosenberg, Hitler's Minister for Economics firmly believed that "the eastern peoples should be relegated to serfdom in support of Ger-man economic advancement."[524] However, despite Rosenberg's beliefs that all eastern peoples should be used as modern serfs, Nazi policy dictated that Jews and partisans were not to be so distinguished. These peoples would be included in the slave labor program for a specific period of time, until their usefulness ended. Partisans would rarely be given the option of work if cap-tured, as they were perceived as "illegal" by the German military and deemed a greater threat.

The German application of labor policies were at their best inconsistent, and at their worst inhumane, with military and civil administrators un-aware of each others' needs. Both entities were unconcerned with mutual support amongst their respective departments in order to accomplish their various objectives. This clear inconsistency also proved detrimental in the formulation of counterinsurgency doctrine, as each branch of service. Each commander operated in his own personal vacuum, separate from adjacent units, and many times unaware of the military situation beyond his area of responsibility.

One of the more ambiguous chain of events during the propaganda war being waged against Jews and Communists was the "hands-off" policy is-sued *ad-hoc*, such as Schenckendorff's 5 July 1942 directive to not be so brutal with the people in countering anti-German feelings.[525] At the same time dur-ing 1941 *Army Group Center's* units were ordered not to retaliate against the civilians *en masse* for partisan attacks, in order to foster good will amongst the people.[526] However, General Pflugbeil's order of 18 July 1941 (which was still in effect) for the area around Bialystok stated: "Seizure of hostages (especially Jews), to be shot at the slightest hint of troublemaking."[527]

Another set of orders issued on 12 July 1942 during *Operation Dreieck* also raise questions as to the logic of those issuing conflicting directives: "Ruthless measures are to be carried out vigorously; unnecessary harshness, particularly the unnecessary burning of houses, is to be avoided."[528] Another part of the new propaganda program was to insure that the resistance members understood that, if they were captured, they would be accorded POW status and thus treated accordingly.[529] However, given the common knowledge of the fates of many POWs this plan was perhaps less than effective in many cases.

Another example of conflicting orders in lieu of the previously mentioned directive was the following, regarding sabotage: "If no culprit is caught, the German *Wehrmacht* will enforce order and security with countermeasures against the general population."[530] This included those failing to harvest food or failing to provide livestock for the army.[531] Both of these actions were clear violations of Geneva and Hague.

Similarly, while directives were issued to display a more "gentle face" towards the people, other orders, such as those issued by "Colonel Koch," commander of the 350th *Infantry Regiment*, directed that the "Jewish question be tackled far more radically. I suggest that all Jews living in rural areas be put under guard in labor camps. Suspect elements must be eliminated."[532] Even General Eberhard von Mackensen, while not counted amongst the most ruthless of German commanders actually issued an order to treat the population sensibly, while still eradicating without mercy those suspected of sabotage or partisan sympathies.[533] Simultaneously the following was also issued to commanders in the field:

> The underhandedness of the partisans, and the proven collusion of the Jewish population, mean that commanders must exercise their power even more intensively and severely than before if set-backs for the troops are to be avoided.[534]

Those officers and officials who saw the problems and attempted to alter the inadequacies fought an uphill battle, especially regarding the treatment of civilians, as stated by Strikfeldt:

> I felt more and more convinced that the achievements of our soldiers would be in vain unless some proper solution could be found for the political, economic and human problems of the occupied zone with its 50–70 million inhabitants.[535]

Richard Breitman also stated the problem regarding conflicting policies:

> Hitler himself issued an order (passed along by radio and read by the British) allowing the use of Jews as forced laborers for the construction of roads in the northern Soviet sector, but in some other cases requests for the use of Jewish labor were denied. The tension and practical needs could lead to serious conflict.[536]

Another facet of the *Freundschaft* (friendship) program was rolling loud-speakers driving through villages, inaugurated during *Operation Maikaefer* in July 1942, and as stated by the operations section of the 203rd *Security Division*:

> Attempts are being made to move inhabitants hiding out in the forests back into the villages, for they have nothing to fear provided they have not participated in partisan activities. It has become clear that the pointless slaughter of livestock or the unjustified burning of villages and shooting of inhabitants, as is often the wont of SD and police units, only succeeds in driving the inhabitants into the arms of the partisans.[537]

The ever conflicting practices of the troops and orders issued by command authority produced confusion, not only among the German soldiers themselves, but also sent conflicting messages to the civilians, which proved detrimental to all concerned in the long run.

II. RACIAL LAWS AMENDED FOR WARTIME NECESSITY

German racial policy was proven to be as flexible as it was restrictive and all- inclusive, as the previously mentioned research of Bryan Mark Rigg in *Hitler's Jewish Soldiers* points out. As the war progressed, Nazi racial policy became interpreted in many different ways, depending upon who was responsible for its translation. Hitler demonstrated this flexibility and his direct involvement in the handling of the racial issue during a meeting in the *Wolfschanze* (Wolf's Lair) in East Prussia in 1944; "where he stated that 'including anti-Bolshevik Russians of Aryan ethnicity will prove crucial in undermining support for Stalin and the Red Army.'"[538] However, in illustrating Hitler's ability to alter his opinion on practically any topic, he also stated: "While we are on the subject, I am skeptical about the participation of all these foreign legions in our struggle on the Eastern Front."[539]

The need to recruit locals in the occupied regions was clear. These people spoke the native languages, knew the primary political personnel, knew the terrain, and understood the basic mentality of the population.[540] Many of these peoples had also suffered under Stalin during his collectivization policies, starving millions to death and sending many more to slave labor camps in Siberia. Tens of thousands were murdered outright by the GRU and NKVD. What should have in fact supported the German cause in converting millions was the fact that Stalin and the Red Army had not properly prepared, or even anticipated a need for a "partisan war."[541]

Although, while not a doctrine for either the tactical or strategic counterinsurgency operational methods, the "Combat Directive for Anti-Partisan Warfare in the East" of 11 November 1942 provided certain defining yet conflicting guidelines. This directive included the handling of POWs, the shooting or hanging of partisans captured, yet was "extremely vague on the issue of partisan deserters, stipulating that they be treated as prisoner-of-war 'according to circumstances."[542] The directive was contradictory in that it stated that both: "Unjust punishment shakes the confidence of the population and creates new partisans...[and] the severity of our measures and the fear of expected punishment must restrain the population from aid or support of the partisans."[543]

Furthering the confusion was the 16 December 1942 Directive issued through *OKW*, "which ordered the most brutal means against women and children as well," and that "any scruples constituted treason against the German people."[544] Additional confusion existed when the commander of the 2nd *Army* ordered restraint in the killing, while the 3rd *Army* commander "authorized any and every means against the partisans, giving the order to shoot all captured partisans, either immediately or after quick interrogation."[545] The evidence shows that the populations responded "gladly to German propaganda" when they were treated well, hence various commanders abridging the policy to suit their personal needs.[546] Most of these actions violated existing international laws.

This area of study becomes relevant when analyzing the racial component of the counterinsurgency war and the doctrine that was developed. Although irregulars (including partisans and guerrillas, for which there has been no distinction produced in the literature until recently) were considered a gray area even by the Allies during the war, the Germans considered it a "black and white" issue.[547]

What were possibly the most frightening aspects of these policies, both economic and extermination was "not the fanatical anti-fanaticism of those who carried out the genocide, but rather the acceptance and toleration of it, indeed the approval and support for it, which came from the leading officials in all the areas of the regime."[548]

One prime example regarding the opinion of the subject peoples is the comment made by Hermann Goering, who "proposed that they kill all the men in the Ukraine...and then send in the SS stallions."[549] In addition, Heinrich Himmler continually lowered the racial restrictions as the need for manpower superseded his racial bigotry.[550] The German perception of Western Europeans was quite different from their perception of Eastern Europeans with few exceptions, such as Galician Poles and ethnic Ukrainians who were considered Aryan.[551] One example of the German perception of the eastern peoples regards POWs:

> It is a tattered, ragged, almighty mish-mash of European and Asiatic races. Only a few wear boots where the leg isn't made out of leather....This, then, is the Red Army soldier of the Soviet paradise. Two worlds colliding, one of cleanliness and order, the other filthy and chaotic in every respect. [The prisoners] are fearful and suspicious, taught for decades as they have been to distrust both outsiders and their own relatives. The senses of many seem completely dulled. Horror, propaganda, fear and then the sudden release of tension after the battle have reduced them almost to the state of animals.[552]

The racial criteria for recruiting soldiers was continuously amended as manpower was needed, although this fact was less prevalent in the west, since those populations were already considered more racially acceptable. However, even the Western Europeans were not considered all-inclusive within the *Volksgemeinschaft*, as stated by Wolff:

> During the early days it was important to place a humane and very caring face on the recruiting effort. I spoke with Himmler about the eventual expansion of SS in general, and he stated that: "We will concern ourselves with the *Waffen SS*," as this was 1941; "and fill out the ranks with those men we know to be suitable. I would prefer to keep the *SD* and *Gestapo* completely German, for security, you understand." Himmler was dedicated to creating a greater Germanic Community, with the SS being seen as the pinnacle of this new order. As you well know, there was some measure of success.[553]

In fact, many of the traditional senior German leaders held a dim view of the new eastern volunteers. Even Schenckendorff judged eleven of his twenty-five *Landesschuetzen-Battalions* as "being worthless."[554] The following report provides a glimpse of what von Schenckendorff referred to:

> The deployment of the *Landesschuetzen-Bataillon* [Battalion] within the compass of the *221st Division* for the operation against Glinka has already shown that with such troops successes will be difficult to achieve. As a consequence of their inadequate combat training, the casualties sustained

by these units are higher than those of front-line troops. Fifty percent of casualties are dead.[555]

The concept of the *Freiwilligen* (military volunteers) and *Hilfswilligen* (*Hiwis*, or labor volunteers)[556] comprised of non-Germans (and in many cases non-Aryans) was handled through the *Truppenamt* (Office of Troops). His concept was created by Lieutenant General Hans von Seeckt and Colonel General Walther Reinhardt following the First World War. Their planning was based upon the experience of Lieutenant General Paul von Lettow-Vorbeck during World War I in East Africa and his use of native forces. This program witnessed an explosion within the ranks of the German forces in both world wars.[557]

Many of the auxiliaries were former prisoners of war or defectors from various nations, including the Soviet Union, although their reliability was always in question. The prevailing belief was that "captured partisans and partisan deserters have a tendency to tell their captors what they thought their captors wanted to hear,"[558] although on many occasions they did provide invaluable intelligence on Red Army and partisan units, members and operations.[559] However, many people were forced into service in violation of the laws.

The volunteers from the USSR alone accounted for between 800,000-900,000 men serving in German uniforms or in the Russian National Peoples' Army (RNNA)[560] and the Russian Army of Liberation (ROA) against their former comrades. Most served in the anti-partisan role under the command of Andrei Vlasov,[561] and the Ukrainian Nationalist Organization (UPA) under Stepan Bandera boasted 300,000 members.[562] In addition, of the 940,000 men serving within the *Waffen SS* and its thirty-eight active divisions (an additional seven were "paper" divisions and divisions of lesser strength), only approximately 250,000 were actually Germanic by birth; the balance being foreign volunteers and conscripts.[563] David Footman states the following regarding the lessening of the racial policy and foreign recruitment:

> It seemed as if a spontaneous anti-Stalin revolution had come into being throughout the occupied area. Within a few months of the start of the offensive some 800,000 ex-red Army personnel were serving in the *Wehrmacht*, a very large population as combatants.[564]

In effect, it would appear that the Germans had successes when the soldiers and events were not influenced by *NSDAP* policy. The propaganda efforts were apparently still successful in the conversions promoting Hitler over Stalin, with certain events supporting those perceptions, as stated by Strikfeldt:

> Unfortunately I have forgotten the name of this excellent officer, who got together a number of Jewish craftsmen from Smolensk and the neighborhood. His workshops were thus able to provide the *Wehrmacht* with much of what was needed, and, incidentally, secure a decent livelihood for the Jewish craftsmen. Our Russian friends remarked that under Stalin such initiative from an individual officer would be unthinkable. "So with you there is still freedom and independence."[565]

"Where the Germans had failed in using their own forces in a successful counter-insurgency role, their hope lay in the recruiting effort of the *Freiwilligen* to assist in combating the irregulars,"[566] despite the fact that Berlin considered these groups a "necessary evil"[567] and not members of the racially based *Volksgemeinschaft* (Peoples' Community).[568] Even POW camps and hospitals were raided to fill the necessary quotas for both labor and military service. Such forced conscription being specifically illegal under Geneva 1929.[569] These groups' applications of racial hatred towards other groups, already targeted by Hitler and the military would sometimes eclipse the atrocities of the Germans.[570] The Lithuanians and Ukrainians were prime examples.

Germany's insincerity in supporting nationalist movements abroad (in contradiction to *NSDAP* policy) is not in question. The facts speak for themselves, such as the statement by Goebbels regarding the ROA: "Goebbels, who was friendly throughout, explained that right from the start he had favored a Russian Liberation Movement: it could always be dissolved should its members take it into their heads to turn against the German Reich."[571]

Part of Germany's problem in targeting those young men fit enough to actively serve against the Red Army and partisans was simple: every man born after approximately 1900 had known nothing but Communism, at least from a cognitive standpoint, or for that matter Stalinism. These persons were similar to the young Germans under National Socialism, as they "willingly acknowledged the permanence and the legitimacy of the Soviet dictatorship."[572]

Another advantage that the Soviets had was the massive numbers of illiterate civilians within the country due to the lack of formal education, hence reading German propaganda was left up to a small minority who may or may not have had a vested interest in accurately sharing the information with their comrades.[573]

The increase in partisan activity during 1943 forced the High Command to increase its foreign recruiting. This was deemed necessary as part of the initial plan to create a viable counterinsurgency doctrine, with the *Waffen SS* creating twenty new units between 1942 and the end of the war.[574] It was in fact the SS, and not the Army, which focused specifically upon the creation of anti-partisan units from the regimental through division level, complete with supporting arms,[575] although the Army and *Luftwaffe Fallschirmjaeger* (Para-troops) also received their complement of volunteers and conscripts.[576]

The SS handling of the foreigners was considered necessary, as the SS were deemed the most effective at providing the appropriate "political edu-cation and indoctrination" of these eastern recruits into the National Social-ist paradigm. Not the least successful tactic in recruitment and inducement for German service was fear of re-capture by the Red Army. In fact, many Germans of eastern or Slavic backgrounds were appointed to these units as instructors and leaders, as they looked Slavic or spoke the various languag-es.[577] There is an irony in just how the former Soviets perceived all of this attention, as stated by Strikfeldt:

> True, there was the ever growing (and to us intolerable) pressure of the party. But to ex-Soviet citizens this "unfreedom" in Germany appeared as freedom itself. That was the big difference. And it was the appeal of this "freedom" that still brought Russians over to our side in spite of all the dis-appointments of 1941.[578]

In order for this new program to succeed the Propaganda Ministry was considered necessary, as explained by Karl Wolff:

> The Propaganda Ministry was already gearing up to take the credit for the recruiting and deployment of these international brigades by November 1941. Josef Goebbels and his disciples at 10 Viktoriastrasse were unaware of the activities regarding recruitment until Herre's letter to OKW[579] and OKH.[580] The Office of Eastern Languages headed by Dr. Eberhardt Taubert [from 1937-41] and the secrecy was exposed on the day of *Barbarossa*. Most of what they accomplished was the creation of interesting propaganda catch phrases that would hopefully turn the population against Stalin. There was some success, yet overall, I would have to say that we failed dismally.[581]

Otto Kumm also gave his perspective on the recruitment problems and the conflict with the existing racial policies:

> If Berlin genuinely cared about winning the war in the east they would have completely. Supported the recruiting plans, and maintained a reign on the *Einsatzgruppen* activities.[582] Hitler's dream was a united Europe that would eclipse and destroy Communism, yet the greatest potential weapon in his inventory was the massive Russian population. Had he taken the

situation seriously and logically analyzed the realities, we would not be discussing this today. It was unbelievably stupid and was, in my opinion, the reason why we lost the war in total.[583]

Waffen SS Major Dr. Fritz Rudolf Arlt worked under the SS Office of Foreign Affairs and Recruitment under Karl Wolff, working with *Wehrmacht Propaganda IV (WPr IV)* under Colonel von Tresckow's direction.[584] Arlt was a university educated intellectual who was briefed on the recruiting plan, as well as the "re-defining" of the racial criteria, and he was instrumental in creating the *Roland* and *Nightingale* anti-partisan and sabotage units comprised of Ukrainians trained by the *Abwehr*.[585]

Arlt believed the racial criteria to be absurd, and he examined the loopholes in the racial regulations.[586] Arlt informed Himmler (as witnessed by Wolff) in 1943 that 3,000,000 men in the Ukraine qualified for service if the "restrictions were lifted or redefined."[587] Arlt was considered "the one humanitarian in a world of misery,"[588] and he was eventually replaced by General Johannes von Blaskowitz for being "too humane."[589] Even Guenther d'Alquen "had tried to convince Himmler that the political and ideological war against the *untermenschen* had failed, reminding the *Reichsfuehrer* that these so-called 'sub-humans' had managed to destroy more than one German Army."[590]

These facts illustrate the apathy with which the supreme leadership treated the partisan as well as the racial problem, which remained one in the same, even when it became absolutely necessary to constantly redefine the racial criteria to serve their own interests. Conflicts continued between military and civil administrators appointed by Hitler either "directly or indirectly," as stated by Breitman: [591]

> Another problem beneath the surface was that some of the generals had bitterly criticized the SS in 1939–40 over atrocities in Poland and other matters, and Himmler and Brauchitsch had been forced to intervene and dampen controversies. In July 1940, Brauchitsch had instructed army authorities not to try and interfere with the way political authorities carried out the racial (Jewish problem in the east. Relations between the army and the SS and police were still far from good.[592]

Even when the orders were issued to utilize the massive numbers of foreign nationals at their disposal, Himmler and Hitler did nothing to assist their field leaders, as stated by Kumm, regarding the Felix Steiner plan for *Operation Citadel* in 1943:[593]

> The idleness of 600,000 men prepared to fight against their former comrades with another 200,000 wasting away in prison camps exemplified the incompetence of the High Command. Felix Steiner was incensed that his

> plan had been shelved, as he was relying upon the Vlasov Army to support
> our forces in the offensive. By the time we actually launched the attack
> Soviet forces outnumbered us heavily and were prepared. It was such a
> waste.[594]

Despite the racial policy and its constant revision for military purposes, the following statistics are impressive: 600,000 former Soviets served with the German Army and *Waffen SS*, with nearly 60,000 serving in the *Luftwaffe*, and 15,000 serving in the *Kriegsmarine* (Navy).[595] This recruitment seemed necessary in the German counterinsurgency plan, yet had mixed results, as stated by Shepherd:

> It seems from official German sources that German manpower engaged in
> security duty in the Soviet Union never exceeded a quarter of a million, but
> hovered for most of the time from 1942 on around the 190,000 mark. Of
> these, only 37,000 at most were suitable for front-line duty. Added to this
> figure were units from Italy and the Axis satellites, of varying but usually
> low quality. Total manpower ranged against the partisans seems never to
> have exceeded 900,000 at any one time, but well over half of these were
> eastern volunteers which were also of usually poor quality.[596]

The record reflects that the volunteer counterinsurgency units performed rather well, although these numbers do not include the tens of thousands serving as civilian support personnel or auxiliaries in rear echelon duties, including concentration camps.[597] These figures are placed into perspective when looking at other sources, such as Mark P. Gingerich:

> The overall racial quality of the Germanic volunteers inducted into the
> *Waffen SS*...(that) according to [SS General Gottlob] Berger, with the sole
> exception of the Flemish, on average 25-30% of the Germanic applicants
> were determined to be racially and physically suitable for service in the
> *Waffen SS*, a higher figure than that reached in Germany itself.[598]

The racial component, which provided the selection criteria for either assimilation or extermination were less applicable regarding foreign labor, in which Reich Armaments Minister Albert Speer's memoirs provide a multitude of examples.[599] Creating a strong anti-Communist coalition in the USSR was deemed critical for success in the early days of counterinsurgency. This assessment was the catalyst for the recruitment of foreign nationals, and German propaganda stressed both history and the persecution over the centuries by Russians (especially focusing upon the two previous decades) against the peoples of Eastern Europe.[600] This propaganda campaign focused heavily upon the discord created by the Bolshevik Revolution, Russian Civil War, and the creation of the Soviet Union.[601]

These events included the recent Stalinist purge of the military, when three of the five marshals, thirteen of nineteen Army commanders, and over half of the 186 division commanders (and in many cases their entire families) were killed or exiled to Siberian mines and labor camps. Even more important were the resulting famines in the Ukraine, Belorussia, Kazakhstan, the Caucasus, and many other regions during years of Stalin's collectivization policies, which would continue even after the war.[602] Perhaps the greatest detriment to the Soviets as a result of the purge was the execution of Marshal Mikhail Nikolayevich Tukhachevsky, the genius during the 1920s and 1930s. He was behind the long range planning for a Soviet partisan defense program in conjunction with the Red Army in case of any future enemy attack.[603]

In addition, the Germans who invaded the Ukraine in 1941 and entered the Academy of Sciences in Kiev found the statistical analysis paperwork compiled during 1932. The report was ordered by Stalin when the crops were harvested, evidence which showed that there had been enough grain to feed the populations for the next two years and four months, and seed the fields for new crops. Stalin had allowed these millions to starve.[604] It was also quite clear that the Soviet government was "more concerned with livestock than human lives."[605] In fact, the people were still living under grain quotas even before the Germans arrived.[606]

The Germans had a golden opportunity to expose and exploit the Stalinist activities in full, including the knowledge that Stalin had "sacrificed millions of lives rather than Soviet prestige,"[607] primarily since exporting the grain brought commercial goods and technology through trade agreements. Feeding the people brought him nothing but a growing population of "potential enemies."[608]

Additionally, the actions of the NKVD,[609] responsible for operating the gulags, mental hospitals, prisons, handling arrests, executions and purges, had hardly endeared all of the Soviet people to Stalin.[610] In many cases, long before the threat of a German appearance, the first outsider a villager saw was the local NKVD representative, including an entourage of armed men performing their not so delicate rituals. As stated by Overy: "In the wave of fear and panic that gripped the Soviet Union in 1942, the NKVD stepped up its search for scapegoats, workers guilty of 'economic misconduct', saboteurs, spies."[611] Even Stalin's own order No. 270, stating that "Soviets who fell into German hands were traitors and would be treated as such upon repatriation" (often including their entire families) was a bonus for the German conversion effort, given the numbers of former Red Army soldiers in captivity.[612]

Another factor supporting a potential German coalition was the fact that the Soviet partisans tended to be quite ruthless with their own populations. Their tactics of forcing young men into service, stealing crops and livestock, executing locals to make political statements, and launching attacks near populated centers in order to provoke a ruthless German response against civilians further alienating the population.[613]

The Germans had a golden opportunity to convince millions to turn from Stalin; people who would "support whichever side offered the best chance of a quiet life."[614] Himmler himself became intrigued with the prospect of forging an army from Stalin's own people, as he was very concerned about the partisan problem, as stated by Wolff:

> The *Reichsfuehrer* was concerned with the problems of partisans, especially in Russia and Yugoslavia, where they were virtually unchecked. Our Hungarian, Romanian, and Bulgarian allies were also experiencing problems with partisans and this was what Himmler said to me: "Wolff, do you believe that we may be successful in trying to create our own units of partisans to work behind enemy lines? Perhaps they could work with the SS commando units...it may work." I spoke to Felix Steiner and later Otto Kumm about this, and they were of the opinion that it would work. The greatest problem was trying to undo the damage already done from the invasion [of Russia] forward with regard to civilian populations, especially the mass executions which had not been handled very well.[615]

Countering the atrocious conduct of the Soviets towards their own people, in order to "win the hearts and minds" of the populations to support a German friendly internal resistance movement proved virtually impossible *en masse*. This is not surprising, considering that "thousands of partisans were rounded up and shot or publicly hanged, with placards placed around their necks, as an example to the rest."[616] Likewise, the Soviet handling of the war including their open propaganda and also fuelled the German hatred, such as the statement by Soviet propaganda master Ilya Ehrenberg in August 1942 in the Red Army journal *Red Star*:

> Now we know. The Germans are not human. Now the word "German" has become the most terrible swear word. Let us not speak. Let us not be indignant. Let us kill. If you do not kill the German, he will kill you....If you have killed one German, kill another. There is nothing jollier than German corpses.[617]

As the plans moved forward Himmler began to re-evaluate the racial policy to suit Germany's critical manpower shortage, and the Office for Tactical

Study headed by the SS and *Abwehr* (Army Intelligence) jointly undertook the planning, as recounted by Wolff:

> The problem had become so critical, especially where morale among the troops was concerned that [SS Major General Felix] Steiner, [SS Lieutenant General von dem] Bach-Zelewski[618] and I decided that with the proper analysis and experienced officers on the project, we could arrive at some solution. Several plans had been tried previously, such as propaganda broadcasts and dropping leaflets by aircraft and artillery shells into suspected partisan areas. This was mostly a waste of time since the partisans fighting us were not really worth trying to convert. We needed to enlist the loyalty of those who had yet been pressed into partisan or Soviet military service. Failing that, the second plan was to develop tactics for soldiers in the field, offering better chances of success while raising their morale, which by 1943 was not as high as we would have liked to think, at least in Russia.[619]

Kumm related his thoughts at that time during this process with Himmler, Wolff, and others, including Major General Hans Doerr:[620] "We needed to know that in the event of success, would the same formula work in Yugoslavia as that applied in Russia? These were all very interesting questions, and we had very little time to attempt trial and error."[621]

The Germans' need for additional manpower, which continuously lowered the racial criteria against the very peoples they were exterminating *because of race*, was only one hypocrisy. The Germans made an extensive effort in the recruitment and training process, only to casually expend these units as "cannon fodder" against superior numbers of heavily-armed and well-supported Red Army troops, a force which they were neither adequately trained nor equipped to confront, thus wasting these invaluable assets. Additionally, the volunteers were not always treated with the respect or military urgency they were due, such as the report dated November 1942, regarding *Ostbatallon* (East Battalion) 604 operating in the Pripet region. The units lacked everything from weapons, medical supplies and footwear, rendering them completely ineffective.[622]

These actions continually diminished not only the ranks of the counterinsurgents, they also illustrated clearly to the volunteers that their lives meant nothing. Whether a gas chamber, firing squad, labor camp or the battlefield, their deaths were imminent, and Communist propaganda used this fact to their advantage:

> Hand-written, printed leaflets targeting the OD and other native units have been found. They encourage the reader to desert with his weapon, appeal to his national honor and also employ the standard scare tactics depicting the grisly revenge which the already advancing Red Army will inflict upon all OD men. There is particular emphasis on "fantasy totals" of Ger-

man dead, as well as the names of OD deserters who are praised for having enticed more of their comrades to desert with their weapons. Of note were a number of personal hand-written letters by bandit chiefs to mayors and other civilians, threatening them with the direst of consequences if they continued working for the Germans. Leaflet raids and distribution have been reported in all *rayons*; lately they are being distributed in the market places.[623]

These measures, according to Shepherd and supported by the German intelligence summaries clearly show that even villages friendly to German troops were often reluctant to assist, or even acknowledge their former acquaintance.[624] As stated in the following:

> The population is in two minds about the troops. On the one hand they know they have nothing to fear from German soldiers; on the other, heavy propaganda activity by the bandits arouses great distrust of the troops, especially in those areas which have felt little of our presence. The fear of being named a traitor by one's neighbor and turned over to the partisans is hindering people from giving precise statements about bandit movements. It was also clear that of all the *starosten* whom we came across, none could name or wanted to name anybody suspected of helping the partisans. It is obvious from this that no *starost* feels that his life is safe.[625]

Mommsen cited another example of the inconsistency of German methodology:

> It is symptomatic that fanatical anti-Semites such as Hans Frank and Wilhelm Kube began to protest against the systematic implementation of the extermination program when it was turned against the reserves of indispensable Jewish labor in the Eastern regions. When the liquidations were not justified by the pretence that they were measures to combat partisans and to weaken the "Jewish-Bolshevik" potential, as was the case with the *Einsatzgruppen*, then they were frequently accounted for by the need to make space for fresh transports.[626]

As this ongoing conflict between various organizations and administrators strained the labor and genocide programs, it also impacted upon the efforts of the counterinsurgency campaign, which required greater manpower, hence the need for foreign auxiliaries.[627] Hitler's various followers were enthusiastic about abiding by his wishes, as they interpreted them at different levels, which in many cases meant that conflicts erupted regarding exactly which policy was to be enforced at any given time. The need to fulfill the wishes of Hitler, the Party, and indeed even their own superiors witnessed officers and soldiers committing far more damage and committing more crimes than were actually necessary in many cases, even to the point of "swelling their 'partisan' body counts with civilian dead."[628]

This was the actual method of Hitler's power, ruling a fragmented and disjointed bureaucracy pursuing their *Fuehrer's* agenda (as they perceived it), as stated by Browning: "Hitler instilled a fanatic faith and unquestioned loyalty, and he held sway over those followers primarily because they believed in the man and his mission. In his ultimate control of power and authority, Hitler was indeed the *Fuehrer*."[629]

III. CONSIDERATIONS

The attitude towards racial segregation before the war, extermination during the war, and the amendments to the racial policy for the war effort would not be applied universally in the counterinsurgency war. All Soviet irregulars would be treated as "Jewish–Bolshevik conspirators" or "bandits" to be dealt with severely, violating the existing international laws of warfare in the case of "suspected" insurgents. Inclusive of the ever shifting applications of political policy in contrast to military necessity, German leaders effectively functioned as their own worst enemy.

The attempt at rectifying the egregious acts from 1941-42 by the initiation of the propaganda recruitment campaigns later proved the point that the senior leadership understood that their murderous policies were failing. It was the additional failure to organize a universal and workable policy of inclusion, and the abandonment of logic, that prevented the military from formulating a lucid counterinsurgency policy. The opportunity of creating a massive anti-Communist revolution and overthrowing the Soviet government with German support was not seriously considered until too late. These applications of intellectually bankrupt social, military and political policies proved to be a fatal self-inflicted wound, given the need for the very manpower they were ultimately destroying. Hitler had wanted to create a new world order. Instead he managed to destroy a continent, altering the history of our world for all time.

Nazi Propaganda poster in support of anti-Communist recruiting within the Soviet Union. U.S. National Archives.

Photograph from the 1 April 1933 Nazi inspired boycott of Jewish businesses. U.S. National Archives.

Above: Arthur Nebe (far left) at funeral of Germans killed by partisans.

Below: Still photo from newsreel on executions in the Ukraine in 1941 at Babi Yar. U.S. National Archives..

Erich von dem Bach Zelewski, founder of the Einsatzgruppem. U.S. National Archives.

Map of German invasion of the Soviet Union on 22 June 1941. U.S. Army War College, courtesy of Dr. Russell F. Weigley.

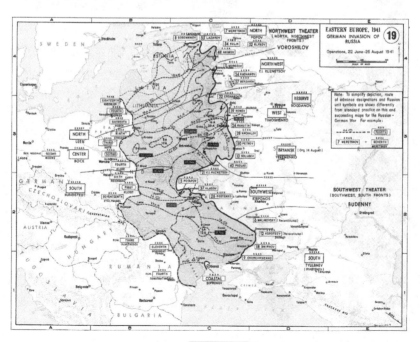

Above: Photo of execution of inmates at Buchenwald in 1943. U.S. National Archives.

Left: Adolf Eichmann, originator of the railroad scheduling method for the Holocaust. U.S. National Archives.

Germans posting a sign warning of partisan activity, ordering drivers to use vehicle convoys for safety. National Archives.

Ukrainian peasants collected for slave labor. National Archives.

German soldiers searching suspected insurgents in October 1941. National Archives.

Above: Execution of Collaborators in Russia 1942. Public Record Office.

Below: (From left to right) Propaganda Minister Josef Goebbels, Deputy Fuehrer Rudolf Hess and Adolf Hitler at rally in 1937. Public Record Office.

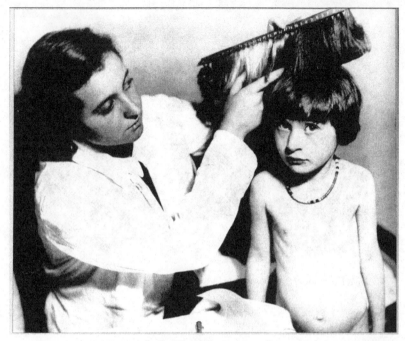

Above: German propaganda method for evaluating ethnically suitable races. U.S. National Archives.

Below: (From left to right) Reinhard Heydrich, Heinrich Himmler and Karl Wolff. U.S. National Archives.

Left: Propaganda poster advertising one of the many anti-Semitic films. Jew Suess was one of the most atrocious. U.S. National Archives.

Below: Locals murdering Jews in their own community in Kaunas, Lithuania on June 28, 1941. Public Record Office.

Left: 1st Lieutenant Karl Lothar Schulz, who launched the initial investigation into the killing of German paratroops in Crete, May 1941. U.S. National Archives.

Left: Luftwaffe Field Marshal Albert Kesselring, commander of the Italian front in 1944. Bundesarchiv Berlin-Lichterfelde.

Below: Field Marshal Gunther von Kluge, who worked with the recruitment of former Soviets into the anti-Communist units. U.S. National Archives.

Below: Field Marshal Wilhelm Keitel. Bundesarchiv Berlin-Lichterfelde.

CHAPTER 4. DEVELOPMENT OF DOCTRINE AND COUNTER-PRODUCTIVITY

This chapter includes interview segments with several men who commanded or participated in German anti-partisan forces. Their experiences and recollections of the difficulties, failures and successes of their efforts proved critical in evaluating the effects of their efforts in the field. German racial and counterinsurgency policy, as well as an analysis of the effectiveness of their various approaches regarding civilians is compared to the literature and sources, and evaluated against the applicable laws.

The counterinsurgency war in the Soviet Union was, according to the experiences of many interviewed who participated, the most nightmarish scenario German troops would encounter on a regular basis. According to Richard Overy (as supported by Karl Wolff's figures),[630] Soviet resistance forces destroyed 65,000 vehicles and 12,000 bridges.[631] Inclusive and supportive of Overy's research is the admission by Wolff, who stated that "between eight and twelve percent of all German losses were attributed to resistance forces throughout Europe," thus posing a great problem for the German military. Much of this damage was inflicted upon the railway networks.[632] Most of this carnage was due to the inability of German forces to deploy enough qualified troops in the necessary areas to check resistance activities. Even the use of indigenous personnel was often deemed insufficient, as stated by the following:

In the course of April 1943 the unrest in the entire divisional area reached dangerous proportions. Valuable economic installations; depots, dairies, distilleries, etc., were everywhere attacked and in places burned down. Raiding and plunder of the villages and the murder of *starosten* and other pro-German inhabitants became the order of the day. The division's attempts to combat this mushrooming threat were severely restricted due to the inadequate forces available.[633]

As stated previously, the original method for handling irregulars was inclusive of the *Einsatzgruppen* missions: rooting out the undesirables and thus hopefully thwarting resistance before it had a chance to organize. This method proved flawed, and as the resistance effort continued to grow in its effectiveness (despite his previous reservations with regard to the handling of civilians and POWs) Schenckendorff issued the following directive on 12 October 1941:

> The enemy is to be utterly annihilated. It is difficult, even for the toughest soldier to decide swiftly between life and death for apprehended partisans and suspects, but the decision must be borne and any personal feeling is to be banished ruthlessly and mercilessly.[634]

Schenckendorff was not unique in his outlook. Field Marshals Walter von Reichenau (known for ruthlessness against civilians), Erich von Manstein, Walter Model, Ferdinand Schoerner (perhaps the most ruthless against civilians, and even his own men), Gunther von Kluge, as well as Generals Hermann Hoth and Ewald von Kleist had issued similar directives.[635]

Many times one commander's directive would either be creatively "interpreted" or simply ignored in order to fulfill a more current agenda. An example are the conflicting orders issued during anti-partisan *Operations Zugspitze* and *Ankara I & II* by German forces during February 1943.[636] During *Ankara I* and *Ankara II* orders had been issued *not* to destroy villages, while during *Operation Zugspitz* orders were issued to destroy structures as necessary, thus confusing the soldiers, civilians, and promoting the correct appearance of a disjointed and misguided command structure.[637] This reality did not escape both the German and Soviet propaganda campaigns, both deemed necessary in combating or recruiting partisans and educating and motivating their respective troops.[638]

The partisans' effectiveness may be evaluated thus: irregulars generally outnumbered the Germans and they had popular support (which is always necessary for a successful resistance movement), as well as the vast regions patrolled by Germans and their auxiliary forces. The opportunities for sabotage and offensive operations were unlimited.[639] The actions of irregulars were often a response to German activity, and often times such actions were the cause of German actions in retaliation. The vicious cycle was self-perpetuating. It was in these actions where the lines of legal and illegal activity were blurred, if not completely erased.

The lack of enough Germans to operate in his capacity is stated in the following *SD* report: "The lack of sufficient security forces means that is not always possible to prosecute the partisan war with the necessary severity. This shakes the confidence of the population and feeds the (partisans') rumor mill."[640]

Simply the fear or belief that partisans were in a certain area could slow the progress of a conventional German unit, thus limiting an advance, allowing Soviet forces more time to prepare a defensive or offensive plan.[641] On many occasions the Germans found themselves outgunned, debilitating them, and thus illustrating the failing German logistic and psychological situation:

> Many times our railway patrols have come to grips with enemy mine layers. On every occasion the bandits have been equipped with machine pistols and our own troops have not. This explains why the enemy's losses are never established, despite the fact that the actions are often fought at extremely close quarters. In the darkness, directly after the moment of surprise has gone, the rifleman hardly ever has a chance to fire a second shot. The regiment wishes to stress the psychological consequences for the troops.[642]

Alexander Dallin summed up the atmosphere for the average German in this environment:

> Among the scant German forces responsible for the security of the vast alien areas, partisan activity, regardless of its military significance or failure, was bound to promote a state of nervousness and insecurity.... The initial impact was greatest on the lower German ranks who came into physical contact with the partisans and the effects of their operations.[643]

The Germans understood that agriculture was the backbone of supporting not only a partisan movement, but also their own forces. The great expanse of territory for which German security forces were responsible (for example Belorussia, which covered 2,000,000 square miles, and *Army Group Center* alone responsible for 145,000 square miles, about the size of Bavaria, Baden-Wuerttemberg, Rhineland and Hessen together)[644] proved impossible to manage militarily, let alone administrate effectively.[645] What the Germans were denied through continued occupation the partisans gained, increasing the spread of partisan controlled territory, which in turn increased the tension and retribution of the Germans. Another dimension was the struggle to convince the populations to support one side or the other. Often political rhetoric and propaganda were used, although fear and the "carrot and stick" approach was the technique most commonly favored. These areas were always points of contention between the two forces.[646]

The men initially selected for this work were usually long-term veterans of the Order Police (*Ordnungspolizei*) and older military veterans. Their commanders were often those officers who decided to embark upon a policy of active counterinsurgency, masking the actual policy of mass murder that would hopefully provide relief for their forces from suspected irregulars. It was also deemed necessary to legitimize the killing as a "counterinsurgency operation" to ease the consciences of the men themselves.

Other counterinsurgency members later in the war would be young soldiers fresh from basic training, or those men deemed unfit for further military front-line service, although up to 1943 Germany placed great emphasis upon creating specific units (German and their allies) for combating the irregular threats. This policy often focused upon promoting good will among the masses that were deemed worthy of salvation and potential assimilation.[647] Such lists were drafted for use in field for determining these qualities, as cited by Richard Rhodes.[648] Another factor was the inability to rotate these men from their duties on a regular basis, which was understood to be important, yet almost impossible under the circumstances:

> Whilst the average age of other security regiments may be not so high, or the signs of strain clear, as they are with *Security Battalion 242*, the sudden loss of a strongpoint is always possible under current conditions. Everything boils down to the fact that...there is no prospect of reinforcement. This means firstly that the demands (on the division) are always increasing, and secondly that there is often no possibility of leave.[649]

The fact that men remained in the field for so long, with so much confusing rhetoric thrown at them in a grueling mental and physical war contributed to the morale breakdown. In any conflict, these circumstances lay the foundation for atrocities being committed, whether by design or accident. It is very likely that many illegal acts were carried out by men who were exhausted, afraid or simply confused.

Special orders had been issued down to specific units on 25 June 1942 and were still in effect, stating that "counterinsurgency training was to continue and be carried out properly," mainly due to the numbers of new troops entering these units.[650] According to Shepherd, this was "a problem which General von Schenckendorff identified across the entire *Army Group Center's* Rear Area."[651]

In fact, in order to reduce the open hostility against German forces, *LI Army Corps* issued a directive taken in the spirit of the 12 July *OKH* directive, ordering its troops to "only punish Communists and ethnic minorities, thus leaving the majority of the populations alone."[652] For an account of German attempts to control excessive Hungarian actions in 1943, the following is interesting:[653]

> The division requests that the Hungarian troops refrain from any evacuation, destruction of villages, or reprisal action in the course of the operations. The division wishes to point out that general burning of villages and measures directed against the population are strictly forbidden by order of the [German] Army group commander.[654]

Germany's allies also perpetrated massacres and violated international law during the war, as the Hungarian experience shows. For example, the research into the counterinsurgency actions has revealed that the Hungarian VIII Corp Commander (name unknown) filed an official complaint to *Army Group Center* regarding the "leniency" of the *221ˢᵗ Security Division*:

> In the course of [*Operation*] *Csaba* (sic) it has been necessary to annihilate villages within the operational area, and resettle their inhabitants. From communication with the *221ˢᵗ Security Division* it had become clear, however, that the divisional command, as the senior field command, opposes this policy. I must emphasize urgently that only the most radical pursuit of this policy will prevent partisans and inhabitants from pouring back in a very short space of time and polluting the area once more.[655]

Many of these counterinsurgency units were formed as part of the *Ordnungsdienst* (Order Service), and were definitely sub-standard when compared to the *SD* and *SS* units,[656] and these conscript and volunteer units also had the highest desertion rates.[657] It is arguable that the low caliber of professional fighting and leadership qualities exhibited by these volunteer and conscript units, as well as "the replacement officers from the west"[658] played a major role in their committing the worst atrocities. Frustration at their enemies combined with poor leadership and long standing prejudices provided the fuel for disaster.[659]

However, not only the foreign recruits demonstrated limited experience in their newly assigned roles, and were recorded with interest.[660] The accepted elites, the paratroops, often had their problems while engaged in the antipartisan role. The *1ˢᵗ Fallshirmjaeger-Ausbildungs-Regiment* (Paratrooper Training Regiment) was staffed with mostly half trained and inexperienced young soldiers and deployed to the Gomel region. The results were less than flattering.[661] In addition, the reassignment of Italian soldiers into the anti-partisan role proved somewhat controversial, if not outright counterproductive:

> The arrival of tens of thousands of troops from the Italian 8th Army during February [1943] did not help one iota. These troops had staggered into the... area after being thrashed in the winter battles in southern Russia, and their morale and discipline were dangerously low; as well as plundering and requisitioning Russian houses and accosting Russian women and girls, they spread defeatist talk and thus reinforce the population's perception that Soviet victory was just a matter of time.[662]

In many cases faulty leadership is the prime factor in military units committing acts which may be perceived as "illegitimate." This is due to soldiers losing confidence in their leaders, hence the fear and frustration borne of uncertainty. This condition and the resulting atrocities were not unique to any particular unit or branch. The myth that the SS and SD were the sole counterinsurgency forces is false, as evidenced by an operation on 29 April 1943 during *Operation Osterhase*:[663]

> In the course of hard, day long fighting it proved possible, thanks to the very well-equipped *Luftwaffe* units which were on hand, to drive the bandits into the forest and cleanse it by evening. After the two bandit camps in the forest were overrun, the enemy, having suffered very heavy losses, fled westward across the swamps.[664]

Part of the problem culminating in atrocities was the difficulty in distinguishing between actual insurgents and innocent civilians, a problem facing not just the average soldier but also his superior leadership, increasing the tensions between soldiers and civilians. Some commanders tried to prevent these problems, as demonstrated by the statement from von Schenckendorff: "The partisan movement is a menace to the lives and property of its own compatriots. The Russian people, the farmers in particular, reject these terror tactics. The current partisan war is a war not for the people, but for Bolshevism."[665]

This inability to distinguish irregulars from noncombatants was primary reason for many crimes to have been committed, even when there were standing orders promoted contrary actions. In Belorussia alone 5,295 villages were destroyed during "legitimate" anti-partisan operations, many times without orders from higher authority.[666] Between July 1941 to 1 March 1942 63,000 "partisans" and 638 Germans had been killed.[667] By May 1942 the numbers of 80,000 "partisans" being killed, versus only 1,094 Germans in *Army Group*

Center's rear area were recorded, providing ample concern regarding the legitimacy of such actions.[668] Another example is that of the *403rd Security Division* registering over a thousand partisans killed without a single German loss during October 1942 alone.[669] Most of these killed were in fact Jews.[670]

The great disparity between the figures of German and "partisan" dead leave nothing to the imagination. Most certainly many of those killed were civilians who were simply in the "wrong place at the wrong time," or were specific targets of the genocide policy and fed into the casualty reports, in order to bolster the legitimacy of the actions.[671] One example is cited by Shepherd regarding the actions and comments of SS Brigadier General Herf:

> Yesterday a *Gauleiter* and General commissar unintentionally and unwittingly broadcast certain secret reports (intended for the *Fuehrer!*) showing that some 480 rifles were found on 6,000 dear "partisans". Put bluntly, all these men had been shot to swell the figure of enemy losses and highlight our own "heroic deeds".[672]

These activities were not universal among all units and commanders, although there were many sadists and butchers, professional soldiers by end large who felt that hunting civilians was perhaps somewhat safer than tackling the Red Army. Shepherd states that:

> The conduct of officers in the *Ostheer's* rear area anti-partisan units was shaped by interactions between *real or perceived* military necessity, ideology, economics, the need for constructive engagement, and the personal perceptions of officers; the second, that perceptions were shaped by a variety of ideological, military, pragmatic, ethical and careerist influences; the third, that the resulting conduct displayed different shades of brutality and restraint.[673]

This belief in their control of the situation and the soundness of their policies was to be eradicated as the Germans became the hunted. The Central Staff of the Partisan Movement was established on 30 May 1942 in Moscow under the direction of General P.K. Ponomarenko (rather late in the war due to Stalin's mistrust of his own people), who was responsible for upgrading the Belorussian partisan movement from an *ad hoc* disorganized paramilitary movement into a full-fledged and equipped military entity supportive of Red Army operations.[674]

This development occurred slowly, with official Soviet figures estimating a partisan strength (mainly through conscription) of between 700,000 and 1,300,000 during the war.[675] This figure does not include separatist an-Communist guerrillas. Contemporary German figures provide the estimates of between 400,000 and 500,000 partisans, while German officials in Western Russia in 1943 claimed only 80,000 partisans in that region, yet these figures only applied to organized resistance groups that could be plainly identified.[676]

Of these estimates, the wartime figure of 52,300 German casualties versus 243,800 "partisan dead" in Western Russia alone (primarily Belorussia and the surrounding areas) is interesting. Another example of irregular statistics are the *201st Security Division's* figures of 2,737 partisan dead versus 109 Germans killed in early 1943, during *Operations Osterhase, Schneehase, Kugelblitz* and *Donnerkeil*,[677] while German casualties all along the front climbed along with partisan strength and morale plummeted.[678] Stalin's call for a partisan war was heeded, and the Soviets forged the most potent resistance groups of the war. As stated by Robert L. O'Connell:

> They became a nation at arms. In their reliance on snipers, and in the partisan campaigns, they did not so much fight the Germans as hunt them. At times they advanced under orders to take no prisoners. As this is characteristic of such struggles, women became involved in the fighting, though on a larger scale than ever before, even flying combat missions, acting as snipers, and participating in human wave assaults. In short, the Russians fought with the desperation of those preyed upon.[679]

The increasing numbers of partisans and their effectiveness, as well as the limitations of propaganda in areas not under German control is stated in the following report from July 1943 from the *221st Security Division*:

> The bandits...are not restricting themselves to destroying economic concerns through attack and sabotage; increasingly they are trying to deprive the occupying troops of crops. Despite our troops' efforts, transportation of food supplies has been disrupted by strong and repeated bandit attacks. Bandit ruled territory has been progressively isolated from neighboring areas. Our own propaganda effort has been largely expelled from such areas. These areas constitute a severe danger, because enemy forces, including airborne troops, can gather there.[680]

German military leaders adopted several methods of attempting to stem the insurgency problems in the Soviet Union, with most methods being adopted and implemented in the field as the enemy threat was presented.[681] The evolution of counterinsurgency doctrine was one of rapid maturation beset by inconsistency, internal conflicts between military, political and regional commanders and administrators, as well as the ever-changing and confusing political and racial doctrine as represented by German propaganda.

With regard to developing a cogent tactical doctrine, the first lesson that must be learned is: just as in conventional warfare, terrain, and weather dictate the pace and scope of counterinsurgency operations. What limits a conventional force will usually assist the irregular, just as an advantage or strength for the insurgent will, on occasion (but not always) be a weakness for his enemy. "An encirclement, considering our own weak forces and our experiences of the previous winter, was out of the question. Attacks were instead on particular points."[682] The irregular can blend into his surroundings, assimilate within the population and become absorbed into the landscape, usually finding safety and support. The conventional uniformed soldier stands out and has no such ability.

Most of the irregulars combating German forces were not the hated "Semitic" peoples, but rather a multitude of ethnic groups fighting as either partisans *or* guerrillas (without the Germans and post-war historians making any distinction), depending upon their ideologies, nationalist ambitions and long term objectives.[683] The ethnic group primarily defined as a viable resistance force were the Slavs, also identified as a "people" to be discriminated against along with the Jews. Slavs were ideally to constitute the bulk of the slave labor force in the east.

Propaganda also targeted Slavs as a people whose "un-cleanliness was notorious from the earliest times," hence reducing their status as human beings in order to morally justify their slaughter.[684] Communists would account for the largest and most effective resistance force in a backlash of unimaginable proportions.[685] It would be this ideological force, an application of illogic and paranoia, as well as opportunism that would throw two socially and politically similar, yet juxtaposed tyrants and their collective populations into the greatest collective mass killing in history.

The counterinsurgent is faced with only three options: ignore the insurgents and their supporters, attempt to convert the insurgents and recruit them, or root out and destroy them. The latter option is very time consuming and frustrating to the men involved, often heightening the dangers to which they are already exposed, as well as creating a sense of despair and hatred. This feeling is often expended upon the suspected civilian support network and the irregulars themselves when captured. One response was to create specific units for the counterinsurgency role, predominantly *Waffen* SS and *Einsatzgruppen* units already engaged in the killing process.[686]

The best explanation for so many actions to become mass murders was desperation and fear, even by soldiers who would normally have been appalled by the *Einsatzgruppen* methods. These factors created the justification many men needed in order to excuse their acts in their own minds, both morally and legally. An example of a mission of complete destruction "justified" by the senior staff of *Wirtschaftskommando "Klinzy"* in Belorussia on 11 July 1943 follows:

> Rayon[687] Mglin has been largely evacuated and burned to the ground. Extensive preparations need making for the crops there to be gathered during the next few weeks, likewise in rayon Slinka twelve villages have been burned down in the course of a military operation.[688]

Another factor was the constant lack of manpower to accomplish the missions, further heightening the tension within the units as partisans increased their activities and their numbers grew. As stated by the intelligence section of the *221st Security Division* during *Operation Klette II* from April to May 1943:[689]

> During April 1943 the unrest in the entire divisional area reached dangerous proportions. Valuable economic installations, depots, dairies, distilleries, etc., were everywhere attacked and in places burned down. Raiding and plunder of the villages and the murder of *starosten*690 and other pro-German inhabitants became the order of the day. The division's attempts to combat this mushrooming threat were severely restricted due to the inadequate forces available.[691]

Other reports also state the reality of both the morale and the military condition of both sides:

> The troops' pride and confidence are suffering, because their paltry numbers, inadequate weaponry and low mobility prevent them from delivering a powerful blow against the bandits. The bandits are in a poor state militarily and could certainly be destroyed if sufficient forces were deployed... the men are willing, as they showed at Kamenka and Lossof, but the current strained situation is creating demands which cannot be met in the long term.[692]

> Last night, quite by accident, the OK in Propoisk uncovered a plot by some *Hilfswillige*, who until then had been reliable, to murder their officers and then, with the OD and bandits massing before Propoisk, to annihilate the other Germans there...(meanwhile) the battalion's strength continues to dwindle without any prospect of reinforcement, and its tasks grow more difficult and numerous. Things cannot continue as they are. The men on watch are being pushed to the limits, and every man down to the lowliest private is afraid in the face of the danger which grows more threatening all the time. No one can explain or understand why our side is so weak and inactive; this is a condition which the German Army has never before experienced...The companies can no longer spare any men for the training courses which have been ordered...the last replacements arrived September 1942.[693]

Erich von dem Bach-Zelewski was one of the first counterinsurgency officers, commanding *Einsatzgruppen* units from July 1941 until October 1942,

as well commanding all anti-partisan forces for the SS in Russia, numbering some 11,000 men with an additional 6,000 Field Police at his disposal.[694]
Bach-Zelewski actually formed the first training program for anti-partisan
operations in September 1941, although this was not as refined a process as it
was to later become.[695] Under Zelewski's command thousands of "suspected
partisans" had been rounded up and executed along with Jews, Gypsies, and
the handicapped. Villages were destroyed on his orders; by 1942 the initial
operations had reached their early zenith, as stated by Overy:[696]

> On a military level the operations were reasonably successful. More than
> two-thirds of the occupied area had no partisan activity of any significance,
> and inhospitable swamp, thousands of partisans were rounded up and shot
> or publicly hanged, with placards placed around their necks, as an example
> to the rest.[697]

The reprisal and operational methods as outlined were either reaction-
ary reflex actions or calculated and methodical liquidation operations. Regardless of either method both were counter-productive due to their inconsistency and ruthless nature. As stated by Colonel General Hans von
Greiffenberg:

> The use of force on the part of the German occupation troops (evacuation,
> taking hostages, punitive expeditions) fell far short of producing the de-
> sired results. Since the Russian partisans hardly adhere to the rules of civi-
> lized warfare, such measures were most likely to provoke reprisals against
> German troops and friendly elements among the local populations.[698]

The traditional German military mindset was not one that readily accepted the concept of "specialized" soldiers in the elitist sense. Those soldiers chosen specifically for such non-traditional operations, such as anti-
partisan interdiction were not initially viewed with admiration, as stated by
James Lucas:

> Considering the aura which today surrounds the camouflaged men of the
> special forces it is surprising to recall that the employment of guerrilla war-
> fare which they operate are aspects of warfare that were repugnant to the
> orthodox military mind as recently as the first decades of this century. The
> conduct of today's special forces would have been incomprehensible to the
> conventional soldiers of former days. The attitude of the German profes-
> sional soldier to special forces was one of total abhorrence.[699]

One problem that arose, becoming counterproductive was the creation
and incorporation of specific anti-partisan units. These units were ruthless
even beyond the expectations of some of the most fervent *Nazi* Party officials.
The *Kaminsky Brigade* was commanded by SS Colonel Bronislav Kaminsky and
designated the 29th *Waffen Grenadier Division der SS 'Russische' Nr. 1*. The *Dirle-*

wanger Brigade was commanded by SS Colonel Oskar Dirlewanger,[700] upgraded from a *Sonderkommando* detachment to a paper division, labeled the 36th *Waffen SS Grenadier Division*. Despite this designation the unit never reached the necessary division strength of 15,000–17,000 men. Both units committed what were undoubtedly the worst atrocities recorded on a regular basis during the war.[701]

German officers and soldiers were not prepared for the kind of war they found themselves involved in; civilians by the millions swarming around them, killing them, and becoming a psychological, materiel and morale burden.[702] German professional officers were taught in detail regarding every aspect of modern warfare, its history, security, logistics, communications, political indoctrination, morale, tactics, strategy, and leadership. Morale became one of the greatest concerns, and many times commanders watched their men become withdrawn after witnessing and especially participating in the killings of civilians, with some actually refusing to participate. As stated by Browning[703] and Breitman:

> Before the first killing, the battalion commander offered his men the option of not taking part. No one would be punished for refraining from mass murder. Yet the overwhelming majority of the middle-aged policemen from Hamburg participated and continued to kill, week after week. Browning concludes that peer pressure and the climate of war led most of them to follow orders despite the availability of an escape to other tasks.[704]

Morale was also affected by other considerations, such as weather and the natural fear of war. As stated by Bartov: "The discipline of the troops has deteriorated during the winter. This is also shown by the increasing numbers of trials. Guard duty has particularly been neglected, spelling danger for the troops."[705] This is also reflected in the following report:

> Recently, heavy losses have had to be sustained due to the troops' negligence and carelessness in their conduct of the full range of necessary security duties. It must be hammered into the troops that they must maintain the sharpest state of alertness, even in those areas where attacks have not recently taken place.[706]

Even the United States Army studied the problems facing the Germans on the Eastern Front following the war, and this information is located in Department of the Army Pamphlets published on this very subject.[707] The Germans were also faced with the problem of soldiers participating or witnessing these events, and later relating them to civilians back home. These events were not considered appropriate, as the "rumors of mass liquidations circulated by soldiers on leave from the front brought details of what they had seen or heard."[708]

This problem was the direct responsibility of the Ministry of Propaganda under Goebbels and the policies outlined by Himmler, which churned out material at a frantic pace to provide justification for the deaths of millions. Himmler's perception of the potential morale problem is stated:

> Himmler was keenly aware that the execution of civilians might have damaging effects on the police executioners-even in 1940 he said he had been warned about this. So Himmler believed that, in addition to orders, the police needed a reason to kill, and they needed social gatherings in the evenings to reduce the strain. Once they had carried out mass murder in response to an allege crime or provocation, it would be easier to get them to follow broader killing orders later... Himmler was convinced that many amongst the German people were too soft to recognize the historical necessity of Nazi Germany's racial policies.[709]

Propaganda, as much as tactical thinking and machine guns was a primary weapon in the counterinsurgency war. The hatreds and carnage took its toll, as stated by Overy: "The law of the jungle might have assisted German fighting spirit in the Soviet campaign, but its morale effects were otherwise entirely negative. The criminalization of warfare produced a growing indiscipline and demoralization amongst German forces themselves."[710]

Conventional German combat doctrine focused upon combined arms assaults, which included armor, aircraft,[711] artillery, dispatch riders,[712] and infantry, with the infantry locating, identifying, and closing with the enemy under cover of the other assets, often resorting to hand to hand combat. The *Waffen SS*, whose commanders competed with the Army for recognition and accolades particularly favored this method of combat.[713] German commanders were forced to address the "new war" and its particular problems.

Secrecy before missions was heavily stressed; men were informed according to rank on a "need to know" basis to ensure security. This was even more important and stressed in the counterinsurgency units.[714] The Germans were not generally instructed in the proper handling of civilian populations, or even how to manage an insurgency, until a firm doctrine for offensive counterinsurgency methods was introduced in early 1943, as stated by Otto Kumm:

> Our professional officers' training, and that of the Army and SS, since more than half the *Waffen SS* were comprised of former Army soldiers, did not include military action against civilian irregular forces. This was not even a concept at this time, since prior to the Second World War there had been static warfare, much like in the First World War. With the new war it was highly mobile, covering ground more quickly, and bringing much more ter-

ritory and more people under our control. Also, another and more dangerous problem was that we now had the Soviet Union to contend with, and
its great mass of territory and people. It should have been foreseen that we
would have future problems with (guerrilla) fighters, but this was simply
an oversight that we tried to remedy too late with too little.[715]

The greatest German flaw was failing to understand the differences between the various peoples of the Soviet Union. Treating all peoples in the
same general manner was their *modus operandi*, without taking into account
the individual as well as collective needs, desires, and ambitions of those
selected populations. Failing to analyze the needs of the various groups and
neglecting to provide security for them, as well as the brutal occupation policies forged the weapons of resistance. The German failure to comprehend
the nature of the various Soviet peoples was summed up by Captain Gregor
Koronov:

> You must understand that when people speak of the Soviet Union and Rus-
> sia, they are not speaking about the same country. Russia is just one of the
> many nations that created the Soviet Union. These soldiers who killed their
> officers and defected did so because they were forced to live under a system
> that they did not want, fighting in an army they did not volunteer for, and
> fighting for a man [Stalin] who had perhaps ordered the executions and
> deportations of people they probably knew. You must also look at the fact
> that these soldiers were White Russians, Belorussians, Ukrainians, and so
> on. What loyalty were they expected to have? I am not surprised that more
> such incidents are not recorded. If this information were to have been re-
> leased by the *Stavka* in Moscow the effect would have been widespread
> panic, and we may have lost the war.[716]

The various peoples tired of Stalinist rule were basically independence
minded nationalists. By harnessing that concept the potential for gathering
allies was clear. One example was the Belorussian population, since many
people felt inclined to fight the Communist partisans "if a nationalist Belorussian government were formed very soon."[717]

The Germans had placed themselves in a position of ultimate failure
long before they began developing a proper counterinsurgency doctrine:
"Where the Germans and other militaries of the world failed in their
counterinsurgency activities was to properly understand the nature of
the insurgent, Eastern or Western European, potential ally or dedicated
adversary."[718] Even more important, they did not care. Hitler had placed the
peoples of the USSR in an unenviable position: that of choosing between
two lethal dictators who were extreme political opposites, yet very similar
in the ruthless application of their respective ideologies.

The Germans were perhaps the worst offenders of logic; attempting to convert as well as subjugate and exploit the very people they were murdering, by infusing propaganda as a fix all remedy. As long as the policies were generally being followed, and their superiors did not take an inordinate amount of interest in their actions, the field officers were usually content to allow the *status quo* to remain undisturbed. This mentality of "out of sight, out of mind" with regard to ones' superiors was a counterproductive policy (as well as illegal). This posture has been a universal phenomenon in militaries throughout history, where subordinates prefer not to be under the constant scrutiny of their superiors.

Coupled with their own ever-changing racial policy and doctrine on how to handle the population, the fluid nature of the war in general, and the abject disregard for international law sealed their fate. The alternating interest in their plight by Hitler compounded the difficulties facing the Germans in the field. Hitler's inability to accept "bad news" or even address issues unpleasant to him were to cost his soldiers and the counterinsurgency effort dearly. Basically, for want of a saddle he killed the horse.

I. REACTIONARY COUNTERINSURGENCY APPLICATIONS

Active counterinsurgency operations were the primary method of trying to reduce the irregular threats, originally starting with the death squads in 1941 to remove suspected threats. These actions forced an upsurge in activity, forcing the Germans to change their method from one of small unit actions against unarmed civilians they perceived as resistance and Red Army supporters, to actively pursuing groups that more heavily armed and better organized units. These operations "produced high body counts among both irregulars and civilians, while feeding the fuel for local resistance recruiters who advertised the atrocities perpetrated against villages."[719]

The initial method for applying the counterinsurgency policy was a two-sided approach. Himmler believed the SS and SD were best suited to the task of murder, which meant eliminating any potential problem to prevent such events from occurring. The German *Ordnungspolizei* under SS Major General Kurt Daluege would be responsible for the civilians behind the front, while supporting the death squads of the *Sonderkommando* and *Einsatzgruppen* units, thus relieving the better trained *Waffen* SS men for front-line duty.[720]

The specific tasking method still presented problems, since officials in Berlin issued orders to field commanders without understanding the complications being experienced, and the unforeseen factors which naturally arose and had to be dealt with accordingly. Many of these unforeseen factors were the constant changing of policy and tactics by the Soviets, who were very adept at field craft and improvisation amongst their forces. They adapted by developing their own doctrine as a response to the German threat. This Soviet development would become the groundwork for insurgency policy long after the war was over in occupied Eastern Europe.[721]

This lack of communication and understanding from above was rampant throughout the German military, and typical of the counterinsurgency units, death squads, and adjacent commands, adding to the confusion. Leon Degrelle discussed this topic:

> Even Gehlen became tired of trying to convince Hitler that there was a better way of dealing with the problem. It was not until Steiner, Wolff, and Gehlen came together with their new plan that we were able to completely take the fight to the partisans successfully. Most of our planning was initiated at the division level and filtered down to the company level, with regimental commanders having great flexibility in the execution of their operations. Still, despite all of the innovations we devised, there was still no substitute for treating the population gently, and this failure was the ultimate mistake.[722]

In order to draw reprisals from the Germans to further their agenda, irregulars would often perform hit and run attacks, withdrawing to villages with the Germans in full pursuit, as previously discussed by Koronov. The end result would be a reprisal mission, thus legitimizing the irregulars' position among the people, even if their deliberate action was the cause of the reprisal.[723] As stated, all inclusive reprisals of this nature were and are a clear violation of the law.

German leaders began using recruited locals as a guerrilla force to counter the partisans, often working in conjunction with military units in anti-partisan sweeps. Given the need for securing static defensive regions the Germans decided to employ an equally important, yet less direct and more stable method of combating resistance. As German forces began to actively engage irregulars more frequently, evaluations regarding these methods were made:

> Following the pattern of large-scale police raids, such anti-partisan actions must converge on a definitive object, achieve complete surprise, and be executed with the utmost thoroughness. Merely combing through a vast for-

est and swamp area for partisans or trying to seal it off will require the use of inordinately large forces and perhaps, may have the effect of pacifying the area temporarily. But the result in the long run will hardly justify the means employed.[724]

The development of doctrine was actually an evolutionary process; from police actions, roundups, hostage taking, and outright murders of suspected irregulars and sympathizers in villages, to small unit actions conducting sweep and clear (also known as search and destroy) operations, finally developing into the large unit assaults on suspected partisan positions by infantry and motorized infantry with artillery and air support. Otto Kumm described his impression of such large-scale operations when they were finally employed by 1943:

> At this time I was serving with *2nd SS Division "Das Reich"* as a company commander and we were ordered to locate and destroy the partisan forces.[725] The problem we had was that we were not accustomed to seeking out an enemy and giving chase, since the Soviet soldiers fought bravely, and usually until they were either killed, captured or out of ammunition. The partisans operated as a hit and run unit, firing a few shots, dropping back, firing again, luring our men into ambushes and trying to penetrate our flanks. Some even carried radios to call artillery and air strikes against us [rare until 1944]. This was not what we were used to. Finally we decided on a tactic of probing forward with a squad, followed by a platoon, which would be flanked by a platoon on each side. Once the partisans fired the center squad would give chase, dropping to fire as the following center platoon rushed through under cover fire. The two flanking platoons were in radio contact with the rest, so depending upon which way the partisans ran the facing platoon would stand fast, whilst the entire formation would pivot around behind the enemy, chasing them into the line of fire of the stationary unit. This plan worked well, and once the enemy were engaged the platoons would call artillery fire behind the partisans preventing escape, forcing them to stand and fight. This is when the heavy weapons would take over and the artillery would be walked back into the partisan unit. It took a few practices to get this down to a proper format, but it proved to be quite effective.[726]

Kumm also expressed his opinion in the value of his own anti-partisan operations as implemented prior to 1943:

> It was like gathering ants by burning their perimeter, forcing them into the ever tightening circle. The few who attempt to leave get burned, while the rest would group together to find some moral security in their closeness. This we exploited by bombing, artillery or machine gun fire, but it was always a costly tactic employed by the partisans. I would have to say that this tactic was definitely the best method of containing and liquidation we ever used.[727]

It must be noted that the actions described by Kumm were completely legal under international law. "Passive" operations were supervised by both the *Abwehr* and *SD Amt IV* (Office IV) who collected intelligence and issued orders to field commanders in rear and forward areas.[728] The practices used were varied, and often in conflict with active operations and adjacent commands. However, the passive method proved more problematic, as the Germans became more defensive in their posture following the setbacks of 1943. Yet the Germans used both active *and* passive methods in a mutually beneficial program, which in fact became doctrine by late 1942, and partisan actions often dictated the method employed by the Germans.

For example, a passive security posture could immediately become "active" should enemy forces engage and withdraw, prompting pursuit. The High Command, not being completely informed or even interested in the needs of the commanders at the front often issued contradictory orders, such as short-term mobile operations to be organized and employed, even if these actions impeded and threatened passive security measures.[729]

German commanders understood the necessity of protecting rear area targets, such as ammunition and troop depots, roads, lines of supply and communication. In order to better protect their assets German commanders looked toward the recruitment of the locals as auxiliaries (*Hilfswilligen*), as well as the *Arbeitseinsatz* effort.[730] These recruits would become more involved as the racial criteria were constantly lowered, with those "best suited" going to field units as *Freiwilligen*.

The recruitment of locals was not always difficult, given that they had often been preyed upon by their own countrymen, and their livestock, farm machinery, and kinfolk were often taken without compensation by the irregulars. These actions were also violations of international law according to Geneva and Hague, and the Germans were astute enough to try and exploit this.[731]

German commanders usually extended better treatment to these "friendly" civilians in order to secure their assistance, placing them on the payroll and providing security from the partisans so many feared.[732] As clearly defined by Geneva, confiscation of personal property is illegal, unless a receipt is given, and the proper financial restitution must be made to the owner, unless said property was previously used against the attacking military force.

Security was the primary concern, and many of the recruits were used as guards on trains and truck convoys, which only moved during the daytime with departure and arrival schedules staggered as to not establish a pattern that could be predicted. These precautions reduced the chance of planned enemy interdiction.[733]

Rail traffic was a particularly favorite target, so the Germans created the security train concept.[734] Two armored gondola cars were place at either end of the locomotives to protect them from heavy weapons fire, while machine gunners and even horse mounted cavalry and motorcycle reconnaissance troops routinely traveled within as a pursuit element in case of contact.[735] For additional security, *flakwierling* (mobile anti-aircraft guns, primarily of the 20mm variety) were mounted on cars with crews, with the total force averaging between forty and fifty soldiers.[736]

Defensive perimeters were established using ditches, single approach roads, wire, and interlocking fields of fire covering killing zones that channeled the enemy into selected fields of fire. These were manned by German troops, with auxiliaries patrolling outside the wire with guard dogs and performing the bulk of the external security patrols.[737] Fortifications included bunkers (often built by slave labor of *Organization Todt* in violation of Hague and Geneva),[738] pillboxes, and mine fields covered by crew served weapons, as well as short to medium range mortars, often supported by 105mm and 88mm guns. German security doctrine also included protecting airfields from attack, as stated by *Luftwaffe* fighter ace and Group Commander Lieutenant General Dietrich Hrabak:

> In Russia we were always aware of the possibility of partisan attacks against our airfields. We had *Luftwaffe* ground soldiers assigned to our fields; never trusting the volunteers, not with the aircraft. I never really had a problem with partisans attacking my airfields in particular, and the only problem I remember having was when we were in the Kurland. The Red Army was attacking and we had to leave rather quickly, but I cannot say for certain if this involved partisans or not. I do know that we took every precaution against partisan sabotage.[739]

II. Preventive Counterinsurgency Applications

German counterinsurgency missions followed an ever-changing, yet very strict process entailing detailed intelligence gathering, operational briefings and post-operational debriefings. This method of mission preparation and analysis is important for any successful operation, where successes and failure may be studied and doctrine may be updated as the situation changes. This method is still in use today by the German, American and British militaries, among others.[740]

Another method of passive counterinsurgency not as widely used (yet often yielded outstanding results) was the attempt at converting the masses to a more manageable and "user friendly" population through humanitarian aid and treatment. His concept would later become known as "winning the hearts and minds." The Germans did manage to convert the peoples of certain regions, including anti-Communist guerrilla groups (especially in the Ukraine, Baltic States, etc.) and disaffected partisans convinced to join the German cause. His was achieved by exploiting the very long-standing problems between rival groups, as mentioned by Degrelle and evidenced by Vlasov's forces.

Many successes were possible by rebuilding churches destroyed during the battles, allowing open worship of their respective faiths (with primary exceptions being Jews and Jehovah's Witnesses). Also effective was allowing the grateful clergy, long underground or exiled by Stalin to re-surface and become influential among their people. Otto Kumm described the process in his own words:

> The amazing part of the effort to convert the masses to our ideology hinged upon how they were treated. On the one hand, we could reduce a village and think that we had solved the problem in that area, only to realize that the problem had just increased in severity. However, when we assisted in the rebuilding of towns, churches, or even allowed the local civil administration to maintain control over their people without a strong military presence, we yielded greater results. This fact was self-evident to those of us in the field. We could not convince our superiors in Berlin to agree to such a method. This was where we failed.[741]

The other area of passive counterinsurgency, which proved quite successful, was propaganda. The utilization of written and verbal communication to penetrate the minds of the resistance and Red Army alike was an ongoing operation. Radio remained an effective method of receiving information, but to transmit propaganda to an opponent effectively was only successful if the target population had access to such devices. Few Soviet citizens were so equipped, and most receiving units were manned and operated by Soviet political officers.

When Lieutenant General Andrei A. Vlasov was captured in 1942, he became only one of dozens of former high-ranking Soviet officers to join the Germans against Stalin, using radio as their medium of choice. These officers were quite disaffected with their leadership and over Stalin's ability to simply throw away lives, sacrificing young men and women for little (if any) positive gain. German propaganda began using these former enemies as propaganda tools directed against their former leader and his subjects.[742] As a result Geneva 1949 was revised to strictly forbid the exploitation and pub-lic display of POWs to serve a political or military objective due to actions such as these. This does not apply to men who convert to the enemy's line of thinking of their own free will, which was the case with Vlasov.

The propaganda campaign directed against the Soviets was quite effec-tive, swelling the ranks of the auxiliaries and volunteers. What prevented this method from being completely successful was the recent memory of past and ongoing atrocities:

> This was particularly true of the Ukraine. True, Hitler envisioned a German land reform conglomerate that would supply the *Reich* with the necessary agricultural produce and slave labor to continue the planting and harvest-ing.[743] However, his failure to take into account the fact that the peoples of the east may not readily exchange one tyrant for another, let alone take up arms in support of his invasion *en masse* proved disastrous.[744]

Germany was faced with a great crisis; how to manage it was the pri-mary concern, and simply killing civilians was not working. The German military, through the specific direction of officers such as Kumm, Wolff, Steiner, Bach-Zelewski, Bittrich, Degrelle, Herbert Gille and others created an entirely new method of waging warfare against irregulars, based upon the conventional German motorized infantry concept. As stated by Kumm:

> Once we were given a plain language of organization and equipment, with tactics outlined, we felt better prepared for tackling the partisan problem. However, we had been improvising with our own methods, and these new tactics were unique; they were handed down as a guideline, not engraved in stone, offering us the opportunity to use the new method in conjunc-tion with the previous method. We were to write reports on our missions and make recommendations. Another unique part of this plan was that everyone, even the lowest rank was to give his input through the chain of command, so that every perspective was covered. It was a wonderful method of waging [counterinsurgency] warfare, but it never resolved the problem of halting the constant flood of partisans that seemed to pop up like mushrooms after a summer rain. Other officers made recommenda-tions that were finally taken seriously and placed into doctrine. This was how important Berlin finally took the partisan problem.[745]

Another method of attempted damage control regarding appeasing the populations was the directive issued from *OKW* and filtered down to various units, such as the *221ˢᵗ Security Division* during *Operations Ankara I* and *Ankara II*[746] during the winter of 1942–43; *Operations Osterhase, Zugspitz, Klette I* and *II*, and *Nachbarhilfe* during the spring of 1943, *Operations Junikaefer* in June 1943 and *Sommerfest* in July 1943, as well as supportive operations. These orders both banned *and* allowed the indiscriminate burning of villages in reprisal, in violation of the existing laws.[747] However, these directives were only as effective as the means available to oversee their enforcement.[748]

III. Analysis of Both Counterinsurgency Methods

The Germans were quite competent at self-analysis with regard to military operations. They supported their analysis by constantly reviewing the after action reports and unit commanders' comments. The updated intelligence gathered would usually provide valuable information. However, they seldom if ever evaluated the legality of their actions. To do so would have been in direct conflict with their orders and the very platform of National Socialism. The greatest detriment to German intelligence gatherers was the inability to collect electronic intelligence. This was due to the fact that most partisan units in the early days did not carry radios, which were expensive and easy to locate with detection equipment.

Several German commanders interviewed provided their personal analysis on the effectiveness of partisan attacks, their own anti-partisan operations and sweeps, as well as a complete evaluation as to "how and why" there were inconsistent success and failure. Leon Degrelle provided his own opinion:

> Partisans were the greatest nightmare we as soldiers faced during the war in the east. With the Red Army we knew their tactics, which were constantly evolving yet based on established procedure, and they adopted our method of *Blitzkrieg* later. However, the partisans were dangerous because they did not wear uniforms and didn't operate as a disciplined, traditional military force. Instead, they functioned as a random hit and run guerrilla group, striking any-where and everywhere without warning. They did suffer from one great flaw; their inability to function outside their own areas of operation, mainly due to their inability to maintain a viable supply and communications network, as well as the fact that were not fully supported by the Red Army until late in 1942-43. Another problem facing the partisans in the east, and not just in Russia, was the fact that despite numbering in the hundreds of thousands, various partisan groups did no always share the same political conviction or ultimate post-war objective, let alone share the same motivation for waging war. Many times partisans would fight each other over limited resources. Sometimes long-standing hatreds would create a problem, igniting infighting as well, such as the conflict between the Georgians and Ukrainians. All of these we tried to use to our advantage. These were the problems we tried to exploit.[749]

The German commanders were also faced with a myriad of problems that were not a concern of their Western Allied counterparts. Setting aside the moral and legal issues regarding their actions, the officers had reason to be concerned with regard to the morale of their men, as well as the mood of the populations. Often it would be the reactions of the civilians or the German commander's perception of their mood that would dictate his actions, if in fact the locals were "user friendly" and considered necessary to the labor or counterinsurgency programs. Leon Degrelle provided an example of how doctrine was developed and propaganda used by judging the actions and mood of the people:

> The political officers would do their best to bring these disaffected factions over to our side, and in many cases it worked. It worked well with the Ukrainians, Bessarabians, Belorussians, and others, because many of these people had suffered under Stalin. However, due to the German method of handling the local populations our own applications for support of these groups were met with an understandable amount of skepticism. It was of course the senseless slaughter of civilians that actually created the partisan problem. We were only able to become successful against the partisans by being able to think like them, understand their motivations and desires; how, where, when, and why they functioned as they did, and try to mentally outmaneuver them. Unfortunately, Berlin did not see the utility in our cause.[750]

The partisans of the Soviet Union were an *ad-hoc* and rather ineffective group during the first year of the German invasion, despite the fact that Red Army and political officers moved into German held territory to recruit and train irregulars.[751] Irregulars that had been long ignored and not fully supported by Stalin with regard to their material value and needs found themselves being considered in a completely different light by the beginning of 1943. Long considered "irrelevant" to the total war effort by Stalin, Red Army commanders and political officers had been reporting on the insurgents' actions that were considered crucial in battles against German forces. So seriously was the partisan support taken, Stalin even eased many of his restrictions following the winter of 1941-42:

> The spring thaw saw the beginnings of Partisan activity throughout the occupied zone, causing grave concern to the front-line commanders and to the civilian administration in the rear. This was not, as some thought at the time, a mere matter of security control. It was one of the fruits of a masterpiece of political innovation by Stalin, who, unlike certain others, was prepared for the time being to put ideology into cold storage. He appealed to Russian love of the country and announced the Great Patriotic War. Warrior heroes of the old Russia; Suvorov, Katuzov, were recalled in honor. In the newly re-opened churches prayers were offered for the victory of Russian arms.[752]

The German failure to address the resistance issues prior to the partisans receiving large-scale materiel support proved to be one of their greatest failures. Richard Overy provides his conclusion on this pivotal moment when the partisan forces became even more lethal, and legitimate:

> By 1943, the partisan movement in the rest of the occupied areas had come of age. The growing confidence of the Red Army and the greater availability of military supplies boosted the partisan organization. The units came to resemble the regular Army. Tanks, heavy artillery, even aircraft were made available. A total of 22,000 trained military experts were sent into the partisan regions, three-quarters of them demolition experts, 8 percent of them radio operators.[753]

The German soldier found himself performing diverse roles for which he was neither trained nor always properly equipped, either with knowledge or hardware to counter the growing insurgency problem. The German soldier was famous for his intensive training. Soldiers were trained to assume command at the next two levels above their rank in case of combat attrition, which was why they were such an effective fighting force. They were not so indoctrinated into the laws of warfare, unlike the military forces of today or their Western Allied counterparts.

However, the development of new ideas and tactics proved the most daunting task of all, but these problems were alleviated by the German ability to interpret the laws of warfare as they saw fit. The policy of propaganda, combined with military methods was expanded upon, and was particularly successful in the anti-partisan campaigns in the short term.[754] Unchanging German policies, even in the light of documented success was, in the end, the most important factor in rendering all those efforts useless. By failing to adhere to international law and building upon a platform of conversion through trust, the German soldier and his nation were doomed from the start.

IV. Conclusion

The actions of *Nazi* Germany constituted a clear violation of international law. With few exceptions, the military response to paramilitary actions often far exceeded the level of response required and acceptable under the laws then in effect.

The military leadership understood the need for implementing a workable counter-insurgency doctrine. What was lacking was a clear understanding of how to effect such a policy that would be deemed both legitimate to the civilians under their control and their own soldiers. What *is* clear was that the NSDAP policies then in effect *were* the prime directive as followed by most German leaders.

What is unclear in many cases is why more of these leaders did not abrogate the racial policy and adopt a more lucid method of handling the civilians, thus reducing the level and violence of irregular activity. It is understood that these commanders would have risked a visit by the *Gestapo*, should their operational methods be questioned. What is not acceptable is that more of the high ranking members of the military (unlike Bittrich and Manteuffel), who understood the law and the necessity of positive action, did not voice these concerns more openly and in concert with like-minded bureaucrats. If Hitler could waver on racial policy to suit his manpower needs, then was it not possible that he could have wavered on the logical application of international law and logic to achieve his aims? Perhaps not, since to do so would have diluted the power of two decades of *Nazi* propaganda and political indoctrination.

Although the answer is clear in hindsight, historians must remember the times and conditions under which the German military operated. Just as the United States military was segregated during the war, according to archaic racial guidelines (which was undoubtedly hypocritical since the US led the war to "save" world democracy), German forces operated under the same type of paradigm, although their behavior was taken to a much greater extreme. It was one thing to segregate people because of color and social prejudice; it was another to kill them because of that prejudice as a matter of state policy.

The rise of resistance always brings a greater armed response from the military in occupation. Hence, the military must use good judgment in handling that resistance, based upon the internal dynamic, direction and force of that resistance, thereby adopting a rational policy of containment and response that maintains at least the "appearance" of legitimacy. People who feel under threat will respond, and people who feel relatively secure in their personal safety will not usually resort to armed violence. In the case of Germany and the subjugated peoples of Europe, especially those in the USSR, they had no choice but to rebel against what they perceived to be a greater threat than the tyranny of Communism.

It must simply be stated that, because soldiers kill civilians in an orderly and systematic fashion during war or occupation, while morally reprehensible, it is not always illegal. In most cases it is the conduct of civilians that regulates the actions of soldiers. In several examples this book has shown that specific and selected regions of the USSR were relatively peaceful while others were hotbeds of unrest; the major difference was in the method of occupation.

For German leaders *en masse* to operate in a much more humane fashion, they would have had to operate in direct violation of German state law. They had the uncomfortable option of breaking German law, and therefore becoming criminals under international law. Few Germans leaders were able to walk the precarious tightrope between these two juxtaposed legal paradigms.

Although the Geneva and Hague Conventions provided the guidelines for universal military and belligerent government conduct during war, it was (and is) the responsibility of individual military leaders to ensure that their actions, and the actions of their troops, do not violate these laws. More important, they should ensure that, regardless of the legitimacy of their actions under the law, those same actions do not violate the laws of human decency. To do so would create insurgent problems where they did not exist before, and would destroy the ultimate political and military objectives of winning "hearts and minds." In the end it all comes under perceived legitimacy. The actions of belligerents, both military and paramilitary must conform to the accepted laws and social mores if they are to be regarded as legitimate, and remain above post conflict scrutiny.

APPENDIX 1. WAFFEN SS AND EINSATZGRUPPEN LEADERS[1]

BY DATES OF COMMAND

Waffen SS Brigade Nr. 1 "Reichsfuehrer-SS"

SS-Brigadier General Karl Demelhuber	24 April–1 November 1941
SS-Senior Colonel Richard Herrmann	1 November–21 December 1941
SS-Brigadier General Wilhelm Hartenstein	21 December 1941–30 November 1942

Waffen SS Brigade Nr. 2 'Reichsfuehrer-SS

SS-Brigadier General Karl von Treuenfeld	24 April 1941–5 July 1941
SS-Colonel Gottfried Klingemann	5 July 1941–25 January 1943

Waffen SS Cavalry Regiment Nr. 1/8ᵗʰ SS Cavalry Brigade "Florian Geyer"

SS-Major General Hermann Fegelein	25 February 1941–19 August 1941*
SS-Colonel Gustav Lombard	19 August–1 September 1941**
SS-Major General Hermann Fegelein	1 September 1941–1 May 1942

*Fegelein was an SS-Colonel; he later took over as commander of 'Florian Geyer' when it became *the 8ᵗʰ Waffen SS Cavalry Division.*

** Lombard was an SS-Major at this time, and later took over the command of the *1ˢᵗ Cavalry Regiment* of *'Florian Geyer'* in 1943. Fegelein was still a colonel at this time, and took over command after Lombard was severely wounded.

SS-Sonderkommando Dirlewanger

SS-Senior Colonel Oskar Dirlewanger	1 August 1940–15 February 1945***

***For a list of all the serving officers of this unit, see MacLean, *The Field Men*, Appendix 5, p. 163.

---

1 See a similar chart in MacLean, *The Field Men*, Appendix 7, p. 165.

APPENDIX 2. ORDER POLICE AND REGIONAL (HIGHER) SS LEADERS FOR THE *EINSATZGRUPPEN*

BY AREAS OF OPERATIONS AND DATES OF COMMAND[2]

NORTHERN RUSSIA

SS-Brigadier General Hans-Adolf Pruetzmann	22 June 1941–30 October 1941
SS-Major General Friedrich Jeckeln	1 November 1941–1 July 1944

CENTRAL AND WHITE RUSSIA

SS-Lieutenant General Erich v.d. Bach-Zelewski	2 June 1941–22 November 1942
SS-Brigadier General Georg Henning v. Bassewitz-Behr 22	November 1942–23 March 1943
SS-Major General Gerett Korsemann	23 March 1943–5 July 1943
SS-Major General Kurt Gottberg	5 July 1943–7 August 1944

SOUTH RUSSIA

SS-Major General Friedrich Jeckeln	22 June 1941–11 December 1941
SS-Lieutenant General Hans Adolf Pruetzmann	11 December 1941–1 July 1944

BLACK SEA/CAUCASUS

SS-Major General Ludolf von Alvensleben	29 October–25 December 1943
SS-Lieutenant General Richard Hildebrandt	25 December 1943–16 September 1944
SS-Lieutenant General Artur Phleps	16–18 September 1944

---

2 See similar chart in ibid. Appendix 6, p. 164.

BIBLIOGRAPHY

PRIMARY SOURCES

United Kingdom

Public Record Office, Kew, Surrey

Special Operations Executive Documents
PRO HS-5/195-Foreign Office and War Office studies on Danube River region guerrilla warfare, October 1940.

Assessment of regional partisan strengths, capabilities.

PRO HS-5/196-SOE counter-sabotage operations in Danube and region.

Cooperation with Red Army and NKVD; liaison with military, 1944.

PRO HS-5/198-SOE operations in the Danube, 1939-44 with Soviet military support.

Foreign Office Documents
PRO FO 371/25240/1 ff. (W 2812/38/48) regarding open prejudice against Jews in Britain; mention of emigration to Palestine. Cites minutes by R.T.E. Latham, 4 April 1940 and J.E.M. Carvell, 8 April 1940.

PRO FO 371/25253/140 (W 8686/8686/48) regarding Latham against anti-Semitism and alien male round-ups; criticizing British policy. Latham minute, 27 June 1940.

PRO FO 371/25252/198 (W 10429/8261/48) regarding United States permitting temporary emigration of Jews as long as Britain agreed to take them back six months after the war ended. MI5 refused on security grounds.

PRO FO 371/55/392 on Ilya Ehrenberg and Soviet Propaganda.

PRO FO 371/4760 in total.

War Office Documents

PRO WO 208/3433-Interrogation report and biography of Hans Bruhn.

List of senior captured German officers in order of capture.

Surrender and interrogation report on Giovani Messe with war record.

PRO WO 208/3504-Captured German Officers' documents, interrogation reports, biographies. Kurt Student (with photograph), Karl Wilhelm von Schlieben, Gerd von Rundstedt, Hermann Bernhard Ramcke, Kurt "Panzer" Meyer, Burkhardt Mueller-Hildebrand, Eugen Koenig, Friedrich von der Heydte, Maximilian von Herff, Ludwig Heilmann, Franz Halder.

PRO WO-208/4413-Capture and interrogation report/biography of Franz Halder, citing his replacement by Kurt Zeitzler.

Capture record and biography of Josef Harpe with photograph.

PRO WO 208/4415-Copy of Kurt Meyer capture and interrogation record.

Copy of Hasso von Manteuffel capture and interrogation record.

Capture and interrogation record of Erich von Lewinsky Gennant von Manstein with report on antiNazi activities and war record, with photograph.

Capture and interrogation report on Eberhard von Mackensen.

Capture record and information on Wilhelm List with photograph.

Newspaper article with photo on the death of Paul von LettowVorbeck.

Capture and interrogation document on Wilhelm von Leeb with photograph, including German document signed by Franz Halder.

PRO WO 208/4416-Post interrogation brief on Gerd von Rundstedt.

Intelligence report and biography of Hans Roettiger with post war photograph and news clipping.

Interrogation report and profile of Lothar Rendulic.

Biography and report on Walter von Reichenau.

Report with photograph of Friedrich Olbricht.

PRO WO 208/4417-Captured German Officers' documents, interrogation reports, biographies. Ferdinand Schoerner (with photograph), Walter von Seydlitz-Kurzbach, Adolf Strauss (four photographs), Kurt Student.

PRO WO 208/4418-Captured German Officers' documents, interrogation reports, biographies. Kurt Zeitzler, Erwin von Witzleben (with photograph), August Winter, Maximilian von Weichs (with photograph), Walter Warlimont, Heinrich Scheel Gennant von Vietinghoff, Erwin Vierow (with photograph).

PRO WO 208/4419-Intelligence reports-summaries of specific officers. Wilhelm Canaris, von Freytag Loringhoven, Oskar Dirlewanger, Erich von dem Bach-Zelewski, Pruetzmann.

PRO WO 208/4448-Captured German Officers' documents, interrogation reports, biographies. Kurt Daluege (with photographs and newspaper articles in German).

PRO WO 208/4449-Captured German Officer's documents, interrogation reports, biographies. Walter Darre (with photograph).

PRO WO 208/4450-Captured German Officers' documents, interrogation reports, biographies. Leon Degrelle (with photographs).

PRO WO 208/4493-Photograph/file on Joachim von Ribbentrop.

PRO WO 208/4503-Interrogation report with photographs and newspaper articles on Dr. Arthur Seyss-Inquart.

Additional PRO Documents

PRO C-2919/12/18

PRO N-11630/96/55

Imperial War Museum, London

Case No. 12, Transcripts of Trial, U.S. Military Tribunal at Nuremberg.

Primary Sources: Germany

Freiburg im Breisgau; Koblenz/Wartime Publications/Memoranda

Gehlen, Reinhard, *Abwehr* documentation; *Organization Gehlen Sammlung*. Freiburg, TF. 235.

Stroop, Juergen, *There is No Longer a Jewish Quarter in Warsaw!* Berlin, Volk und Reich Verlag, 1944.

Wolff, Karl, *Persoenlich Kriegstagebuch, 1939-1945*. Unpublished. File B 120/589

Zentralle Stelle der Landesjustzverwaltungen, Ludwigsburg

Az II 202, case nos. AR-Z 9/63, Z 104/82, Z 86/84, AR-Z 27/61, AR-Z 37/69, AR-Z, 197/67, AR 946/61, AR 1258/68, AR 1780/66, AR 2353/65, AR 2394/65, SA 44a Z 20/60.

Bundesarchiv Berlin-Lichterfelde

Files NS 19/2406, 2605; R 20/1-2, 4-8, 10-18, 25-9, 32, 60, 214; R 70 SU/13, 14, 18, 21, 22, 26, 31, 108, 116.

Bundesarchiv Koblenz/Militaerarchiv Freiburg im Breisgau (BA-MA)

Personnel Records (*indicates Koblenz location only)

Hans Frank	N-1110**
Arthur Seyss-Inquart	N-1180
Adolf Hitler	N-1128
Kurt Zeitzler	N-63
Wilhelm Staedel	N-1252
Heinrich Himmler	N-1126
Konstantin von Neurath	N-1310
Karl Wever	N-1203
Joachim von Ribbentrop	N-1163
Karl Wolff	NL-1465* (also listed as NL-163 Koblenz)
Alfred Jodl	N-69
Fritz-Dietloff *Graf* v.d Schulenburg	N-1301
Dietrich Bonheoffer	N-1308
Albert Speer	NL-1340*
Ludwig Beck	N-28
Carl Goerdeler	NL-1113*
Hans Doerr	N-29
Wilhelm *Ritter* von Leeb	N-14(also listed at NL-301 Koblenz)
Wilhelm Keitel	N-54
Eberhard von Mackensen	N-581

Walter Model	N-6
Wilhelm List	N-33
Maximilian Weichs	N-19
Hermann von Witzleben	N-23
Erwin von Witzleben	N-231
Karl Gaisser	N-279
Josef Goebbels	N-1118
Ernst Koestring	N-123
Hans von Seeckt	N-247
Walter Reinhardt	N-86
Paul von Lettow-Vorbeck	N-103
August von Mackensen	N-39
Franz Halder	N-220
Dr. Rudolf Himze	N-331
Ferdinand Schoerner	N-60
Fedor von Bock	N-22
Helmuth Stieff	N-114
Wilhelm Willemer	N-342
Erich von Manstein	N-507
Oskar Niedermayer	N-122
Hermann Hoth	N-503
Wolfgang Foerster	N-121
Wolfgang Kapp	N-1309
Bernd *Freiherr* Freytag von Loringhoven	N-525

**This file was only available at one time in 1999; afterward it disappeared from the Freiburg archive, ostensibly for microfilming. Searches at the other locations have not produced the file. Very suspicious.

Additional Personnel Files in Freiburg im Breisgau

RH7/704, 707, 714; 853H/AS46467; 12278H/AS49246; 8709H/AS32213; 888H/ 47779

1616H/AS35747; 546H/AS63343; 10239H/AS96; 943H/AS62045; 673H/AS28303796
    H/Bem.s.aH6/26aMsG109; 2577H/AS32860; 6900H/AS60275.

Army Group Files located at RH 19 II/123-24, 139, 153, 163-66, 170, 170D, 171-78, 383.

Army Files located at RH 20-9/373; RH 20-18/1279-1281; RH 21-2/374, 403, 489, 521,
    541, 558, 564, 574, 584, 713, 718-20, 725-27, 732, 901, 908.

Army Group Rear Area Files located at RH-22/2-13; 170-71; 185-88; 224-36; 215; 237K,
    238K; 243-44; 247-51; 298.

Division Files located at RH 26-5/7-11; RH 26-6/8-52, 56, 57K, 59-60, 62-72, 86-104, 109-11, 114-16; RH 26-9/81-2, 85-90; RH 26-35/88-9, 95-6, 103-05; RH 26-50/85; RH 26-72/79, 85-92, 98, 100-05; RH 26-93/38-9; RH 26-96/33; RH 26-201/5-9K, 10-12; 18-19; RH 26-203/1-7; RH 26-207/13-29; RH 26-213/3-4, 69, 11-13; RH 26-221/10-2; 13a-b, 14-35, 36K, 37-80, 83-95, 98, 101, 104; RH 26-227/36-76, 96-101, 107-112, 130-50; RH 26-251/13, 15-19, 81-2; RH 26-253/46; RH 26 254/6-7; RH 26-258/40-1, 85; RH 26-281/2,4,6-14, 25a-b, 29, 31, 33; RH 26 285/4-5, 7-8, 10, 12, 15, 17, 18-21, 42, 44, 46; RH 26-286/2-5, 8-9, 10, 14, 16; RH 26-299/124; RH 26 339/5,7,16, 18, 36, 38-9; RH 26-403/2-4, 7; RH 26-444/6-12, 17-9; RH 26-454/5-28, RH 26-707/213, 15, 15D, 16-9, 21; RH 27-11/91, 95-8; RH 31/554-71, 75-77, 80, 84-6, 88-90, 92-5, 602-03, 767-69, 771-76, 87, 95-6, 807, 14, 16-21, 24-7, 30-4, 37, 48-9, 70.

Bundesarchiv Zentralle Nachweisstelle, Kornelimuenster

RH 26-6 G; RH 26/227 G; RH 26/253 G; RH 26-254 G; 7265H/AS32004; 4201L/AS18826; 8082H/AS38847; 8388H/AS31949; 8389H/AS1914.

Additional Primary Sources as Published

Die Geheimen Tagesberichte der Duetschen Wehrmachtfuehrung im Zweiten Welt Krieg, 1939–1945.

_____. Band 2, 1. Mai 1940-28. Februar 1941 (Osnabrueck: Biblio Verlag, 1993).

_____. Band 3, 1. Maerz 1941-31. Oktober 9141 (Osnabrueck: Biblio Verlag, 1992).

_____. Band 4, 1. November 1941-31. Mai 1942(Osnabrueck: Biblio Verlag, 1992).

_____. Band 5, 1. Juni 1942-30. November 1942 (Osnabrueck: Biblio Verlag, 1991).

_____. Band 6, 1. Dezember 1942-31. Mai 1943 (Osnabrueck: Biblio Verlag, 1989).

_____. Band 7, 1. Juni 1943-31. August 1943 (Osnabrueck: Biblio Verlag, 1988).

Mueller, Norbert, Deutsche Besatzungspolitik in der UdSSR 1941-1944. Dokumente (Cologne: Pahl-Rugenstein, 1980).

University and National Libraries and Archives in the United States

University of North Carolina at Chapel Hill, William Royal Davis Library

Handbook of the Organisation Todt-by the Supreme Headquarters Allied Expeditionary Force Counter-Intelligence Sub-Division MIRS/MR-OT/5/45. Reprint of March 1945 London edition (Biblio Verlag: Osnabrueck, 1992).

Die Organisation Todt im Einsatz 1939-1945: Dargestellt Nach Kriegsschauplaetzen auf Grund der Feldpostnummern. 1. Teil, Klaus Boehm, ed. (Biblio Verlag: Osnabrueck, 1987).

Yale University Library/Archive, New Haven, CT

The Avalon Project at Yale University Law School: Convention Between the United States of America and Other Powers, Relating to Prisoners of War; July 27, 1929."

Articles 1-8 of the Geneva Convention of 1929.

The Hague Convention of 18 October 1907 regarding Laws of Land Warfare.

United States National Archives

Microfilm Selections

BDC (Berlin Documentation Center) A-3343, SSO-023: Bach-Zelewski personnel record.

BDC A-3343, SSO-134: Kurt Daluege's SS personnel record.

M-1019 Roll 23: Post-war interrogation of *Waffen SS Oberstgruppenfuehrer* Josef 'Sepp' Dietrich.

M-1019 Roll 39: Post-war interrogation of *Waffen SS Brigadefuehrer* Otto Kumm.

M-1019 Roll 80: Post-war interrogation of *Waffen SS Obergruppenfuehrer* Karl Wolff.

M-1270 Roll 23 & Roll 24: Interrogation Reports of *Generalleutnant* Reinhard Gehlen, *Generaloberst* Edmund Gleise von Horstenau (0482), Gehlen Interrogation Files, Albert Goering (et al.).

Captured German Documents-Series are listed as follows:
H 11-8/24; 65002/20, 21-26, 28, 33, 35, 37, 38, 53; 75825; T-312 in total.

T-III H371/4B, 4C; 65002/30.

T-77 microfilms WilD file nos. (T-77/WilD)/311 336, 345, 347, 349-52, 354, 358-81, 94, 846-459, 876-78; 733, 34-5, 48-53; 811, 16, 18, 42-3, 53-7, 61-5; 1082, T-175, 233-6, T-313/22041/1, 3; 27358/4; 28499/58, 85; 37075/58, 91, 113, 133, 141, 158; 43407/36; 75118/34a; 30233/65, 66; 30260/4; 37075/90, 162, 167, 169; 85387; 28499/88, T-315/13914/4-6; 14424/1-2, 4; 14878/3-5; 15701/1-3; 15954/4, 14; 16182/1-6, 8; 16748/7-22; 19344/1-6; 19403/1-2, 5; 19661/1; 20179/1-6, 8-11; 21708/622041 /8; 22441/7; 22639/1-5; 22866/1-4; 26009/8; 27358/1-2; 27797/1-6; 27973/ 4; 29027; 29087/2, 9; 29196/1-3; 29241/2-3; 29380/1-7; 30137/5; 30260/1-2; 32103/2; 32104; 33300/1-8; 34026/1-4; 34132/7; 35155/2, 4; 35222/2-3; 35307/1-3; 35408/1-2;

35770/1-3, 5; 35950/1-2; 36050; 36509/1-10; 37966/4; 37996/9-10; 38204/1-6; 38424/1-3; 39100/1-4; 41762/1-7; 42150/1-2; 429186/1-3; 43060/2, 4; 43405/1, 3-4; 43494; 43887/1-2, 4; 44225/1-2; 44418/6; 45546; 77827/1; 77842/1-3; WK VII/527.

National Archives Manuscript Collections

MS #B-250 "Answers to Questions Concerning Greece, Crete and Russia," compiled by General Walter Warlimont.

MS #B-271 "Questions Asked General Guderian' and "Answers Given by General Guderian," supplied by Heinz Guderian.

MS #B-334 "Balkans Campaign 1941," by General von Vietinghoff.

MS #B-525 Supplements to the Study, "The Balkan Campaign" (Invasion of Yugoslavia), supplied by General von Greiffenberg.

MS #C 065g "Military Events in the Balkans, 1941," by Helmuth Greiner.

MS #C-65I "Operation Barbarossa," By Helmuth Greiner.

MS #C-101 "The Relationship between the German Campaign in the Balkans and the Invasion of Russia," by General Mueller-Hildebrand.

MS #P-030 "The German Campaign in the Balkans, 1941: A Model of Crisis Planning," by General Mueller-Hildebrand.

MS #P-030b "The Improvisation of an Operation: German Preparations for Operations Against Yugoslavia in 1941," by General Mueller-Hildebrand.

Additional Captured German Documents

OKW — Uebernahme Kroatiens und des serbischen Gebietes durch Italiener und Bulgaren, Abteilung Landesverteidigung.

Weisungen Nr. 25, Yugoslavien, OKW/137.

OKW (Operations Division)

Aufmarsch "Barbarossa" 1941, H-22.219.

Aufmarschanweisungen "Barbarossa" 1941, H-22/220.

Barbarossa', Band 2, vom 29.4.41 bis 26.9.41, H-22/353.

Schematische Kriegsgliederung, Op. Abt. III.

Army Group South (Operations Planning/Reports)

Aufmarschanweisungen 'Barbarossa', Heeres Gruppe Sued, Ia, Anlagen Nr. 1, 45 u.76 z.

Kriegstagebuch, Teil I, Gen. St. d.H. Op. Abt. 13-603,6.

Heeresgruppe Sued Kriegstagebuch, Teil I, 2.2.41-21.6.41, W-1784-A.

Kriegstagebuch der Heeresgruppe Sued, Abt. Ia, WB-1784-B.

Second Army

Armee-Oberkommando 2, Kriegstagebuch 28.3.41-24.4.41, E- 246/1.

Armee-Oberkommando 2, Ia. Anlage zum Kriegstagebuch Yugoslavien; Erfahrungsberichte, 12.5.41-3.6.41, E- 187/7.

Armee-Oberkommando 2. Anlage zum Kriegstagebuch Yugoslavien, Armee befehle, 5.4.41-2.6.41, E-187/8.

Armee-Oberkommando 2, Waffenstillstandsverhandlungen, 14.4.42-20.6.41, E-188/3.

2 AOK Handakte, Ia, Oberstleutnant i.Gi. Feyerabend, E-252/2.

Anlage zum Kriegstagebuch Yugoslavien, Gefechtsberichte 5.4.41-16.4.41, Armee-Oberkommando 2, Ia, 16690/285.

Anlage zum Kriegstagebuch Yugoslavien, 5.4.41-20.6.41. Armee-Oberkommando 2, Ia, 16690/268.

Armee-Oberkommando 2, Ia, Nr. 1008/41 (geheime) 16690/287.

Armeebefehle-Bespr. M.d. Kdr. Gen. Aufmarschanweisung Yugoslavien, Gliederung der 2. Armee, 4.4.41-11.5.41, Balkan.

Twelfth Army

Der Balkanfeldzug der 12. Armee. Generalfeldmarschall List-Ein strategischer. Ueberlick, Ernst Wisshaupt schreiben, E-60/3.

Balkanfeldzug der 12. Armee 1941-Bilderbericht, 15078/1.

English Translations of Captured Documents

Fuehrer Directives and Other Top Level Directives of the German Armed Forces, 1939-41, ONI, Washington, DC, 1948.

The Private War Journal of *Generaloberst* Franz Halder, Chief of the General Staff of *OKH*, 14 August 1939-24 September 1942, volumes V, VI, and VII.

Count Ciano Papers (Rose Garden) 1940-43.

US State Department Declassified Documents

Blau, George E., *The German Campaign in Russia: Planning and Operations (1940–42).* Washington, D.C. Department of the Army Pamphlet no. 20–261a (1955).

Blackstock, Paul W. *Indications of Soviet Plans and Intentions in German-Soviet Relations,* Western European Branch. No date.

Department of the Army Pamphlet no. 20-291, *Effects of Climate on Combat in European Russia,* Washington, D.C., Department of the Army, Department of Defense (February, 1952).

_____. Pamphlet no. 20-292, *Warfare in the Far North,* Washington, D.C., Department of the Army, Department of Defense (October, 1951).

_____. Pamphlet no. 20-231, *Combat in Russian Forests and Swamps,* Washington, D.C., Department of the Army, Department of Defense (July, 1951).

_____. Pamphlet no. 20-230, *Russian Combat Methods in World War Two,* Washington D.C., Department of the Army, Department of Defense (November, 1950).

Howell, Edgar M. *The Soviet Partisan Movement 1941-1944,* Washington, D.C.: Dept. of the Army Pamphlet no. 20-244 (October, 1956).

Media Sources

Great Britain Newspapers

The Scottish Mail on Sunday, "The Picture that Finally Proves Konrad Kalejs is a Nazi Killer," 9 January 2000, pp. 8-9.

Manchester Guardian, 17 Oct. 1939.

United States Newspapers

The New York Times Magazine, 5 Dec. 1944.*Wilmington Star News.* (UPI) "Ex-Nazi Officer Gets 5 Years." 25 July 1997, Sec. A-1, p. 2. Wilmington, North Carolina.

_____. "Ex-Vichy Official to Stand Trial." 27 January 1997, Sec. A-1, p. 2. Follow up of 30 January 1997, Sec. A-1, p.1.

Television Documentaries

Britain

"Hitler's Forgotten Millions," directed by David Okuefuna. London, Channel 4, 1999. Documentary on the history of black and mixed race persons in Nazi Germany. German and English with English sub-titles.

British Broadcasting Company, "Real Lives: Albert Goering," broadcast on 5 December, 1998. London, Channel 4. Documentary on the brother of Reichsmarschall Hermann Goering.

_____. Documentary, "The Death Train," October Films Production, 1997. Channel 4 Broadcast on 18 December 1998.

United States

Danger Central: "Spy Web-The GRU." History Channel documentary, broadcast on 31 August 2000, USA.

SECONDARY SOURCES

Books

Aly, Goetz. "Endloesung". Voelkerverschiebung und der Mord an den europaeischen Jude (Frankfurt am Main: Fischer, 1996).

Anderson, Truman O. "Die 62. Infanterie-Division: Repressalien im Heeresgebiet Sued, Oktober bis Dezember 1941," in Hannes Heer and Klaus Naumann (eds.). Vernischtungskrieg. Verbrechen der Wehrmacht, 1941 bis 1944 (Hamburg: Hamburger Edition, 1995).

Arad, Yitzhak, Yisrael Gutmann and Abraham Margaliot (eds.). Documents on the Holocaust: Selected Sources on the Destruction of the Jews of Germany and Austria, Poland, and the Soviet Union, translated by Lea Ben Dor; introduction by Steven T. Katz (Lincoln, NE: University of Nebraska Press; London, Jerusalem: Yad Vashem, 1999).

Arad Yitzhak, Shmuel Krakowski and Spector (eds.) The Einsatzgruppen Reports (New York, Jerusalem: Yad Vashem 1989).

Armstrong, John A. (ed). Soviet Partisans in World War II (Madison: University of Wisconsin Press, 1964).

Bar-On, Zvi, "On the Position of the Jewish Partisan in the Soviet Partisan Movement," First International Conference on the History of the Resistance Movements (New York: Pergamon Press, 1960), pp. 215-247.

Barnett, Correlli. Hitler's Generals (London: Weidenfeld & Nicolson, 1989).

Bartov, Omer, Hitler's Army: Soldiers, Nazis and War in the Third Reich (New York: Oxford University Press, 1992).

_____. The Eastern Front, 1941-45: German Troops and the Barbarisation of Warfare (Basingstoke: Macmillan, 1985).

_____. "Wem gehoert die Geschichte? Wehrmacht und Geschichtswissenschaft," in Hannes Heer and Klaus Naumann (eds.), Vernichtungskrieg. Verbrechen der Wehrmacht. 1941 bis 1944 (Hamburg: Hamburger Edition, 1995), pp. 601-19.

Baur, Hans. Hitler at My Side (Houston: Eichorn Publishing, 1987).

Berenbaum, Michael and A. Peck (eds.), The Holocaust and History (Bloomington: Indiana University Press; and Washington D.C.: United States Holocaust Museum, 1998).

Berenbaum, Michael (ed.), "The Uniqueness and Universality of the Holocaust," in Mosaic of Victims (New York: New York University Press, 1990).

Bessel, Richard and E.J. Feuchtwanger (eds.), Social Change and Political Development in Weimar Germany (London: Croom Helm, 1981).

Best, Geoffrey. Humanity in Warfare (London: Weidenfeld & Nicolson, 1980).

Black, Peter R., Ernst Kaltenbrunner: Ideological Soldier of the Third Reich (Princeton, NJ: Princeton University Press, 1984).

Bracher, Karl Dietrich, The German Dictatorship: The Origins, Structure and Consequences of National Socialism (London, New York: Penguin Books, 1970, 1988).

Bradley, James and Ron Powers. Flags of Our Fathers (New York: Bantam- Doubleday Dell Publishers, 2000).

Breitman, Richard, Official Secrets: What the Nazi's Planned-What the British and Americans Knew (New York, London: Hill & Wang Publishing, 1998).

Broszat, Martin, Hitler and the Collapse of Weimar Germany (Munich, London: Berg, 1987).

_____. The Hitler State: The Foundation and Development of the Internal Structure of the Third Reich, translated by John W. Hiden (London; New York: Longman, 1981).

Broszat, Martin and Klaus Schwabe (eds.), Die deutschen Eliten und der Weg in den Zweiten Weltkrieg (Munich: C.H. Beck Verlag, 1989).

Browning, Christopher R., Ordinary Men: Reserve Police Battalion 101 and the Final Solution in Poland (New York: Harper Perennial, 1992).

_____. The Path to Genocide: Essays on Launching the Final Solution (Cambridge: Cambridge University Press, 1992).

_____. Fateful Months: Essays on the Emergence of the Final Solution (New York: Holmes & Meier, 1985).

Buchbender, Ortwin. Das toenende Erz. Deutsche Propaganda gegen die Rote Armee Im Zweiten Weltkrieg (Stuttgart: Seewald, 1978).

Bullock, Alan, Hitler: A Study in Tyranny. 2nd edition (London: Oldham Books, 1962, 1964).

Burleigh, Michael & Wolfgang Wippermann, The Racial State: Germany 1933-1945 (Cambridge: Cambridge University Press, 1991).

Burrin, Philippe, Hitler and the Jews: The Genesis of the Holocaust (London: Edward Arnold, 1994).

Caplan, Jane and Thomas Childers, Re-evaluating the Third Reich (New York: Berg, 1993).

Carr, Edward Hallett, German Soviet Relations between the Two World Wars, 1919-1939, reprint of 1952 OUP edition (New York: Harper & Row, 1966).

Carr, William, Arms, Autarky and Aggression (London: Edward Arnold, 1979).

_____. Hitler: A Study in Personality and Politics (London: Edward Arnold, 1978).

Cesarani, Craig. The Final Solution: Origins and Implementation (London: Routledge, 1994).

Chesnoff, Richard Z., Pack of Thieves: How Hitler and Europe Plundered the Jews and Committed the Greatest Theft in History (New York: Anchor Books, 1999).

Combs, William L., The Voice of the SS: A History of the SS Journal, "Das Schwarze Korps" (New York: Peter Lang, 1986).

Conquest, Robert, Stalin: Breaker of Nations (New York, London: Weidenfeld & Nicolson, 1991).

_____. The Harvest of Sorrow: Soviet Collectivisation and the Terror (New York, London: Hutchinson, 1986).

_____. The Great Terror: Stalin's Purge of the Thirties (Harmondsworth: Penguin Books, 1971).

Conway, J.S., The Nazi Persecution of the Churches, 1933-1945 (London: Weidenfeld & Nicolson, 1968).

Conway, Martin, Collaboration in Belgium: Leon Degrelle and the Rexist Movement, 1940-1944 (New Haven: Yale University Press, 1994).

Cooper, Matthew, The Phantom War: The German Struggle Against the Soviet Partisans, 1941-1944 (London: MacDonald & Jane's, 1979).

Cooper, Matthew, The German Army 1933-1945: Its Political and Military Failure (London: Scarborough House, 1978).

Crew, David F., Nazism and German Society 1933-1945 (London: Routledge, 1994).

Dallin, Alexander German Rule in Russia, 1941-1945: A Case Study in Occupation Policies, 2nd edition (London, Boulder, CO: Macmillan, 1981).

Dallin, Alexander and Ralph Mavrogordato, "The Kaminsky Brigade: A Case Study of Soviet Disaffection," Alexander and Janet Rabinowitch (eds.), Revolution and Politics in Russia: Essays in Memory of B.I. Nicolaevsky (Bloomington: University of Indiana Press, 1972), pp. 243-80.

_____. "Partisan Psychological Warfare and Popular Attitudes," in John A Armstrong (ed.), Soviet Partisans in World War II (Madison: University of Wisconsin Press, 1964), pp. 197-337.

Davis, Brian L., Waffen SS, 2nd edition (New York, Poole: Blandford, 1987).

Degrelle, Leon, Campaign in Russia: The Waffen SS on the Eastern Front (New York, London: Crecy, 1985).

_____. Epic: The Story of the Waffen SS (Torrence, CA: Institute for Historical Review, 1983).

Demeter, Karl, The German Officer Corps in Society and State: 1650-1945 (London: Weidenfeld & Nicolson, 1965).

Deutscher, Issac, Stalin: A Political Biography, 2nd edition (London: Oxford University Press, 1966).

DeWitt, Hurt and Wilhelm Moll. "The Bryansk Area," in John A. Armstrong (ed.), Soviet Partisans in World War II (Madison: University of Wisconsin Press, 1964), pp. 458-516.

Erickson, John, "Soviet Women at War," John and Carol Gerrard (eds.), World War 2 and the Soviet People: Selected Papers from the Fourth World Congress for Soviet and East European Studies (London, New York: St. Martin's Press, 1993), pp. 50-76.

Fainsod, Merle, Smolensk Under Soviet Rule (London: Macmillan, 1959).

Feig, Konnilyn G. Hitler's Death Camps: The Sanity and Madness (New York, London: Holmes & Meier Publishers, Inc., 1979).

Fein, Helen. Accounting for Genocide: National Responses and Jewish Victimization during the Holocaust (New York, London: Free Press, 1979).

Fest, Joachim C. The Face of the Third Reich, 3rd edition Translation by Michael Bullock (London: Weidenfeld & Nicolson, 1970).

Fischer, Conan, The Rise of the Nazis (Manchester, New York: Manchester University Press, 1995).

Fischer, Fritz, From Kaiserreich to Third Reich: Elements of Continuity in German History, 1871-1945 (London, New York: Unwin-Hyman, 1979).

_____. Germany's Aims in the First World War (London: Chatto & Windus, 1967).

Fleischauer, Ingeborg, "Die sowjetische Aussenpolitik und die Genese des Hitler-Stalin-Paktes," in Bernd Wegner, et al, Zwei Wege nach Moskau: Vom Hitler-Stalin-Pakt I zum Unternehemen Barbarossa (Munich, Zurich: P. Piper GmbH & Co., 1991), pp. 19-39.

Foerster, Juergen, "Wehrmacht, Krieg und Holocaust," in Rolf-Dieter Mueller and Hans-Erich Volkmann (eds.), Die Wehrmacht: Mythos und Realitaet (Munich: Oldenbourg, 199), pp. 948-63.

_____. "The Relation between Operation Barbarossa as an Ideological War of Extermination and the Final Solution," in David Cesarani (ed.), The Final Solution: Origins and Implementation (London: Routledge, 1994). Pp. 85-102.

_____. "Zum Russland-Bild der Militaers 1941-1945," in Hans-Erich Volmann (ed.), Das Russlandbild im dritten Reich (Cologne: Boehlau, 1994), pp. 141-63.

_____. "Hitlers Entschiedung fuer den Krieg gegen die Sowjetunion," im Horst Boog, et al, Der Angriffe auf die Sowjetunion, 2nd paperback edition (Frankfurt am Main: Fischer, 1991), pp. 27-68.

_____. "Das Unternehmen "Barbarossa" als Eroberungs und Vernichtungskrieg," in ibid. pp. 498-538.

_____. "Das nationalsozialistische Herrschaftssystem und der Krieg gegen die Sowjetunion," in Reinhard Ruerup (ed.), Der Krieg gegen die Sowjetunion 1941-1945: eine Dokumentation (Berlin: Argon, 1991), pp. 28-45.

_____. "Hitlers Wendung nach Osten. Die deutsche Kriegspolitik 1940-1941," in Bernd Wegner, et al, Zwei wege nach Moskau: Vom Hitler-Stalin-Pakt bis zum Unternehmen Barbarossa (Munich, Zurich: P. Piper & Co., 1991), pp. 113-32.

_____. "Die Sicherung des 'Lebensraumes'," in Horst Boog, et al, Der Angriff auf die Sowjetunion (Frankfurt am Main: Fischer, 1991), pp. 1227-87.

Foot, Michael R.D., SOE in France: An Account of the Work of British Special Operation Executive in France, 1940-1944, reprint of 1966 edition (London: HMSO, 1966).

Footman, David, Civil War in Russia (London: Faber & Faber, 1961).

Fraenkel, Heinrich and Roger Manvel, The Canaris Conspiracy: The Secret Resistance to Hitler in the German Army (New York: Heinemann, 1969).

_____. Der 20 Juli (Berlin: Ullstein, 1964).

Friedlaender, Saul, Nazi Germany and the Jews: Years of Persecution, 1933-1939 (London: Phoenix Giant, 1997).

_____. Memory, History, and the Extermination of the Jews of Europe (Bloomington: Indiana University Press, 1993).

Galay, Nicholas, "The Partisan Forces," B.H. Liddell-Hart (ed.), The Red Army, 1918 to 1945: The Soviet Army, 1946 to the Present (New York: Peter Smith, 1968), pp. 153-176.

Gerlach, Christian. Kalkulierte Morde. Die deutsche Wirtschafts und Vernichtungs-politik in Weissrussland 1941 bis 1944 (Hamburg: Hamburger Edition, 1999).

_____. Krieg, Ernaehrung, Voelkermord. Forschungen zur deutschen Vernichtungspolitik im Zweiten Weltkrieg (Hamburg: Hamburger Edition, 1998).

_____. "Deutsche Wirtschaftsinteressen, Besatzungspolitik und der Mord an den

Juden in Weissrussland 1941-1943," in Ulrich Herbert (ed.), Nationalsozialistische Vernichtungspolitik 1939-1945. Neue Forschungen und Kontroverse (Frankfurt am Main: Fischer, 1998), pp. 263-91.

Gerrard, John and Carol, "Bitter Victory," John and Carol Gerrard (eds.), World War 2 and the Soviet People: Selected Papers from the Fourth World Congress for Soviet and East European Studies (New York, London: St. Martin's Press, 1993), pp. 1-27.

Geyer, Michael. " 'Es muss daher mit schnellen und drakonischen Massnahmen durchgegriffen arden': Civitella in val di Chiana am 29. Juni 1944," in Hannes Heer and Klaus Naumann (eds.), Vernichtungskrieg. Verbrechen der Wehrmacht, 1941 bis 1944 (Hamburg: Hamburger Edition, 1995), pp. 208-38.

Goebbels, Josef, Die Tagebuecher von Josef Goebbels: Im Auftrage des Instituts fuer Zeitgeschichte und mit Unterstuetzung des Staatlichen Archivdienstes Russlands (1995-1998)

_____. Teil I, Band 8, April-November 1940, Herausgegeben von Elke Froehlich, Bearbeitet von Jana Richter (Munich, 1998).

_____. Teil I, Band 9-Dezember 1940-Juli 1941, Herausgeben von Elke Froehlich; Bearbeitet von Manfred Kittel (Munich, London, Paris, 1998).

_____. Teil II, Band 10- Oktober-Dezember 1943, Herausgeben von Elke Froehlich; Bearbeitet von Volker Dahm (Munich, London, Paris, 1994).

_____. Teil II, Band 11, Januar-Maerz 1944, Herausgaben Elke Froehlich; Bearbeitet von Dieter Marc Schneider (Munich, London, Paris, 1994).

_____. Teil II, Band 12, April-Juni 1944, Herausgegeben von Elke Froehlich, Bearbeitet von Hartmut Mehringer (Munich; London; Paris, 1995).

_____. Teil II. Diktate, Band 13, Juli-September 1944, Herausgaben von Elke Froehlich; Bearbeitet von Jana Richter (Munich; London; Paris, 1995).

_____. *Teil II, Band 14, Oktober-Dezember 1944,* Herausgegeben von Elke Froehlich; Bearbeitet von Jana Richter und Hermann Graml (Munich; London; Paris, 1996).

_____. *Teil II, Band 15, Januar-April 1945,* Herausgegeben Elke Froehlich, Bearbeitet von Maximilian Gcshaid (Munich; London; Paris, 1995).

_____. *The Goebbels Diaries 1942-1943,* edited and translated by Louis P. Lochner (London; Garden City, NJ: Hamish Hamilton, 1948)

Goldhagen, Daniel Jonah, *Hitler's Willing Executioners: Ordinary Germans and the Holocaust* (London: Little, Brown & Co., 1996).

Hassell, Ulrich von, *The Von Hassell Diaries, 1938-44: The Story of the Forces Against Hitler Inside Germany* (London: Hamish Hamilton, 1947).

Heaton, Colin D. *German Anti-Partisan Warfare in Europe, 1939-1945* (Atglen, PA: Schiffer Publishing, Ltd., 2001)

"Belgian Volunteer in the Waffen SS," *Military History.* Vol. 23, No. 8 (November 2006), ISSN-0889-7328, pp. 46-53. Weider Publications, Leesburg, VA.

Heer, Hannes, "Killing Fields: Die Wehrmacht und der Holocaust," in Hannes Heer & Klaus Naumann (eds.), *Vernichtungskrieg. Verbrechen der Wehrmacht* (Hamburg: Hamburger Edition, 1995), pp. 57-77.

_____. "Die Logik des Vernichtungskrieges. Wehrmacht und Partisannenkampf," in ibid, pp. 104-38.

Herbert, Ulrich. *National Socialist Extermination Policy* (Oxford: Berghan Books, 1999).

_____. *Hitler's Foreign Workers: Enforced Foreign Labour in Germany under the Third*

Reich, translated by William Templar (Cambridge; New York: Cambridge University Press, 1997).

_____. *Best: Biographische Studien ueber Radikalismus, Weltanschauung und Vernunft, 1903-1989* (Bonn: J.H.W. Dietz Verlag, 1996).

Herwarth, Hans von. *Zwischen Hitler und Stalin: Erlebte Zeitgeschichte 1931 bis 1945* (Frankfurt: Ullstein, 1985).

Hesse, Erich. *Der Sowjetrussische Partisankrieg 1941-1944 im Spiegel Deutscher Kampfanweisungen und Befehle*, 2nd edition (Giettingen: Muster-Schmidt, 1993).

Hilberg, Raul. "Wehrmacht und Judenvernichtung," in Walter Manoschek (ed.), *Die Wehrmacht im Rassenkrieg* (Vienna: Picus, 1996), pp. 23-38.

_____. *The Destruction of the European Jews*, 3 vols. (New York, London: Holmes & Meier Publishers, Inc., 1985).

Hildebrand, Klaus, *The Foreign Policy of the Third Reich* (Berkeley: University of California Press, 1973).

Hillgruber, Andreas. *Hitlers Strategie und Kriegsfuehrung 1940-41* (Frankfurt: 1952).

_____. "Das Russland-Bild Fuehrenden deutschen Militaers vor Beginn des Angriff auf die Sowjetunion," in Bernd Wegner, et al, *Zwei Wege nach Moskau: Vom Hitler-Stalin-Pakt I zum Unternehmen Barbarossa* (Munich, Zurich: P. Piper GmbH & Co., 1991), pp. 167-84.

Hitler, Adolf, translation by Ralph Manheim, introduction by D.C. Watt, *Mein Kampf* (London: Hutchinson, 1969).

_____. T. Taylor (ed.), *Hitler's Secret Book* (New York: Grove Press, 1961).

_____. *Mein Kampf* (Munich: Volk Verlag, 1936).

Homze, Edward L., *Foreign Labour in Nazi Germany* (Princeton, NJ: Princeton University Press, 1967).

Hondros, Ernest Demetrious, *Occupation and Resistance: The Greek Agony, 1941-44* (New York: Pantheon, 1983).

Jaeckel, Eberhard, "On the Purpose of the Wannsee Conference," James S. Pacy and Alan P. Wertheimer (eds.), *Perspectives on the Holocaust: Essays in Honor of Raul Hilberg* (Boulder, CO: Westview Press, 1995).

_____. "Germany's Way into the Second World War," M. Laffan (ed.), *The Burden of German History, 1919-45* (London: Methuen, 1988), pp. 174-181.

_____. Translation and introduction by Franklin L. Ford, *Hitler's World View: A Blue Print for Power* (Washington, D.C., Cambridge, MA: Wesleyan University Press, 1981).

Joll, James, *Europe Since 1870: An International History* (New York: Weidenfeld & Nicolson, 1973).

Steven T. Katz, *The Holocaust in Historical Context*, vol. 1 (New York: Oxford University Press, 1994.

Keitel, Wilhelm, *In the Service of the Reich: The Memoirs of Field Marshal Keitel, Chief of the German High Command, 1938-1945*, introduction and epilogue by Walter Gorlitz; translated by David Irving, reprint of 1966 3rd ed. (New York: 1979).

_____. *Generalfeldmarschall Keitel: Verbrecher oder Offizier?: Erinnerungen, Briefe, Dokumente des Chefs OKW*; Hrsg. Von Walter Goerlitz (Goettingen: Musterschmidt-Verlag, 1961).

Kellett, Anthony. *Combat Motivation* (Boston: Kluwer Boston, 1982).

Kershaw, Ian, *Hitler 1936-1945: "Nemesis"* (New York, Harmondsworth: Penguin, 2002).

_____. *Hitler 1889-1936: "Hubris"* (New York, London: W.W. Norton & Co., 1998).

_____. *The Nazi Dictatorship: Problems and Perspectives of Interpretation*, 2nd edition (London: Edward Arnold, 1993).

_____. *Profiles in Power: Hitler* (New York: Longman, 1991).

_____. *The Hitler Myth: Image and Reality in the Third Reich* (New York; Oxford: Clarendon Press, 1987).

_____. "How Effective Was Nazi Propaganda?" David Welch (ed.), *Nazi Propaganda: The Power and the Limitations* (London: Croom Helm, 1983), pp. 180-205.

_____. "Ideology, Propaganda, and the Rise of the Nazi Party," Peter Stachura (ed.), *The Nazi Machtergreiftung* (London, 1983), pp. 162-81.

_____. "Alltaeglisches und Ausseralltaeglisches: ihre Bedeutung fuer die Volksmeinung 1933-1939," in Detlev Peukert & Juergen Reulecke (eds.), *Die Reihen fast geschlossen. Beitrage zur Geschichte unterm Nationalsozialismus* (Wueppertal: Hammer, 1981), p. 273.

Kesselring, Albert, *The Memoirs of Field Marshal Kesselring*; forward by Kenneth Macksey (London; Novato, CA: Presidio Press, 1988).

Kettenacker, Lothar, "Hitler's Impact on the Lower Middle Class," David Welch (ed.), *Nazi Propaganda: The Power and the Limitations* (London: Croom Helm, 1983), pp. 10-28.

Klein, Peter (ed.), *Die Einsatzgruppen in der besetzten Sowjetunion 1941/42. Die Taetigkeits und Lageberichte des SD* (Berlin: Gedenk und Bildungsstaette hause der Wannsee Konferenz, 1997).

Korfes, Sigrid Wegner, "Botschafter Friedrich Werner Graf von der Schulenberg und die Vorbereitung von 'Barbarossa,'" in Wegner et al, *Zwei Wege nach Moskau Vom Hitler-Stalin-Pakt bis zum Unternehmen Barbarossa* (Munich, Zurich: P. Piper & Co, 1991).

Krausnick, Helmut, Hans Bucheim, Martin Broszat, Hans –Adolf Jacobsen (et al.), *Anatomy of the SS State*, translation by Richard Barry, Dorrian Long and Marian Jackson; introduction by Elizabeth Wiskemann (London, New York: Harper-Collins, 1968).

Kroener, Bernhard R., "Die Personellen Ressourcen des Dritten reiches im Spannungsfeld zwischen Wehrmacht, Buerokratie und Kriegswirtschaft 1939-1942," in *Das Deutsche Reich und der Zweite Weltkrieg, Band 5/1. Organisation und Mobilisierung des deutschen machtbereichs 1939-1942* (Stuttgart: Deutsche Verlags-Anstalt, 1988).

Lange, Horst. *Tagebuecher aus dem Zweiten Weltkrieg: Herausgegeben und Kommentiert von Hans Dieter Schaefer* (Mainz: von Hase & Koehler Verlag, 1979).

Laska, Vera (ed.), *Women in the Resistance and the Holocaust: Voices of Eyewitnesses. Contributions to Women's Studies no. 37* (Westport, CT: The Free Press, 1983).

Latzel, Klaus, *Deutsche Soldaten-nationalsozialistischer Krieg? Kriegserlebnis Kriegserfahrung 1939-1945* (Munich: Ferdinand Schoeningh, 2000).

____. "Tourismus und gewalt: Kriegswahrnehmungen in Feldpostbriefen," in Heer & Naumann (eds.), *Vernichtungskrieg. Verbrechen der Wehrmacht, 1941 bis 1944* (Hamburg: Hamburger Edition, 1995), pp. 447-59.

Laqueur, Walter Zeev (ed.), *The Second World War: Essays in Military and Political History* (London: Weidenfeld & Nicolson, 1982).

Lee, M. M. and Michalka, W., *German Foreign Policy, 1917-1933* (Leamington Spa: Berg, 1987).

Linz, Susan J. (ed.), *The Impact of World War II on the Soviet Union* (Totowa, NJ: Rowman & Allan Held, 1985).

Littlejohn, David, *The Patriotic Traitors: A History of Collaboration in German Occupied Europe, 1940-45* (London: Heinemann, 1972).

Lokowski, Richard, "Zwischen Professionalismus und Nazismus: Die Wehrmacht Des Dritten Reich vor dem Ueberfall auf die UdSSR," in Bernd Wegner, et al, *Zwei Wege nach Moskau: Vom Hitler-Stalin-Pakt bi zum "Unternehmen Barbarossa"* (Munich, Zurich: P. Piper GmbH & Co., 1991), pp. 149-66.

Longerich, Peter, *Politik der Vernichtung: Eine Gesamtdarstellung der nationalsozialistischen Judenverfolgung* (Munich: Peiper Verlag, 1998).

Loza, Dmitrii Fedorovich. *Fighting for the Soviet Motherland: Recollections from the Eastern Front Hero of the Soviet Union/Dmitrii Loza* (Lincoln: University of Nebraska Press, 1998).

Lucas, James, *Das Reich: The Military Role of the 2nd SS Division* (London: Arms & Armour Press, 1991).

_____. *Kommando: German Special Forces of World War Two* (London: Arms & Armour Press, 1985).

Lukacs, John, *The Hitler of History* (New York: Vintage, 1997).

Lumins, Valdis O., *Himmler's Auxiliaries* (Chapel Hill, NC: University of North Carolina Press, 1991).

MacLean, French, *The Field Men: The SS Officers Who Led the Einsatzkommandos-the Nazi Mobile Killing Units* (Atglen, PA: Schiffer Publishing Ltd., 1999).

Magenheimer, Heinz. *Hitler's War: Germany's Key Strategic Decisions, 1940-1945*, translated by Helmut Boegler (London: Arms & Armour Press, 1998).

Manchester, William, *The Arms of Krupp* (New York, London: Joseph, 1969).

Mazower, Mark, "Militaerische Gewalt und nationalsozialistische Werte: Die Wehrmacht im Griechenland im 1941 bis 1944," in Heer & Naumann (eds.), *Vernichtungskrieg. Verbrechen der Wehrmacht, 1941 bis 1944* (Hamburg: Hamburger Edition, 1995), pp. 157-90.

_____. *Inside Hitler's Greece: The Experience of Occupation, 1941-44* (New Haven, CT., London: Yale University Press, 1993).

McClure, Brooks, "Russia's Hidden Army," Franklin Mark Osanka (ed.), *Modern Guerrilla Warfare: Fighting Communist Guerrilla Movements* (New York: Free Press; London: Collier-Macmillan, 1962), pp. 80-98.

Medvedev, R.A., *Let History Judge: The Origins and Consequences of Stalinism* (New York, London: Macmillan, 1972).

Messenger, Charles, *Hitler's Gladiator: The Life and Times of Obergruppenfuehrer and Panzergeneral-Oberst Der Waffen SS Sepp Dietrich* (London: Brassey's Inc., 1988).

Michalka, Wolfgang (ed.) et al. *Der Zweite Weltkrieg: Analyse, Grundzeuge, Forschungsbilanz* (Munich: Piper, 1989)

Mommsen, Hans, *From Weimar to Auschwitz* (New Jersey: Princeton University Press, 1991).

_____. "The Realization of the Unthinkable: The 'Final Solution of the Jewish Question' in the Third Reich," in Gerhard Hirschfeld (ed.), *The Policies of Genocide: Jews and Soviet Prisoners of War in Nazi Germany* (London: Allen & Unwin, 1986), pp. 97-144.

_____. "National Socialism: Continuity and Change," in Walter Laqueur (ed.), *Fascism: A Readers Guide. Analysis, Interpretations, Bibliography* (Berkeley, CA: University of California Press, 1976), pp. 179-204.

Mommsen, Wolfgang J. "Neither Denial nor Forgetfulness Will Free Us from the Past," in James Knowlton and Truett Cates (eds.), *Forever in the Shadow of Hitler?* (Atlantic Highlands, N.J.: Humanities Press, 1993), pp. 202-15.

Mosse, George L., *Toward the Final Solution: A History of European Racism* (Madison: University of Wisconsin Press, 1978).

Mueller, Norbert, *Europa unterm Hakenkreuz, Die Okkupationspolitik des deutschen Faschismus, 1938-1945. Die faschistische Okkupationspolitik in den zeitweilig besetzen Gebieten der Sowjetunion, 1941-44* (Berlin: Deutsche Verlag, 1991).

_____. *Wehrmacht und Okkupation 1941-1944. Zur Rolle der Wehrmacht und ihrer Fuehrungsorgane im Okkupationsregime des faschistischen deutschen Imperialismus auf sowjetischen Territorium* (East Berlin: Deutsche Militaerverlag, 1971).

Mueller, Rolf-Dieter and Gerd R. Ueberschar. *Hitler's War in the East 1941-1945 : A Critical Assessment* (Oxford: Berghan, 1997).

_____. *Kriegsende 1945: Die Zerstoerung des Deutschen Reiches* (Frankfurt am Main: Fischer Taschenbuch Verlag, 1994).

Mueller, Rolf-Dieter, "Von der Wirtschaftsallianz zum kolonialen Ausbeutungskrieg," in Horst Boog et al (eds.), *Der Angriff auf die Sowjetunion* (Frankfurt am Main: Fischer, 1991), pp. 141-245.

_____. "Das Scheitern der wirtshcaftlichen 'Blitzkriegstrategie'," in ibid, pp. 936-1029.

_____. "Die Rekrutierung sowjetischer Zwangsarbeiter fuer did deutsche Kriegswirtschaft," in Ulrich Herbert (ed.), Europa und der der "Reicheinsatz" (Essen: Klartext-Verlag, 1991), pp. 234-50.

Mueller, Rolf-Dieter and Hans-Erich Volkmann, "Die Wehrmacht: Historische last und Verantwortung. Die Historiographie im Spannungsfeld von Wissenschaft und Vergangenheitsbewaeltigung," in R-D Mueller & H-E Volkmann (eds.), *Die Wehrmacht: Mythos und Realitaet* (Munich: Oldenbourg, 1999), pp. 3-35.

Mulligen, Timothy P. *The Politics of Illusion and Empire: German Occupation Policy in the Soviet Union, 1942-1943* (New York: Praeger, 1988).

Munoz, Antonio J., *Forgotten Legions: Obscure Combat Formations of the Waffen SS* (New York: Paladin Press, 1991).

Newland, Samuel J. *Cossacks in the German Army, 1941-1945.* London, US Army War College: Frank Cass & Co. Ltd, 1991.

Niclauss, Karl-Heinz, *Die Sowjetunion und Hitlers Machtergreifung: Eine Studie die deutsch-russischen Beziehungen der Jarhe 1929 bis 1935*, Band 29; Bonner Historische Forschungen (Bonn: Ludwig Roehrscheid Verlag, 1966).

Noakes, Jeremy and Geoffrey Pridham (eds.), *Nazism: 1919-1945: Foreign Policy, War and Racial Extermination: A Documentary Reader*, 3 vols. (Devon: University of Exeter, 1991).

O'Connell, Robert L., *Of Arms and Men: A History of War, Weapons and Aggression* (New York: O.U.P., 1989).

Ogorreck, Ralf. *Die Einsatzgruppen und die "Genesis der Endloesung"* (Berlin: Metropol, 1996).

O'Neill, R.J. *The German Army and the Nazi Party* (London: Corgi, 1968).

Orlovsky, Daniel, "Political Clientalism in Russia: The Historical Perspective," T.H. Rigby and Bohdan Harasymiw (eds.), *Leadership Selection and Patron-Client Relations in the USSR and Yugoslavia* (London, Boston, MA: Allen & Unwin, 1983), pp. 174-99.

Osanka, Franklin Mark (ed.), *Modern Guerrilla Warfare: Fighting Communist Guerrilla Movements* (New York: Free Press; London: Collier-Macmillan, 1962).

Overy, Richard James, *Russia's War* (London, New York: Penguin, 1997).

_____. *Why the Allies Won* (London: W.W. Norton & Co., 1995).

Padfield, Peter, *Himmler: Reichsfuehrer-SS* (New York, London: Macmillan, 1990).

Paret, Peter (ed.), *The Makers of Modern Strategy from Machiavelli to the Nuclear Age* (New Jersey: Princeton University Press, 1986).

Peukert, Detlev, "The Genesis of the 'Final Solution' from the Spirit of Science," David Crew (ed.), *Nazism and the German Society: 1933-1945* (London; New York: Routledge, 1994), pp. 274-96.

_____. *Inside Nazi Germany: Conformity, Opposition and racism in Everyday Life* (London: Penguin, 1993).

Quarrie, Bruce, *Hitler's Samurai: The Waffen SS in Action* (Wellingborough: Patrick Stephens, 1984).

Rauss, Erhard and Oldwig von Natzmer. *The Anvil of War: German Generalship on the Eastern Front*, Peter G. Tsouras (ed.) (London: Greenhill Books, 1994).

Reed, Mary E., "The Anti-Fascist Front of Women and the Communist Party in Croatia: Conflicts Within the Resistance," Tova Yedlin (ed.), *Women in Eastern Europe and the Soviet Union*, New York: Praeger, 1980), pp. 128-39.

Reitlinger, Gerald, *The SS: Alibi of a Nation, 1922-1945* (London: The Viking Press, 1981).

_____. *The House Built on Sand: Conflicts of German Policy in Russia* (London: Cox & Wyman, 1962).

Rhodes, Richard, *Masters of Death: The SS Einsatzgruppen and the Invention of the Holocaust* (New York: Alfred A. Knopf, 2002).

Rich, Norman, *Hitler's War Aims: Ideology, the Nazi State, and the Course of Expansion*, 2 Vols. (London, New York: W.W. Norton & Co., 1973).

Richter, Tim C. "Die Wehrmacht und der Partisannenkrieg in den besetzten Gebieten der Sowjetunion," in R-D Mueller & H-E Volkmann (eds.), *Die Wehrmacht: Mythos und Realitaet* (Munich: Oldenbourg, 1999), pp. 837-57.

Rigby, Thomas Henry, Archie Brown and Peter Reddaway (eds.), *Authority, Power and Policy in the USSR: Essays Dedicated to Leonard Shapiro*, 2nd edition (London: Macmillan Press, 1983).

Rigby, Thomas Henry, "A Conceptual Approach to Authority, Power and Policy in the Soviet Union," T.H. Rigby, Archie Brown and Peter Reddaway (eds.), *Authority, Power and Policy in the USSR: Essays Dedicated to Leonard Schapiro* (London: Macmillan Press, 1980), pp. 9-31.

Rigg, Bryan Mark, *Hitler's Jewish Soldiers: The Untold Story of Nazi Racial Laws and Men of Jewish Descent in the German Military.* (Lawrence: University of Kansas Press, 2002).

Roseman, Mark, *The Wannsee Conference and the Final Solution: A Reconsideration* (New York: Henry Holt & Co., 2002).

Rosenbaum, Alan S. (ed.), *Is the Holocaust Unique? Perspectives on Comparative Genocide*, 2nd edition (Boulder, CO: Westview Press, 2001).

_____. *Prosecuting Nazi War Criminals* (Boulder, CO: Westview Press, 1993).

Rosenberg, Dr. Alfred, *Future Roads for German Policy* (Berlin: Reich und Volk Verlag, 1932).

Rosinski, Herbert, *The German Army*, introduction (ed.) by Gordon Craig (London: Pall Mall Press, 1966).

Ruble, Blair and Edward Bubis, "The Impact of World War II on Leningrad," Susan J. Linz (ed.), *The Impact of World War II on the Soviet Union* (Totowa, NJ: Rowman & Allanheld, 1985), pp. 189-206.

Ryan, Cornelius. *The Last Battle*, reprint edition (New York: Touchstone Books, 1995).

Sajer, Guy, *Forgotten Soldier*, 2nd edition (Baltimore: Nautical and Aviation Press, 1988).

Schlabrendorff, Fabien *Graf* von, *The Secret War Against Hitler*, translation by Hilda Simon, forward by Terence Prittie (London: Hodder & Stoughton, 1966).

Schramm, Percy Ernst, Helmuth Greiner, Andreas Hillgruber, and Hans-Adolf Jacobsen (eds). *Kriegstagebuch des Oberkommandos der Wehrmacht: (Wehrmacht-fuehrungsstab), Vols. 2.1-4.2, 1942-1945* (Frankfurt am Main: Bernard & Graefe fuer Wehrwesen, 1961-65).

Schulte, Theo. *The German Army and Nazi Polices on Occupied Russia* (Oxford, Providence, RI: Oxford University Press, 1989).

Sollum, A.H., "Nowhere Yet Everywhere," Franklin Mark Osanka (ed.), *Modern Guerrilla Warfare: Fighting Communist Movements* (New York: Free Press; London: Collier-Macmillan, 1962), pp. 15-24.

Speer, Albert, *Inside the Third Reich* (London, New York: Weidenfeld & Nicolson, 1975).

Spielvogel, *Hitler and Nazi Germany: A History*, 3rd ed. (New Jersey: Prentice Hall, 1996).

Stachura, Peter (ed.), *The Nazi Machtergreifung* (London: Allen & Unwin, 1983).

Stalin, Joseph, *The Great Patriotic War of the Soviet Union* (New York: Modern Languages Publishing House, 1945).

Steenberg, Sven, *Vlasov*. Translation by Abe Farbtsein (New York: Knopf, 1970).

Steinhoff, Johannes and Peter Pechel, with Dennis Showalter and Helmut D. Schmidt, *Voices from the Third Reich: An Oral History* (New York: Alfred Regnery, 1994).

Stewart, George, *The White Armies of Russia: A Chronicle of Counter-Revolution and Allied Intervention*, reprint of 1933 edition (New York: Bantam, 1970).

Stoakes, Geoffrey, *Hitler and the Quest for World Dominion: Nazi Ideology and Foreign Policy in the 1920s* (Leamington Spa: Berg, 1986).

Streit, Christian. *Keine Kameraden: Die Wehrmacht und die Sowjetischen Kriegsgefangenen 1941-1945*, 4th edition (Bonn: Dietz, 1997).

Strik-Strikfeldt, Wilfried, translation and forward by David Footman, *Against Stalin and Hitler: Memoir of the Russian Liberation Movement, 1941-45* (New York, London: Macmillan. 1970).

Swain, Geoffrey, "The Comintern and Southern Europe, 1938-1943," Tony Judt (ed.), *Resistance and Revolution in Mediterranean Europe, 1949-1948* (London: Routledge, 1989), pp. 29-52.

Sydnor, Charles W., *Soldiers of Destruction: The SS Death's Head Division, 1933-1945* (New Jersey: Princeton University Press, 1990).

Thayer, Charles W., *Guerrilla* (New York: Harper & Row, 1963).

Time-Life Publications, *The Apparatus of Death* (Alexandria, VA: Time-Life Books, Inc., 1991).

_____. *Conquest of the Balkans* (Alexandria, VA: Time-Life Books, Inc., 1990).

_____. *The SS* (Alexandria, VA: Time-Life Books, Inc., 1989).

Tolz, Vera, "New Information About the Deportation of Ethnic Groups in the USSR during World War 2," John and Carol Gerrard (eds.), *World War 2 and the Soviet People: Selected Papers from the Fourth World Congress for Soviet and East European Studies* (New York, London: St. Martin's Press, 1993), pp. 161-179.

Trevor-Roper, Hugh R. *Hitler's Table Talk 1941-44* (London: Weidenfeld & Nicolson, 1953).

_____. 3rd revised edition (New York: Enigma Books, 2000).

_____. *The Last Days of Hitler*, 4th edition (London: Macmillan, 1972).

Tsouras, Peter G. (ed.), *Fighting in Hell: The German Ordeal on the Eastern Front* (London, Mechanicsburg, PA: 1995).

_____. *The Great Patriotic War* (London; Novato, CA: Greenhill Books-Presidio Press, 1992).

Ueberhorst, Horst, *Elite fuer die Diktatur: Die Nationalpolitischen Erziehungstalten 1933-1945-Ein Dokumentarbericht* (Duesseldorf: Droste Verlag, 1969).

Ueberschar, Gerd R. and Wolfram Wette, *Der deutsche Ueberfall auf die Sowjetunion. "Unternehmen Barbarossa 1941,"* (Frankfurt am Main: Taschenbuecher, 1991.

Ueberschar, Gerd R. (ed). *Militaergeschichte Verlag-Beitraege zur Militaer und Kriegsgeschichte-Militaergeschichte: Probleme-Thesen-Wege* (Stuttgart: Deutsche Verlags-Anstalt, 1982).

Uhle-Wettler, Franz, *Hoehe und Wendepunkte: Deutscher Militaer Geschichte* (Mainz: von Hase & Koehler, 1984).

Ulam, Alan B., *Stalin: The Man and His Era*, 2nd edition (New York: Praeger, 1973).

Umbreit, Hans, "Strukturen deutscher Besatzungspolitik in der Anfangsphase des deutsch-sowjetische Krieges," in Bernd Wegner, et al, *Zwei Wege nach Moskau: Vom Hitler-Stalin-Pakt bi zum Unternehmen Barbarossa* (Munich, Zurich: P. Piper GmbH & Co., 1991), pp. 237-50.

_____. "Das unbewaeltigte Problem. Der Partisanenkrieg im Ruecken der Ostfront," in –Juergen Foerster (ed.), *Stalingrad: Ereignis-Wirkung-Symbol* (Zurich: Piper, 1992), pp. 130-50.

Walzer, Michael, *Just and Unjust Wars: A Moral Argument with Historical Illustrations* (New York: Basic Books, 1977).

Wegner, Bernd. *Zwei Wege nach Moskau: Vom Hitler-Stalin-Pakt bis zum Unternehmen Barbarossa* (Munich, Zurich: R. Piper GmbH & Co. 1991).

_____. "Der Krieg gegen die Sowjetunion 1942/43," in horst Boog et al, *Das Deutsche Reich und der Zweite Weltkrieg Bd. 6: Der Globale Krieg. Die Ausweitung zum Weltkrieg und der Wechsel der Initiativ 1941-1943* (Stuttgart: Deutsche Verlags- Anstalt, 1990), pp. 761-1102.

Weinberg, Gerhard, *Germany, Hitler and World War II* (Madison: University of Wisconsin Press, 1995).

_____. "The Yelnya-Dorogobuzh Area of Smolensk Oblast," in John A. Armstrong (ed.), *Soviet Partisans in World War II* (Madison: University of Wisconsin Press, 1964), pp. 389-457.

_____. *Hitlers Zweite Buch* (New York: 1961).

Wette, Wolfrum, " 'Rassenfeind'. Antisemitismus und Antislawismus in der Wehrmachtpropaganda," on Walter Manoschek (ed.), *Die Wehrmacht im Rassenkrieg* (Vienna: Picus, 1996), pp. 58-72.

Wilhelm, Hans-Heinrich. *Die Einsatzgruppe A der Sicherheitspolizei und des SD 1941/42* (Frankfurt am Main: Peter Lang, 1996).

_____*Rassenpolitik und Kriegfuehrung. Sicherheitspolizei und Wehrmacht in Polen und der Sowjetunion* (Passau: Wissenschaftverlag Rother, 1991).

Williamson, Gordon K., *The SS: Hitler's Instrument of Terror: The Full Story from Street Fighters to the Waffen SS* (Osceola, WI: Motorbooks International, 1994).

Yedlin, Tova (ed.), *Women in Eastern Europe and the Soviet Union* (New York: Praeger, 1980).

Yerger, Mark C., *Knights of Steel: The Structure, Development, and Personalities of the 2. SS-Panzer.* (Self Published by Mark C. Yerger, 1994).

Zaloga, Steven J. and Leland S. Ness. *Red Army Handbook, 1939-1945* (Stroud: Sutton Publishing, 1998).

Zeidler, Manfred, "Deutsch-Sowjetische Wirtschaftsbeziehung im Zeichen des Hitler-Stalin-Paktes," in Bernd Wegner, et al, *Zwei Wege nach Moscow,* pp. 93-110.

Peer Reviewed Journals

Bacon, Edwin, " 'Glasnost' and the Gulag: New Information on Soviet Forced Labour around World War II," *Soviet Studies,* vol. 44, no. 6 (1992), pp. 1069-86.

Bajohr, Stefan, "Weisslicher Arbeitsdienst im Dritten Reich: Ein Konflikt Zwischen Ideologie und Oeconomie," *Vierteljahrschaefte Fuer Zeitgeschichte,* vol. 28, no. 3 (1980), pp. 331-57.

Bartov, Omer, "The Conduct of War: Soldiers and the Barbarization of Warfare," *Journal of Modern History,* vol. 64, no. 4 (December 1992) 532-45.

Beller, Steven, " 'Your Mark is Your Disgrace': Liberalism and the Holocaust," *Contemporary European History,* vol. 4, no. 2 (1995), pp. 209-21.

Bergman, Jay, "The Idea of Individual Liberation in Bolshevik Visions of the New Soviet Man," *European History Quarterly,* vol. 27, no. 1 (January 1997), pp. 57-92.

Bradford, Richard H., review of Johann Ewald, "Treatise on Partisan Warfare," *The Journal of Military History,* vol. 57, no. 1 (January 1993), pp. 141-2.

Breitman, Richard, "Himmler's Police Auxiliaries in the Occupied Soviet Territories," located at the Simon Wiesenthal Centre/Museum of Tolerance online at www.motlc.wiesenthal.com (03/08/2002).

_____. Ibid. "A Nazi Crusade?" (03/08/2002).

Broszat, Martin, "Soziale Motivation und Fuehrer-Bindung im Nationalsozialismus," *Vierteljahreshefte fuer Zeitgeschichte,* no. 18 (1970), pp. 392-409.

Brower, Daniel L. "Collectivized Agriculture in Smolensk: The Party, the Peasantry, and the Crisis of 1932," *The Russian Review,* vol. 36, no. 2 (April 1977), pp. 151-66.

Buchler, Yehoshua, "Kommandostab Reichsfuehrer-SS: Himmler's Personal Murder Brigades in 1941," *Holocaust and Genocide,* vol. 1, no. 1 (1986), pp. 11-25.

Burleigh, Michael, "Between Enthusiasm, Compliance and Protest: The Churches, Eugenics and the Nazi 'Euthanasia' Programme," *Contemporary European History,* vol. 3, no. 3 (1994), pp. 253-63.

Carr, William, "A Final Solution: Nazi Policy Towards the Jews," *History Today*, vol. 35, no. 11 (November, 1985), pp. 665-9.

Cherniavsky, Michael, "Corporal Hitler, General Winter and the Russian Peasant," *Yale Review*, no. 51 (1962), pp. 547-558.

Cohen, Stephen, "Stalin's Terror as Social History," *Russian Review*, vol. 45, no. 4 (October 1986), pp. 375-384.

Conquest, Robert, "What is Terror?" *Slavic Review*, vol. 45, no. 2 (Summer 1986), pp. 235-7.

Cottam, K. Jean, "Soviet Women in Combat in World War II: The Rear Services, Resistance Behind Enemy Lines, and Military Political Workers," *International Journal of Women's Studies*, vol. 5, no. 4 (1982), pp. 363-78.

Childers, Thomas, "The Social Basis of the National Socialist Vote," *Journal of Contemporary History*, vol. 11, no. 4 (October 1976), pp. 17-42.

Dalrymple, Dana G. "The Soviet Famine of 1932-1934," *Soviet Studies*, vol. XV, no. 3 (January 1964), pp. 250-84.

Ellman, Michael, "A Note on the Number of 1933 Famine Victims," *Soviet Studies*, vol. 43, no. 2 (1991), pp. 375-9.

Erickson, John, "The Soviet Response to the Surprise Attack: Three Directives, 22 June 1941," *Soviet Studies*, vol. XXIII, no. 4 (April 1972), pp. 519-53.

_____. "The Soviet Union at War (1941-1945): An Essay on Sources and Studies," *Soviet Studies*, vol. XIV, no. 3 (January 1963), pp. 249-74.

Fitzpatrick, Sheila, "Stalin and the Making of a New Elite, 1928-1939," *Slavic Review*, vol. 38, no. 2 (1979), pp. 377-402.

Friedberg, Maurice, "The USSR and Its Émigrés," *The Russian Review*, vol. 27, no. 2 (April 1968), pp. 131-48.

Gingerich, Mark P., "*Waffen SS* Recruitment in the Germanic Lands, 1940-41," *The Historian*, vol. 59, no. 4 (Summer 1997), pp. 818-30.

Ginsburgs, George, "Laws of War and War Crimes on the Russian Front During World War II: The Soviet View," *Soviet Studies*, vol. XI, no. 3 (January 1960), pp. 253-85.

_____. "The Soviet Union as a Neutral, 1939-1941," *Soviet Studies*, vol. X, no. 1 (July 1958), pp. 12-35.

Girnius, Kestutis, "The Collectivisation of Lithuanian Agriculture, 1944-1950," *Soviet Studies*, vol. XL, no. 3 (July 1988), pp. 460-78.

Gregor, Neil, "Big Business and the '*Blitzkriegwirtschaft*'; Daimler-Benz AG and the Mobilisation of the German War Economy, 1939-42," *Contemporary European History*, vol. 6, no. 2 (1997), pp. 193-208.

Gumz, Jonathan, "German Counterinsurgency Policy in Independent Croatia, 1941-1944," *The Historian*, vol. 61, no. 1 (Fall 1998), pp. 33-50.

Hachtmann, Ruediger, "Industriearbeiten in Der Deutschen Kriegswirtschaft 1936 bis 1944/45," *Geschichte und Gesellschaft*, vol. 19, no. 3 (1993), pp. 332-66.

Heilman, Leo, "Organised Looting: The Basis of Partisan Warfare," *Military Review*, vol. 45, no. 2 (1965), pp. 61-68.

Herbert, Ulrich, "Labour and Extermination: Economic Interest and the Primacy of *Weltanschauung* in National Socialism," *Past and Present*, no. 138 (February 1993), pp. 144-95.

Hillgruber, Andreas, "Revisionismus-Kontinuitaet und Wandel in der Aussenpolitik der Weimarer Republik," *Historische Zeitschrift*, no. 237 (1983), pp.

Johnston, Robert H., "The Great Patriotic War and the Russian Exiles in France," *The Russian Review*, vol. 35, no. 3 (July 1976), pp. 303-21.

Katz, Zev, "Party-Political Education in Soviet Russia, 1918-1935," *Soviet Studies*, vol. VII, no. 3 (January 1956), pp. 237-47.

Kent, George O., "Pope Pius XII and Germany: Some Aspects of German-Vatican Relations, 1933-1943," *American History Review*, vol. 70, no. 1 (October 1964), pp. 59-68.

Kershaw, Ian, " 'Working Towards the Fuehrer': Reflections on the Nature of the Hitler Dictatorship," *Contemporary European History*, vol. 2, no. 2 (1993), pp. 103-18.

Kettenacker, Lothar, "The Anglo-Soviet Alliance and the Problem of Germany," *Journal of Contemporary History*, vol. 17 (no number) (1982), pp. 435-58.

Knox, MacGregor, "Conquest, Foreign and Domestic in Fascist Italy and Nazi Germany," *Journal of Modern History*, vol. 56 (1984), pp. 1-57.

Koch, Hans-Joachim Wolfgang, "Hitler's 'Programme' and the Genesis of Operation Barbarossa," *The Historical Journal*, vol. 26, no. 4 (1983), pp. 891-920.

_____. "Hitler and the Origins of the Second World War-Second Thoughts on the Status of Some of the Documents," *The Historical Journal*, vol. 11, no. 1 (1968), pp. 125-43.

Kohn, Hans, "Germany and Russia," *Current History*, vol. 38, no. 221 (January 1960), pp. 1-5.

Koutaisoff, E. "Soviet Education and the New Man," *Soviet Studies*, vol. V, no. 2 (October 1953), pp. 103-37.

Kowalewski, David, "Protest for Religious Rights in the USSR: Characteristics and Consequences," *The Russian Review*, vol. 39, no. 4 (October 1980), pp. 426-41.

Kroener, Bernhard R., "Der erforene Blitzkrieg. Strategische Planungen der deutschen Fuehrungen gegen die sowjetunion und die Ursachen ihres Scheiterns," *The Historical Journal*, vol. 26, no. 4 (1983), pp.891-920.

Krop, J.F., "Jews Under the Nazi Regime," *Annals of the American Academy of Social Science*, vol. 245 (1946), pp. 28-32.

Kumanyev, G.A., "On the Soviet People's Partisan Movement in the Hitlerite Invader's Rear, 1941-1944," *Revue Internationale d' Histoire Militaire*, no. 47 (1980), pp. 180-88.

Liber, George, "Urban Growth and Ethnic Change in the Ukrainian SSR, 1923-1933," *Soviet Studies*, vol. XLI, no. 4 (October 1989), pp. 574-91.

Mason, Tim, "The Workers' Opposition in Nazi Germany," *History Workshop Journal*, issue 11 (Spring 1981), pp. 120-37.

_____. "Labour in the Third Reich, 1933-1939," *Past and Present*, no. 33 (1966), pp. 112-41.

McCann, James M. "Beyond the Bug: Soviet Historiography of the Soviet-Polish War of 1920," *Soviet Studies*, vol. XXXVI, no. 4 (October 1984), pp. 475-93.

Michaelis, Meir, "Fascism, Totalitarianism and the Holocaust: Reflections on Current Interpretations of National Socialist Anti-Semitism," *European History Quarterly*, vol. 19, no. 1 (January 1989), pp. 85-103.

Miller, Frank J., "The Image of Stalin in Soviet Russian Folklore," *The Russian Review*, vol. 39, no. 1 (January 1980), pp. 50-67.

Milton, S., "Images of the Holocaust-Part I," *Holocaust and Genocide Studies*, vol. 1 (1986), pp. 27-61.

_____. "Images of the Holocaust-Part II," *Holocaust and Genocide Studies*, vol. 1 (1986) 193-216.

Moskoff, William, "Soviet Higher Education Policy during World War II," *Soviet Studies*, vol. XXXVIII, no. 3 (July 1986), pp. 406-15.

Mulligan, Timothy, "Reckoning the Cost of the People's War: The German Experience in The Central USSR," *Russian History/Histoire Russe*, vol. 9, no. 1 (1982), pp. 27-48.

Nariewicz, Olga, "Soviet Administration and the Grain Crisis of 1927-28," *Soviet Studies*, vol. 20, no. 2 (1968), pp. 235-41.

_____. "Stalin, War, Communism and Collectivisation," *Soviet Studies*, vol. 18, no. 1 (1966), pp. 20-37.

Noakes, Jeremy, "Social Outcasts in Nazi Germany," *History Today*, vol. 35 (December 1985), pp. 15-9.

Olcott, Martha Brill, "The Collectivization Drive in Kazakhstan," *The Russian Review*, vol. 41, no. 2 (April 1981), pp. 122-42.

Orlow, Dietrich O., "The Conversion of Myths into Political Power: The Case of the Nazi Party," *The American Historical Review*, vol. 72, no. 3, (April 1967), pp. 906-24.

Overy, Richard J., "Germany, 'Domestic Crisis' and War in 1939," *Past and Present*, vols. 114-117 (1987), 138-68.

_____. "Hitler's War and the German Economy: A Reinterpretation," *Economic History Review*, vol. 35 (1982), pp. 272-92.

Pohl, Dieter, "Die Holocaust-Forschung und Goldhagens Thesen," *Vierteljahreshefte fuer Zeitgeschichte*, no. 45 (1997), pp. 1-48.

Polonsky, Antony, "Stalin and the Poles," *European History Quarterly*, vol. 17, no. 4 (October 1987), pp. 435-92.

Posthumus, J.H., "The Structure of the Occupational Government," *The Annals of the American Academy of Social and Political Science*, vol. 245 (May 1946), pp. 1-2.

Raack, R.C., "Stalin's Plans for World War II," *Journal of Contemporary History*, vol. 26, no. 2 (April 1991), pp. 215-27.

Reese, Roger, "The Impact of the Great Purge on the Red Army: Wrestling with the Hard Numbers," *Soviet and Post Soviet Review*, vol. 19, no. 1-3 (1992), pp. 71-90.

_____. "A Note on the Consequence of the Expansion of the Red Army on the Eve of World War II," *Soviet Studies*, vol. XLI, no. 1 (January 1989), pp.

Ro'I, Yaacov, "The Task of Creating the New Soviet Man: 'Atheistic Propaganda' in the Soviet Muslim Areas," *Soviet Studies*, vol. XXXVI, no. 1 (January 1984), pp. 26-44.

Schauff, Frank, "Company Choir of Terror: The Military Council of the 1930s-The Red Army Between the XVIIth and XVIIIth Party Congresses," *Journal of Slavic Military Studies*, vol. 12, no. 2 (June 1999), pp. 123-63.

Sella, Amnon, "Red Army Doctrine and Training on the Eve of the Second World War," *Soviet Studies*, vol. XXVII, no. 2 (April 1975), p. 245-64.

Shapiro, Jane P., "Soviet Historiography and the Moscow Trials: After Thirty Years," *The Russian Review*, vol. 27, no. 1 (January 1968), pp. 68-77.

Smith, Arthur L., "The German General Staff and Russia, 1919-1926," *Soviet Studies*, vol. VIII, no. 2 (October 1956), pp. 125-33.

Sokolov, B.V. "The Cost of War: Human Losses for the USSR and Germany, 1939-1945," *Journal of Slavic Military Studies*, vol. 9, no. 1 (March 1996), pp. 152-93.

Spring, D.W. "The Soviet Decision for War Against Finland, 30 November 1939," *Soviet Studies*, vol. XXXVIII, no. 2 (April 1986), pp. 207-26.

Steinberg, Jonathan, "Third Reich Reflected: German Civil Administration in the Occupied Soviet Union, 1941-4," *The English Historical Review*, vol. CX (June 1995), pp. 620-51.

Streit, Christian, "Partisans, Resistance, Prisoners of War," *Soviet Union-Union Sovietique*, vol.18, no. 1 (1991), pp. 260-76.

Taylor, Pauline B., "Treason, Espionage, and Other State Crimes," *The Russian Review*, vol. 23, no. 3 (July 1964), pp. 247-58.

Thurston, Robert W., "Social Dimension of Stalinist Rule: Humour and Terror in the USSR 1935-1941," *Journal of Social History*, vol. 24 (1991), pp. 541-62.

_____. "Fear and Belief in the USSR's Great Terror," *Slavic Review*, vol. 45, no. 2 (1986), pp. 213-34.

Tumarkin, Nina, "The Invasion and War as Myth and Reality," *Soviet Union/Union Sovietique*, vol. 18, no. 1-3 (1991), pp. 277-96.

_____. "Religion, Bolshevism, and the Origins of the Lenin Cult," *The Russian Review*, vol. 40, no. 1 (January 1981), pp. 35-46.

Turner, Henry Ashby, "Big Business and the Rise of Hitler," *The American Historical Review*, vol. 75 (1969), pp. 56-70.

Viola, Lynne, "The Peasant Nightmare: Visions of the Apocalypse in the Soviet Countryside," *Journal of Modern History*, vol. 62, no. 4 (December 1990), pp. 747-70.

Vonk, K., "The Transportation System," *Annals of the American Academy of Social and Political Science*, vol. 245 (1946), pp. 70-8.

Welch, David, "Manufacturing a Consensus: Nazi Propaganda and the Building of a 'National Community' (*Volksgemeinschaft*)," *Contemporary European History*, vol. 2, no. 1 (1993), pp. 1-15.

_____. "Propaganda and Indoctrination in the Third Reich: Success or Failure?" *European History Quarterly*, vol. 17, no. 4 (1987), pp. 403-22.

Wilenchik, Witalij, "Die Partisanenbewegung in Weissrussland 1941-1944," *Sonderdruck aus: Forschungen zur osteuropaeischen Geschichte*, vol. 34 (1984), pp. 195-201.

Wimberg, Ellen, "Socialism, Democratism and Criticism: The Soviet Press and the National Discussion of the 1936 Draft Constitution," *Soviet Studies*, vol. 44, no. 2 (1992), pp. 313-32.

Winkler, Heinrich August, "German Society, Hitler and the Illusion of Restoration, 1930-33," *Journal of Contemporary History*, vol. 11, no. 4 (October 1976), pp. 1-16.

Zawodny, J.K. "Soviet Partisans," *Soviet Studies*, vol. XVII, no.3 (January 1966), pp. 368-77.

Journals Consulted

Bacon, Edwin, "Soviet Military Losses in World War II," *Journal of Slavic Military Studies*, vol. 6, no. 4 (December 1993), pp. 613-33.

Berghahn, Volker R., "NSDAP und 'Geistige Fuehrung' der *Wehrmacht* 1939-1945," *Vierteljahreshefte fuer Zeitgeschichte*, no 17 (1969), pp. 17-71.

_____. "Militaer, industrialisierter Kriegfuehrung und Nationalsozialismus," *Neue Politische Literatur*, vol. XXVI, no. 1 (1981), pp. 20-41.

Browning, Christopher R., "Wehrmacht Reprisal Policy and the Mass Murder of Jews in Serbia," *Militaergeschichtliche Mitteilungen*, vol. 33, no. 1 (1983), pp. 311-49.

Cimbala, Stephen J. "Intelligence, C3 and the Initial War Period," *Journal of Soviet Military Studies*, vol. 4, no. 3 (September 1991), pp. 397-447.

Clemens, Walter C., "The Burden of Defense: Soviet Russia in the 1920s," *Journal of Slavic Military Studies*, vol. 9, no. 4 (December 1996), pp. 786-99.

Daugherty, Leo J. III, "The Reluctant Warriors: The Non-Russian Nationalities in the Service of the Red Army During the Great Patriotic War 1941-1945," *Journal of Slavic Military Studies*, vol. 6, no. 3 (September 1993), pp. 426-45.

_____. "The *Volksdeutsche* and Hitler's War," *Journal of Slavic Military Studies*, vol. 8, no. 2 (June 1995), pp. 296-318.

Dunn, Walter S. "Deciphering Soviet Wartime Order of Battle: In Search of a New Methodology," *Journal of Soviet Military Studies*, vol. 5, no. 3 (September 1992), pp. 405-25.

van Dyke, Carl, "The Timoshenko Reforms: March-July 1940," *Journal of Slavic Military Studies*, vol. 9, no. 1 (March 1996), pp. 69-96.

Frankson, Anders, "Summer 1941," *Journal of Slavic Military Studies*, vol. 13, no. 3, (September 2000), pp. 131-44.

Gebhardt, James F. "The Petsamo-Kirkenes Operation (7-30 October 1944): A Soviet Joint and Combined Arms Operation in Arctic Terrain," *Journal of Soviet Military Studies*, vol. 2, no. 1 (March 1989), pp. 49-86.

Gerard, Beth M. "Mistakes in Force Structure and Strategy on the Eve of the Great Patriotic War," *Journal of Soviet Military Studies*, vol. 4, no. 3 (September 1991), pp. 471-86.

Glantz, David M. (ed.), "Forgotten Battles of the German-Soviet War (1941-45), Part I," *Journal of Soviet Military Studies*, vol. 12, no. 4 (December 2000), pp.149-97.

_____. "Forgotten Battles of the German-Soviet War (1951-45), Part 4: The Winter Campaign (5 December 1941-April 1942): The Demyansk Counter-Offensive," *Journal of Slavic Military Studies*, vol. 13.no. 3 (September 2000), pp. 145-64.

_____. "Forgotten Battles of the German-Soviet War (1941-45), Part 3: The Winter Campaign (5 December 1941-April 1942): The Moscow Counter- Offensive," *Journal of Slavic Military Studies*, vol. 13, no. 2 (June 2000), pp. 139-85.

_____. "Forgotten Battles of the German-Soviet War (1941-45), Part II," *Journal of Slavic Military Studies*, vol. 13, no. 1 (March 2000), 172-237.

_____. "Attache Assessments of the Impact of the 1930s Purge on the Red Army," *Journal of Soviet Military Studies*, vol. 2, no. 3 (September 1989), pp. 417-38.

_____. "A Collection of Combat Documents Covering the First Three Days of the Great Patriotic War," *Journal of Soviet Military Studies*, vol. 4, no. 1 (March 1991), pp. 112-46.

_____. "A Collection of Combat Documents Covering Soviet Western Front Operations: 24-30 June 1941," *Journal of Soviet Military Studies*, vol. 4, no. 4 (June 1991), pp. 120-45.

_____. "Combat Documents of the Soviet Northwestern Front 24 June-1 July 1941-'Operational Report no. 04 from Northwestern Front Headquarters, Dated 24 June 1941, 1000, on the Course of Combat Actions of Front Forces', Series 'G'," *Journal of Soviet Military Studies*, vol. 5, no. 1 (March 1992), pp. 115-57.

_____. 'Soviet Mobilization in Peace and War, 1924-1942: A Survey', *Journal of Soviet Military Studies*, vol. 5, no. 3 (September 1992), pp. 323-62.

_____. 'The Kharkov Operation, May 1942: from the Archives, Part I', *Journal of Soviet Military Studies*, vol. 5, no. 3 (September 1992), pp. 451-93.

_____. 'The Kharkov Operation, May 1942, Part II: Southwestern Front Combat Operations', *Journal of Soviet Military Studies*, vol. 5, no. 4 (December 1992), pp. 611-86.

_____. "The Failures of Historiography' Forgotten Battles of the German-Soviet War (1941-1945)," *Journal of Slavic Military Studies*, vol. 8, no. 4 (December 1995), pp. 768-808.

Goff, James M. "Evolving Soviet Force Structure, 1941-1945: Process and Impact," *Journal of Soviet Military Studies*, vol. 5, no. 3 (September 1992), pp. 363-404.

Gorter-Gronvik, Waling T. and Mikhail N. Suprun, "Ethnic Minorities and Warfare at the Arctic Front 1939-45," *Journal of Slavic Military Studies*, vol. 13, no. 1, (March 2000), pp.127-42.

Hayward, Joel, "Hitler's Quest for Oil: The Impact of Economic Considerations on Military Strategy, 1941-42," *The Journal of Strategic Studies*, vol. 18, no. 4 (December 1995), pp. 94-135.

Heer, Hannes, "Der Freispruch. Zu Joerg Friedrichs Essay 'Das Gesetz des Krieges'," *Mittelweg 36*, vol. 12, no. 1, (1994), pp. 54-61.

Korol, V.E. "The Price of Victory: Myths and Reality," *Journal of Slavic Military Studies*, vol. 9, no. 2 (June 1996), pp. 417-26.

Krausnick, Helmut, "Kommissarbefehl und 'Kriegsgerichtbarkeitserlass Barbarossa' in neuer Sicht," *Vierteljahreshefte fuer Zeitgeschichte*, vol. 25 (1977), pp. 682-738.

Kreidel, Hellmuth, "Jagd auf Grischin. Deutsche Gegenmassnahmen gegen den Polk Grischin 1942/43 im Heeresgebiet Mitte," *Wehrkunde*, vol. 5 (1956), pp. 45-7.

_____. "Partisanenkampf in Mittelrussland," *Wehrkunde*, vol. 4 (1955), pp. 380-5.

Latzel, Klaus, "Vom Kriegserlebnis zur Kriegserfahrung. Theoretische und methodische Ueberlegungen zur erfahrungsgeschichtlichen Untersuchung von Feldpostbriefen," in *Militaergeschichtliche Mitteilungen* no. 56 (1997), pp. 1-30.

Lazowick, Yaacov, "Rollbahn Mord: The Early Activities of Einsatzgruppe C," *Holocaust and Genocide Studies*, no. 2 (1987), pp. 221-41.

Maslov, Alexander A. "Tried for Treason against the Motherland: Soviet Generals Condemned after Release from German Captivity," *Journal of Slavic Studies*, vol. 13, no. 2 (June 2000), pp. 86-138.

_____. "Forgiven by Stalin-Soviet Generals Who Returned From German Prisons in 1941-45 and Who Were Rehabilitated," *Journal of Slavic Military Studies*, vol. 12, no. 2 (June 1999), pp. 173-219.

_____. "The Unbroken: Soviet Generals/Defenders of the Ukraine Who Perished in Fascist Captivity," translated by Robert R. Love, FMSO, Ft. Leavenworth, USA, *Journal of Slavic Military Studies*, vol. 7, no. 2 (June 1994), pp. 292-98.

_____. "The Soviet General Officer Corps, 1944-1945: Losses in Combat," *Journal of Slavic Military Studies*, vol. 8, no. 3 (September 1995), pp. 580-611.

_____. "How Were Soviet Blocking Detachments Employed?" *Journal of Slavic Military Studies*, vol. 9, no. 2 (June 1996), pp. 427-35.

_____. "Concerning the Role of Partisan Warfare in Soviet Military Doctrine of the 1920s and 1930s," *Journal of Slavic Military Studies*, vol. 9, no. 4 (December 1996), pp. 885-94.

Main, Steven J. "The Arrest and 'Testimony' of Marshal of the Soviet Union M.N. Tukhachevsky (May-June 1937)," *Journal of Slavic Military Studies*, vol. 10, no. 1 (March 1997), pp. 151-95.

Messerschmidt, Manfred, "Das Verhaeltnis von Wehrmacht und NS-Staat und die Frage der Traditionsbildung," *Aus Politik und Zeitgeschichte*, no. 17 (1981), pp. 11-23.

Naumann, Klaus, "Wenn ein Tabu bricht. Die Wehrmachtausstellung in der Bundes-Republik," *Mittelweg*, no. 36 (Feb./Mar. 1996), pp. 11-24.

Reent, Aleksandr P. and Aleksandr E. Lysenko, "World War II Through the Prism of a Christian *Weltanschauung*," *Journal of Slavic Military Studies*, vol.13, no. 1 (March 2000), pp. 113-26.

_____. "Ukrainians in Armed Formations of the Warring Sides during World War II," *Journal of Slavic Military Studies*, vol. 10, no. 1 (March 1997), pp. 210-36.

Samuelson, Lennart, "Mikhail Tukhachevsky and War-Economic Planning: Reconsiderations on the Pre-war Soviet Buildup," *Journal of Slavic Military Studies*, vol. 9, no. 4 (December 1996), pp. 804-47.

Savushkin, Robert, "In the Tracks of a Tragedy: On the 50th Anniversary of the Start of the Great Patriotic War," *Journal of Soviet Military Studies*, vol. 4, no. 2 (June 1991), pp. 213-51.

Schauff, Frank, "Company Choir of Terror: The Military Council of the 1930s-The Red Army Between the XVIIth and XVIIIth Party Congresses," *Journal of Slavic Military Studies*, vol. 12, no. 2 (June 1999), pp. 123-63.

Searle, Alaric, "The Employment of the Red Army 4th Airborne Corps in the Viaz'ma Operation (February-March 1942)," *Journal of Slavic Military Studies*, vol. 12, no. 2 (June 1999), pp. 245-50.

_____. 'J.F.C. Fuller, "Tukhachevsky and the Red Army, 1923-1941: The Question of the Reception of Fuller's Writings in the Soviet Union," *Journal of Slavic Military Studies*, vol. 9, no. 4 (December 1996), pp. 848-84.

Suggs, William H. "In Search of the Bogatyri: The Need for a New Myth in the Soviet Army," *Journal of Soviet Military Studies*, vol. 4, no. 3 (September 1991), pp. 506-12.

Witt, Donald Cameron, "Who Plotted Against Whom? Stalin's Purge of the Soviet High Command Revisited," *Journal of Soviet Military Studies*, vol. 3, no. 1 (March 1991), pp. 46-65.

Weinberg, Gerhard L., "Review Note: The Chapter on Russo-German Relations in Volume IV of Documents on German Foreign Policy 1918-1945," *Journal of Central European Affairs*, vol. 12, no. 51 (April 1952), pp. 70-4.

Tarleton, Robert E., "What Really Happened to the Stalin Line? Part I," *Journal of Soviet Military Studies*, vol. 5, no. 2 (June 1992), pp. 187-219.

_____. "What Really Happened to the Stalin Line? Part II," *Journal of Slavic Military Studies*, vol. 6, no. 1 (March 1993), pp. 21-61.

Zaccor, Albert M. "Guerrilla Warfare on the Baltic Coast: A Possible Model for Baltic Defense Doctrines Today?" *Journal of Slavic Military Studies*, vol. 7, no. 4 (December 1994), pp. 682-702.

Zarubinsky, O.A. "The 'Red' Partisan Movement in Ukraine During World War II: A Contemporary Assessment," David M. Glantz (ed.), *Journal of Slavic Military Studies*, vol. 9, no. 2 (June 1996), pp. 399-416.

Non-Peer Reviewed Periodicals

Bell, Kelly, "Costly Capture of Crete," *World War II*, vol. 14, no. 1, ISSN 0898-4204 (May 1999), pp. 50-6.

Belyakov, Vladimir, "No Retreats Allowed," *World War II*, vol. 7, no. 3, ISSN 0898-4204 (September 1992), pp. 22-9, 70-1.

Bullock, David L., "Reds Versus Whites," *Military History*, vol. 9, no. 2, ISSN-0889-7328, (June 1992), pp. 42-9.

Chalabian, Antranig, "Personality," *Military History*, vol. 12, no. 2, ISSN 0889-7328 (June 1995), pp. 10-2, 16.

Clearwater, John, "Undercover," *World War II*, vol. 13, no. 6, ISSN-0898-4204 (February, 1999), pp. 60-4.

D' Angelo, Rudy A., "Perspectives," *World War II*, vol. 3, no. 3, ISSN 0898-4204 (September 1999), p. 18.

Deac, Wilfred P., "Undercover," *World War II*, vol. 13, no. 3, ISSN 0898-4204 (September 1998), pp. 18-24, 70-2.

_____."City Streets Contested," *World War II*, vol. 9, no. 3, ISSN 0898-4204 (September 1994), pp. 32-44, 66.

Denkhaus, Raymond A., "Armament," *World War II*, vol. 8, no. 2, ISSN 0898-4204 (July 1993), pp. 14, 68-9.

Dodge, Nicholas, "Revolutionary Upheaval Survived," *Military History*, vol. 11, no. 5, ISSN 0889-7328 (December 1994), pp. 54-61.

Fonner, D. Kent, "Personality," *Military History*, vol. 12, no. 7, ISSN 0889-7328 (March 1996), pp. 10-2, 16.

Fournie, Daniel A., "Intrigue," *Military History*, vol. 14, no. 7, ISSN 0889-7328 (March 1998), pp. 12, 65.

Frisch, Franz A.P. and Wilbur D. Jones, Jr., "A Panzer Soldier's Story," *World War II*, vol. 10, no. 3, ISSN 0898-4204 (September 1995), p. 50.

Greenberg, Lawrence M., "Rolling Advance Stymied," *World War II*, vol. 6, no. 2, ISSN 0898-4202 (July 1991), pp. 26-33.

Guttman, Jon, "Genocide Delayed," *World War II*, vol. 8, no. 1, ISSN 0898-4204 (May 1993), pp. 44-52.

Heaton, Colin D. "Belgian Volunteer in the Waffen SS," *Military History*, vol. 23, No. 8. ISSN-0889-7328 (November 2006), pp. 46-53.

Huchthausen, Peter A., "Perspectives," *World War II*, vol. 12, no. 4, ISSN 0898-4204 (November 1997), p. 70.

Kleinwald, James, "No Relief for Stubborn Volunteers," *World War II*, vol. 7, no. 1, ISSN 0898-4204 (May 1992), pp. 30-6.

Lew, Christopher, "Undercover," *World War II*, vol. 11, no. 2, ISSN 0898-4204 (July 1996), pp. 8, 20.

Lindsey, Brian, "Personality," *World War II*, vol. 14, no. 2, ISSN 0898-4204 (July, 1999), pp. 68-76.

McTaggart, Pat, "Winter Tempest at Stalingrad," *World War II*, vol. 12, no. 4, ISSN 0898-4204 (November, 1997), pp. 30-6.

_____. "Soviet Encirclement Thwarted," *World War II*, vol. 8, no. 5, ISSN 0898-4204 (January 1994), p. 34.

Murphy, Jeffrey A., "Personality," *Military History*, vol. 12, no. 4, ISSN 0889-7328 (October 1995), pp. 20, 24, 28, 80, 81.

Noyles, Harry F., III, "Sergeant's Odyssey," *World War II*, vol. 8, no. 3, ISSN 0898-4204 (September 1993), p. 46.

Smith, Robert Barr, "Final Verdict at Nuremberg," *World War II*, vol. 10, no. 4, ISSN 0898-4204 (November 1995), pp. 38-44, 83, 88

_____. "Nuremberg: Final Chapter for the Thousand Year Reich," *World War II*, vol. 10, no. 4 ISSN 0898-4204 (November 1995), pp. 38-46.

Stolfi, Russell H.S., "10th Panzer's Lightning Eastern Front Offensive," *World War II*, vol. 12, no. 3, ISSN 0898-4204 (September 1997), pp. 34-40.

Stout, Robert Joe, "Undercover," *World War II*, vol. 5, no. 6, ISSN 0898-4204 (March 1991), pp. 12-6.

Szymczak, Robert, "Bolshevik Wave Breaks at Warsaw," *Military History*, vol. 11, no. 6, ISSN 0889-7328 (February 1995), pp. 54-61, 90.

Taylor, Barry, "Personality," *Military History*, vol. 8, no. 2, ISSN 0889-7328 (August 1991), pp. 8, 12-6.

Weeks, Albert L., "Perspectives," *World War II*, vol. 13, no. 4, ISSN 0898-4204 (November 1999), pp. 12-24.

_____. "Personality," *World War II*, vol. 12, no. 4, ISSN 0898-4204 (November 1997), pp. 8-10, 78.

_____. "Undercover," *World War II*, vol. 10, no. 3, ISSN 0898-4204 (September 1994), pp. 8-10, 14-6.

Zabecki, David T., "Personality," *World War II*, vol. 12, no. 1, ISSN 0898-4204 (May 1997), pp. 8-12, 69.

Ph.D. Theses/Dissertations

Anderson, Truman O., "The Conduct of Reprisals by the German Army of Occupation in the Southern USSR, 1941-1943," University of Chicago PhD thesis, 1994.

Corum, James Sterling, "The Reichswehr and the Concept of Mobile War in the Era of Hans von Seeckt," Queen's University of Kingston Ph.D. thesis, May 1992.

Foglesong, David Scott, "America's Secret War against Bolshevism: United States Intervention in the Russian Civil War, 1917-1920," University of California, Berkeley Ph.D. thesis, 1991.

Gingerich, Mark P., "Toward a Brotherhood of Arms: Waffen SS Recruitment of Germanic Volunteers, 1940-1945," University of Wisconsin Ph.D. thesis, 1992.

Giziowski, Richard John, "The Moral Dilemmas of Leadership: The Case of German General Johannes Blaskowitz," Illinois State University Ph.D. thesis, 1992.

Gerlach, Christian, "Die deutsche Wirtschafts und Vernichtungs Politik im Weissrussland 1941-1944," Technical University of Berlin PhD thesis, 1997.

Gordon, Gary, "Soviet Partisan Warfare 1941-44: The German Perspective," University of Iowa Ph.D. thesis, 1972.

McHugh, Michael Caldwell, "With Malice toward None: The Punishment and Pardon of German War Criminals, 1945-58," Miami University Ph.D. thesis, 1992.

Pronin, Alexander, "Guerrilla Warfare in the German-Occupied Soviet Territories, 1941-1944," Georgetown University Ph.D. thesis, 1965.

Shepherd, Ben, "German Army Security Units in Russia, 1941-1943: A Case Study," University of Birmingham, Institute for German Studies, UK, 2000.

Slepyan, Kenneth D., "The People's Avengers: Soviet Partisans, Stalinist Society and the Politics of Resistance, 1941-1944," University of Michigan, 1994.

Unpublished Works

Hill, Alexander, "Between Two Fires: Explaining Local Responses to German Occupation and the Soviet Partisan Movement on the Territory Occupied by the German Army Group North 1941-1944," paper presented to Soviet Industrialisation Project Series, University of Birmingham, 1999.

Consulted Material from Russia

(Courtesy of Dr. Ken Slepyan, Dr. Reina Pennington, Lt. Col. Leonidas Maximciuc)

Partizanskaia Mest,' organ of the 5th Leningrad Partisan Brigade.

Partizanskaia Pravda, organ of the United Partisan Detachments of the Southwestern Districts of Orel Oblast.

Pravda, various dates.

Izvestiia TsK KPSS: "Iz istorii Velikoi Otechestvennoi voiny," Series 7-11 (1990) no. 6

Main Archive of the Russian Federation (GARF)
(Courtesy of Reina Pennington and Dr. Ken Slepyan)

Fond 6093: Records of State Radio

Fond 7021: Records of the Extraordinary State Commission on the Determination
and Investigation of the Atrocities of the German-Fascist Invaders.

Fond 8355: Records of Osoaviakhim (Auschwitz).

Fond 8581: Record of the Soviet Information Bureau

Central Museum of the Armed Forces of the USSR (TsMVS)
Fond 4: Documents and Objects from the Soviet Partisan Movement.

Russian Centre for the Preservation and Study of Documents of
Recent History (RTsKhIDNI) (Courtesy of Dr. Ken Slepyan)
Fond 17: Records of the Central Committee.

Fond 69: Records of the Central Staff of the Partisan Movement.

Scientific Archive of the Institute of History of Russia, Department
of Manuscripts (NA IIR ORF) (Courtesy of Ken Slepyan)
Fond 2: Records of the Commission on the History of the Great Patriotic War-The
Partisan Movement.

Soviet Document Collections and Memoirs (All translations courtesy of Lt.
Col. Leonidas Maximciuc; all documents courtesy of Dr. Ken Slepyan).
KPSS. o vooruzhenykh silakh Sovetskogo Soiuza: Sbornik dokumentov. Moscow,
1958.

Krym v period Veilikoi Otechestvennoi voiny, 1941-1945 gg. Simferopol, 1973.

Stranitsy narodnogo podviga: Kalininskaia oblast' v gody Velikoi Otechestvenoi
voiny. Moscow, 1974.

Kurskaia oblast' v period Velikoi Otechestvennoi voiny Sovetskogo Soiuza,1941-1945
gg.: Sbornik dokumentov i materialov. 2 vols. Kursk, 1960.

Leningrad v Velikoi Otechestvennoi voine Sovetskogo Soiuza: Sbornik dokumentov
i materialov. 2 vols. Leningrad, 1944-1947

Orlovskaia oblast' v gody Velikoi Otechestvennoi voiny, 1941-1945 gg.: Sbornik
dokumentov i materialov. Orel, 1960.

Partizanskaia bor'ba s nemetsko-fashistksimi okkupantami na territorii Smolenshchiny. Smolensk, 1962.

Sumskaia Oblast' v period Velikoi Otechestvennoi voiny, 1941-1945 gg.: Sbornik dokumentov i materialov. 2nd ed. Kiev, 1988.

Velikaia Otechestvennaia voina, 1941-1945: Slovar' spravochnik. Moscow, 1988.

Vsenarodnoe partizanskoe dvizhenie v Belorusii v gody Velikoi Otechestvennoi voiny: Dokumenty i materialy. 4 vols. Minsk, 1967-1972.

V tylu vraga: Bor'ba partizan i podpol'shchikov na okkupirovnnoi teritorii Leningradskoi oblasti, 1942-1944 gg.: Sbornik dokumentov. 3 vols. Leningrad, 1981-1985.

Za rodnuiu Kareliiu: Partizany i podpol' shchiki vospominaniia, dokumenty. Petrozavodsk,1990.

Additional U.S. Material Consulted

Ohio State University (Courtesy of Timothy A. Wray).
Cornelius Ryan Papers, Box 67, Folder 16.

National Archives Microfilm Publication Collection
RG (Record Group)-242/Roll 112/frame 2637747 (hereafter cited as RG-242/112/2637747), Eriegnismeldung UdSSR, No. 48, dated 10 August 1941.

RG- 242, T-175/180/2715184-96: Various documents on the SS Officer Candidates Course at Bad Toelz in 1942.

RG-242, T-454/100/699.

RG-242, T-501/21103-5, Nuremberg Document L-180 on *Einsatzgruppe A*, Gesamtbericht bis zurn 15 Oct. 1941. International Military tribunal, Trial of Major War Criminals Before the International Military Tribunal, 42 vols. (Washington, DC 1949).

RG-242, T-580/Roll 219/Ordner 60: Letter from Heydrich to Daluege dated 12 February 1940.

RG-242, T-580/Roll 220/Ordner 61: *Nachlass* Daluege, 'Jewry and Penal Punishment'.

RG-242, T-580/Roll 222/Ordner 66: *Nachlass* Daluege; Letter from Karl Wolff to Kurt Daluege, Reinhard Heydrich and Theodor Eicke, dated 25 August 1939.

RG-242, T-580/Roll 228/Ordner 91. Report on the German Order Police in *Nachlass* Daluege.

RG-238, M-1270/Roll 1/422-23: References to Bach-Zelewski's career and post-war interrogation, dated 30 October 1945.

T-311, Rolls 167-70; T-313 Roll 488; T-314 Roll 1457; T-315 Roll 2154; T-501 Rolls 247, 249, 264, 265; T-733 Roll 7: Unit records for *1st, 2nd, 3rd, 4th, 9th, 10th,* and *12th Waffen SS Panzer* Divisions.

Television Documentaries & Newspapers Consulted-Various Dates

Great Britain

Daily Record & Mail, 12 September, 1939; 2, 3 January, 1940.

Manchester Guardian, and 5 January, 1940.

Forward. 16 September 1939; 9 & 16 March 1940.

The Times (London). 2-3 July 1934; 10 October 1934; 19 June 1936; 1 July 1936; May-July 1940.

The World at War. Thames television presentation (London: BBC, 1983).

The Partisans of Vilna. Documentary Film. Washington D.C.: Euro-American Home Video, 1987.

The Daily Record and Mail, Dates of 2, 5, 8, 13, 14,15, 23 September 1939.

The Guardian. 30 November, 1998, 'Return to Auschwitz: Day Trip to the Death Camps', pp. 2-3.

The Sunday Times Magazine, Barbara Wyllie, Paulina Bren and Sam Lowenberg, et al. 22 November 1998, 'Goering's List,' pp. 44-52.

Jewish Chronicle (London), 28 February; 14 March 1941; 22 November 1940; 31 May 1940; 2 August & 26 July; 11 & 25 October 1940; 10, 24, 31 January; 28 February, 7 March, 15 April, 22 August 1941; 20 March, 17 & 31 July, 25 September 1942.

United States

American Jewish Yearbook, vol. 45, Philadelphia, PA.1943/5704.

Germany

Frankfurter Zeitung, Die Welt, Bild am Sonntag, Voelkischer Beobachter (Berlin); April September 1940; January 1941; December 1942.

_____. (Munich) January-May 1940.

Secondary Sources Consulted

Books

Ackermann, Josef, 'Heinrich Himmler,' Ronald Smelser and Rainer Zitelmann (eds.), *The Nazi Elite* (London; New York: Macmillan Press, 1993).

Ailsby, Christopher, *SS: Hell on the Eastern Front: The Waffen SS War in Russia, 1941-1945* (Osceola, WI: Motorbooks International, 1998).

Ainsztein, Reuben, Jewish *Resistance in Nazi Occupied Eastern Europe: With a Historical Survey of the Jew as a Fighter and Soldier in the Diaspora* (London: Elek, 1974).

Andreyev, Catherine, *Vlasov and the Russian Liberation Movement: Soviet Reality and Émigré Theories* (Cambridge: Cambridge University Press, 1987).

Angrick, Anrej. "'Da Haette man schon ein Tagebuch fuehren muessen.' Das Polizeibataillon 322 und die Judenmorde im Bereich der Heeresgruppe Mitte Waehrende des Sommers und Herbstes 1941," in Helge Grabitz, et al (eds.), *Die Normalitaet des Verbrechens: Bilanz und Perspektiven der Forschung zu den nationalsozialistischen Gewaltverbrechen* (Berlin: Edition Hentrich, 1994), pp. 325-85.

Armstrong, John A., *Ukrainian Nationalism*, 3rd edition (Littleton, CO: Ukrainian Academic Press, 1990).

Barber, John and Mark Harrison, "The Image of Stalin in Propaganda and Public Opinion During World War 2," John and Carrol Gerrard (eds.), *World War 2 and the Soviet People: Selected Papers from the Fourth World Congress for Soviet and East European Studies* (New York; London: St. Martin's Press, 1993), pp. 38-49.

_____. *The Soviet Home Front: A Social and Economic History of the USSR in World War II* (London: Longman, 1991).

Barkai, Avraham. *Nazi Economics, Ideology, Theory and Policy* (Leamington Spa: Berg; New Haven, CT: Yale University Press, 1990).

Baynes, N.H. (ed.), *Documents on German Foreign Policy, 1918-1945, Series C (1933-1937)*

The Third Reich: First Phase, 5 vols. (London: HMSO, 1957).

_____. *Documents on German Foreign Policy, 1918-1945, Series D (1937-1945), The Third Reich: First Phase*, 9 vols. (London: HMSO, 1957).

Berghahn, Volker R. and Martin Kitchen (eds.). *Germany in the Age of Total War* (London: Croom Helm, 1981).

Bessel, Richard, *Political Violence and the Rise of Nazism* (New Haven, CT: Yale University Press, 1984).

Bidermann, Gottlob Herbert, *...und litt an meiner Seite: dabei im Inhalt'Krim-Kurland mit der 132. Infanterie Division 1939-1945* (Reutlingen: Steinach-Verlag, 1995).

Birn, Ruth Bettina. "Two Kinds of Reality? Case Studies on Anti-Partisan Warfare during the Eastern Campaign," in Bernd Wegner (ed.), *From Peace to War. Germany, Soviet Russia and the World, 1939-1941* (Oxford: Berghahn, 1997).

_____. *Die Hoehren SS und Polizeifuehrer. Himmlers Vertreter im Reich und in den besetzten Ostgebieten* (Duesseldorf: Droste, 1986).

Bonwetsch, Bernd. "Sowjetische Partisanen 1941-1944. Legende und Wirklichkeit des 'allgemeinen Volkskrieges'," in Gerhard Schulz (ed.), *Partisanen und Volkskrieg. Zur Revolutionierung des Krieges im 20. Jahrhundert* (Goettingen: Vandenhoek & Rupprecht, 1985). pp. 92-124.

Bramsted, Ernest K., *Goebbels and National Socialist Propaganda, 1925-1945* (Ann Arbor: University of Michigan Press, 1965).

Browder, George. *Hitler's Enforcers: The Gestapo and the SS Security Service in the Nazi Revolution* (New York; London: O.U.P., 1996).

_____. *Foundations of the Nazi Police State: The Formation of Sipo and SD.* (New York, London: Peter Lang, 1988, 2nd printing Louisville: University Press of Kentucky, 1990).

_____. *The Path to Genocide: Essays on Launching the Final Solution* (Cambridge: Cambridge University Press, 1995).

_____. "Harald Turner und die Militaerverwaltung in Serbien 1941-1942," in Dieter Rebentisch and Karl Teppe (eds.), *Verwaltung contra Menschenfuehrung im Staat Hitlers*

(Goettingen: Vandenhoek & Rupprecht, 1986), pp. 351-73.

_____. *Fateful Months: Essays on the Emergence of the Final Solution* (New York; London: Holmes & Meier, 1985).

_____. *The Final Solution and the German Foreign Office: A Study of Referat D III of Abteilung Deutschland, 1940-43* (New York; London: Holmes & Meier, 1978).

Brustein, William, "Blue-Collar Nazism: The German Working Class and the Nazi Party," Conan Fischer (ed.), *The Rise of National Socialism and the Working Classes in Weimar Germany* (Oxford: O.U.P., 1996), pp. 137-61.

Buccheim, Hans, "Instrument of Domination," Martin Broszat, et al (eds.), *Anatomy of the SS State* (London, New York: Cambridge University Press, 1968).

Bullock, Alan, "Hitler and the Origins of the Second World War," E.M. Robertson (ed.), *The Origins of the Second World War* (London: Macmillan, 1967).

Carr, William M., "National Socialism: Foreign Policy and the Wehrmacht," W. Laqueur (ed.), *Fascism* (London, New York: Macmillan, 1979).

_____. *A History of Germany, 1815-1945* (London: Edward Arnold, 1969).

Carter, Stephen K., *Russian Nationalism* (London: John Speirs, 1990).

Cecil Robert. *Hitler's Decision to Invade Russia, 1941* (London: Davis-Poynter, 1975).

_____. *The Myth of the Master Race: Alfred Rosenberg and Nazi Ideology* (London: Batsford, 1972).

Childers, Thomas. *The Formation of the Nazi Constituency, 1919-1933* (London, Croom Helm, 1986).

_____. *The Nazi Voter: The Social Foundations of Fascism in Germany, 1919-1933* (Chapel Hill, London: University of North Carolina Press 1983).

Conquest, Robert, *The Nation Killers: The Soviet Deportation of Nationalities.* (London: Macmillan, 1970).

Corni, Gustavo. *Hitler and the Peasants: Agrarian Policy in the Third Reich, 1930-1939* (New York; Oxford: Berg, 1990).

Davidowicz, L.S. *The War Against the Jews, 1933-45* (London: Weidenfeld & Nicolson, 1975).

Davies, R.H., M. Harrison and S.G. Wheatcroft (eds.), *The Economic Transformation of the Soviet Union, 1913-1945* (New York: Cambridge University Press, 1994).

Deutsch, H.C., *Hitler and His Generals: The Hidden Crisis January-June, 1938.* (Minneapolis: University of Minnesota Press, 1974).

DeWitt, Kurt. "Organization and Control of the Partisan Movement," in John A. Anderson (ed.), *Soviet Partisans in World War II* (Madison: University of Wisconsin Press, 1964), pp. 73-139.

Dicks, Henry V., *Licensed Mass Murderers: A Socio-Psychological Study of Some SS Killers* (Sussex: Sussex University Press & Chatto-Heinemann, 1972).

Dietrich, Otto. *The Hitler I Knew* (London: Methuen, 1957).

Dixon, Aubrey C. and Otto Heilbrunn, *Communist Guerrilla Warfare* (London: Allen & Unwin, 1954).

Domarus, Max, *Hitler: Speeches and Proclamations, 1932-1945: The Chronicle of a Dictatorship: The Years 1939 to 1940*, 3 vols. (New York; London: I.B. Tauris, 1990).

Dressen, Willi & Ernst Klee (eds.), *"Gott mit uns." Der deutsche Vernichtungskrieg im Osten 1939-1945* (Frankfurt am Main: Fischer, 1989).

Dunn, Walter S. Jr., *Hitler's Nemesis: The Red Army, 1930-1945* (Westport, CT: Greenwood Press, 1994).

Eckman, Lester and Chaim Lazar, *The Jewish Resistance: The History of the Jewish Partisans in Lithuania and White Russia During the Nazi Occupation, 1940-1945* (New York: Sheingold Publishers, 1977).

Ellis, Frank, "Army and Party in Conflict: Soldiers and Commissars in the Prose of Vasily Grossman," John and Carol Gerrard (eds.), *World War 2 and the Soviet People: Selected Papers from the Fourth World Congress for Soviet and East European Studies* (New York; London: St. Martin's Press, 1993), pp. 180-201.

Erickson, John, *The Road to Berlin: Continuing the History of Stalin's War with Germany* (Boulder, CO: Westview Press, 1983).

_____. *Stalin's War with Germany* (London: Weidenfeld & Nicolson, 1983).

_____. *The Road to Stalingrad: Stalin's War with Germany*. 2 Vols. (New York, Harper & Row, 1975).

Erickson, John and E.J. Feuchtwanger (eds). *Soviet Military Power and Performance* (London: Macmillan, 1979).

Erlich, A., *The Soviet Industrialisation Debate 1924-1928* (Cambridge, MA: Harvard University Press, 1967).

Eschenberg, T., *The Road to Dictatorship: Germany, 1918-1933*, 2nd edition (London: Oswald Wolff, 1964).

Evans, Richard J., *In Hitler's Shadow: West German Historians and the Attempt to Escape from the Nazi Past* (New York; London: I.B. Tauris, 1989).

_____. *Rethinking German History* (London: Allen & Unwin, 1987).

Ewald, Johann, *Treatise on Partisan Warfare*, translated and introduced by Robert A. Selig and David Curtis Skaggs (Westport, CT: Greenwood Press, 1991).

Farquharson, John E., *The Plough and the Swastika: The NSDAP and Agriculture in Germany, 1928-45* (Beverly Hills, CA: Sage Publications, 1976).

Farquharson, John E. and John W. Hiden, *Explaining Hitler's Germany: Historians and the Third Reich* (London: Batsford, 1983).

Fein, Helen. (ed). *Genocide Watch* (London; New Haven, CT: Yale University Press, 1992).

_____. *Current Research in Anti-Semitism*, vol. 1 (Berlin: de Gruyter, 1987).

Fest, Joachim C., *Hitler* (London: Weidenfeld & Nicolson, 1974).

Feuchtwanger, E.J., *From Weimar to Hitler* (London; New York: Macmillan, 1995).

Fischer, Conan, *The Rise of National Socialism and the Working Class in Weimar Germany* (Oxford: Providence, 1996).

_____. *The German Communists and the Rise of the Nazis* (Basingstoke: Macmillan, 1991).

_____. *Stormtroopers: A Social, Economic and Ideological Analysis 1929-35* (London: Allen & Unwin, 1983).

Fleming, Gerald. *Hitler and the Final Solution* (London: Hamish Hamilton, 1985).

Foerster, Friedrich Wilhelm. *Europe and the German Question* (London: Allen & Unwin, 1941).

Foot, Michael R.D., *Resistance* (London: Paladin, 1978).

_____. *Resistance: An Analysis of European Resistance to Nazism, 1940-1945*, 2nd edition (London: Eyre Methuen, 1976).

_____. *Aneuran Bevan: A Biography, 1897-1945*, vol. I. 2nd edition (London: Granada, 1984).

Friedman, Philip, "Jewish Resistance to Nazism: Its Various Forms and Aspects," in Jong, Dr. L. de, *First International Conference on the History of the Resistance Movements* (New York: Methuen, 1960), pp. 195-214.

Gallately, Robert, "Enforcing Racial Policy in Nazi Germany," Caplan and Childers (eds.), *Re-evaluating the Third Reich* (New York: Holmes & Meier, 1993).

_____. *The Gestapo and German Society: Enforcing Racial Policy* (New York; London: Clarendon, 1990).

Galtung, Johan. *Hitlerismus, Stalinismus Reaganismus: drei Variationen einem Thema von Orwell* (Baden-Baden: Nomos, 1987).

Geary, Dick. *Hitler and Nazism* (London; New York: Routledge, 1993).

Gessner, Klaus. "Geheime Feldpolizei die Gestapo der Wehrmacht," in Hannes Heer and Klaus Naumann (eds.), *Vernichtungskrieg. Verbrechen der Wehrmacht, 1941 bis 1944* (Hamburg: Hamburger Edition, 1995), pp. 343-58.

_____. *Geheime Feldpolizei. Zur Funktion und Organisation der faschistischen Wehrmacht* (Berlin: Militaerverlag der DDR, 1986).

Getty, J. Arch, *Origins of the Great Purges: The Soviet Communist Party Reconsidered, 1933-1938* (Cambridge: Cambridge University Press, 1985).

Getty, J. Arch and R. Manning, *Stalinist Terror* (Cambridge: Cambridge University Press, 1993).

Geyer, Michael and J.W. Boyer (eds.), *Resistance Against the Third Reich, 1933-1990* (Chicago, London: University of Chicago Press, 1994).

Gilbert, Martin. *Second World War* (London: Weidenfeld & Nicolson, 1989).

_____.*The Holocaust: The Jewish Tragedy* (London: Weidenfeld & Nicolson,1986).

_____. *The Final Journey: The Fate of the Jews in Nazi Europe* (London: Allen & Unwin, 1979).

Gill, Graeme, *The Origins of the Stalinist Political System* (Cambridge: Cambridge University Press, 1990).

Gordon, Sarah. *Hitler, Germans and the "Jewish Question"* (New Jersey; Oxford: Princeton University Pres, 1984).

Graml, Hermann, Hans Mommsen (et al.), *The German Resistance to Hitler*, translation by Peter and Betty Ross (London: Batsford, 1970).

Grenkevich, Leonid D. *The Soviet Partisan Movement 1941-1944* (London: Frank Cass, 1999).

Grunfeld, Frederic V. *The Hitler File: A Social History of Germany and the Nazis, 1918-45*, introduction by H.R. Trevor-Roper (London: Weidenfeld & Nicolson, 1974).

Gunther, H., *The Culture of the Stalin Period* (London: Macmillan, 1990).

Gvozdenovic, Dusan, *The Great Patriotic War of the Soviet Union, 1941-1945: A General Outline* (Moscow: Progress Publishers, 1974).

Hagen, Mark von, *Soldiers in the Proletarian Dictatorship: The Red Army and the Soviet Socialist State, 1917-1930* (Ithaca, NY: Cornell University Press, 1990).

Haimson, Leopold, *"Civil War and the Problem of Social Identities in Early Twentieth Century Russia," Party, State, and Society in the Russian Civil War* (Bloomington: University of Illinois Press, 1989), pp. 2447.

Halder, Franz. *Hitler as War Lord* (London: Putnam, 1950).

Hale, Oren J., *The Captive Press in the Third Reich* (Princeton, NJ: Princeton University Press, 1964).

Hamilton, Richard F., *Who Voted for Hitler?* (Princeton, NJ: Princeton University Press,1982).

Hammel, Klaus. "Kompetenzen und Verhalten der Truppe im rueckwaertigen Heeresgebiet," in Hans Poeppel, et al (eds.), *Die Soldaten der Wehrmacht* (Munich: Herbig, 1998), pp. 178-229.

Hanfstaengl, Ernst, *Hitler: The Missing Years* (London: Eyre & Spottiswoode, 1957).

Harris, Nathaniel. *Hitler* (London: Batsford, 1989).

Harrison, Mark, *Soviet Planning in Peace and War: 1938-1945* (New York: Cambridge University Press, 1985).

Hasch, Wolfgang & Gustav Friedrich, "Der Partisankrieg der Sowjetunion und die deutschen gegenmassnahmen im Zweiten Weltkrie," in Hans Poeppel et al (eds.), *Die Soldaten der Wehrmacht* (Munich: Herbig, 1998), pp. 230-55.

Haslam, Jonathan, *The Soviet Union and the Struggle for Collective Security in Europe, 1933-1939* (London: Macmillan, 1984).

_____. *Soviet Foreign Policy, 1930-33: The Impact of Depression* (London: Macmillan, 1983).

Haupt, G.M. and J.J. Marie. *Makers of the Russian Revolution* (London: Allen & Unwin, 1974).

Hawes, Stephen and Ralph White (eds.), *Resistance in Europe: 1941-1945* (London: Allen Lane, 1975).

Headland, Ronald. *Messages of Murder: A Study of the Reports of the Einsatzgruppen of the Security Police and the Security Service* (East Rutherford, NJ: Farleigh Dickinson, 1992).

Heer, Hannes and Klaus Naumann, 'Einleitung', in Heer & Naumann (eds.), *Vernichtungskrieg. Verbrechen der Wehrmacht, 1941 bis 1944* (Hamburg: Hamburger Edition, 1995), pp. 25-36.

Heilbrunn, Otto, *Partisan Warfare* (New York: Praeger, 1967).

Henri, Ernst. *Hitler Over Europe?* (London: Dent, 1934).

Herbert, Ulrich (ed.). *Nationalsozialistische Vernichtungspolitik 1939-1945. Neue Forschungen und Kontroverse* (Frankfurt am Main: Fischer, 1998).

_____. "Neue Antworten und Fragen zur Geschichte des Holocaust," in ibid, pp. 9-66.

_____. *Hitler's Foreign Workers* (Cambridge: Cambridge University Press, 1997).

Hiden, John W. and John. Farquharson, *Explaining Hitler's Germany: Historians and the Third Reich* (London: Batsford, 1983).

Hildebrand, Klaus, Reich, Nation State, Great Power' Reflections on German Foreign Policy, 1871-1945 (London: German Historical Institute, 1995).

_____. *German Foreign Policy from Bismarck to Adenauer: The Limits of Statecraft* (London: Unwin-Hyman, 1989).

_____. *The Third Reich.* Translation by P.S. Falla, The Third Reich (London; Boston: Allen & Unwin, 1984).

_____. *The Foreign Policy of the Third Reich* (Berkeley: University of California Press, 1973).

Hillgruber, Andreas. "Der Ostkrieg und die Judenvernichtung'," in Gerd R. Ueberschaer & Wolfram Wette (eds.), *Der deutsche Ueberfall auf die Sowjetunion. "Unternehmen Barbarossa" 1941* (Frankfurt am Main: Fischer, 1991) pp. 185-205.

_____. *1933 wie die Republik der Diktatur erlag Volker Rittberger (Hrog) mit Betraegen* (Stuttgart: W. Kohlhammer, 1983).

_____. *Germany and the Two World Wars* (London; Cambridge, MA: Harvard University

Press, 1981).

_____. *Deutschlands Rolle in der Vorgeschichte der beiden Weltkriege* (Goettingen: Vandenhoeck & Ruprecht, 1967).

Hitler, Adolf. *Hitler: Speeches and Proclamations 1932-1945: The Chronicle of a Dictatorship* (London: I.B. Tauris, 1990).

Hobsbawm, Eric, *The Age of Extremes: The Short Twentieth Century* (London: Michael Joseph, 1994).

_____. *Bandits* (London; New York: Penguin, 1969).

Hoffmann, Joachim. *Stalins Vernichtungskrieg 1941-1945*, 2nd edition (Munich: Verlag fuer Wissenschaft, 1995).

_____. "Die Kriegfuehrung aus der Sowjetunion," in Horst Boog et al (eds.), *Der Angriff auf die Sowjetunion*, 2nd edition (Frankfurt am Main: Fischer, 1991), pp. 848-964.

Huntington, S.P. *The Soldier and the State* (Cambridge, MA: Harvard University Press, 1957).

Hueppauf, Berns, "Der entleerte Blick hinter der kamera," in Heer & Naumann (eds.), *Vernischtungskrieg. Verbrechen der Wehrmacht, 1941 bis 1944* (Hamburg: Hamburger Edition, 1995), pp. 504-27.

Huttenbach, H.R., *Soviet Nationality Policies: Ruling Ethnic Groups in the USSR* (London; New York: Mansell, 1990).

Ignatov, P.K., *Partisans of the Kuban*, translation by J. Fineberg (London: Hutchinson & Co., 1945).

Jacobsen, Hans Adolf (ed.), *July 20, 1944: The German Opposition to Hitler as Viewed by Foreign Historians, an Anthology* (Bonn: Press & Information Office of the federal Government, 1969).

_____. "Kommissarbefehl und Massenexekution sowjetischer Kriegsgefangener," in Hans Buccheim (ed.), *Anatomie des SS-Saates*, vol. 2 (Munich: Deutsche Taschenbuch-Verlag), pp. 135-232.

Jaeckel, Eberhard. *Hitler in History* (Hanover, NH; London: Brandeis University Press by University Press of New England, 1984).

Jahn, Peter, "Rassenfurcht und Antibolshewismus: Zur Entstehung und Wirkung von Feindbildern," in Pater Jahn & Reinhard Ruerup (eds.), *Erobern und Vernichten. Der Krieg gegen die Sowjetunion 1941-1945. Essays* (Berlin: Argon, 1991), pp. 47-64.

Joes, Anthony James. *Guerrilla Warfare: A Historical, Biographical, and Bibliographical Sourcebook* (Westport, CT: Greenwood Publishing Group, 1996).

_____. *Guerrilla Conflict Before the Cold War* (New York: Praeger, 1996).

Kagan, Jack and Dov Cohen, *Surviving the Holocaust with the Russian Jewish Partisans* (New York; London: Valentine Mitchell, 1998).

Kaiser, D., *Economic Diplomacy and the Origins of the Second World War: Germany, Britain, France, and Eastern Europe, 1933-1939* (Princeton, NJ: Princeton University Press, 1980).

Kater, M.H., *The Nazi Party: A Social Profile of Members and Leaders* (Cambridge, MA; London: Harvard University Press, 1983).

Keesings Contemporary Archives. *A Weekly Diary of World Events, 1941-42* (London: Keesing, 1941-42).

_____. (London: Keesing, 1943-46).

Kele, Max H., *Nazism and Workers: National Socialist Appeals to German Labour. 1919-1933* (Chapel Hill: University of North Carolina Press, 1972).

Kershaw, Ian. *Weimar: Why did Germany Fail?* (London: Weidenfeld & Nicolson, 1990).

_____. *Popular Opinion and Political Dissent in the Third Reich, Bavaria 1933-1945* (Oxford: Oxford University Press, 1983)

Kershaw, Ian and Moshe Lewin (eds.), *Stalinism and Nazism: Dictatorships in Comparison.* (Cambridge: Cambridge University Press, 1997).

Klink, Ernst and Horst Boog, "Die Militaerische Konzeption des Krieges gegen die Sowjetunion," in Boog, et al, *Der Angriff auf die Sowjetunion*, 2nd paperback edition (Frankfurt am Main: Fischer, 1991), pp. 246-395.

_____. "Die Operationsfuehrung." in ibid, pp. 541-847.

Klinkhammer, Lutz and Hans-Heinrich Wilhelm. *Die Truppe des Weltanschauungskrieges. Die Einsatzgruppen der Sicherheitspolizei und des SD 1938-1942*, vols. 1-2 (Stuttgart: Deutsche Verlags-Anstalt, 1981).

Klinkhammer, Lutz, "Der Partisanenkrieg der Wehrmacht 1941-1944," in R-D Mueller & H-E-Volkmann (eds.), *Die Wehrmacht: Mythos und Realitaet* (Munich: Oldenbourg, 1999), pp. 815-36.

Koch, Hans-Joachim Wolfgang. *In the Name of the Volk: Political Justice in Hitler's Germany* (London: I.B. Tauris, 1998).

_____. (ed.). *Aspects of the Third Reich* (Basingstoke: Macmillan, 1985).

_____. *The Hitler Youth: Origins and Development, 1922-45* (London: Macdonald and Jane's, 1975).

Kuczynski, J., *Germany: Economic and Labour Conditions under Fascism* (Boulder, CO: Westview Press, 1976).

Kroener, Bernhard R., "Strukturelle Veraenderungen in der Militaerischen Gesellschaft des Dritten Reiches," in Michael Prinz & Rainer Zitelmann (eds.), *Nationalsozialismus und Modernisierung* (Darmstadt: Wiss. Buchgesellschaft, 1994), pp. 267-96.

Kwiet, Konrad, "Auftakt zum Holocaust: Ein Polizeibataillon im Osteinsatz," in Wolfgang Benz (ed.), *Der Nationalsozialismus. Studien zu Ideologie* (Frankfurt am Main: Fischer, 1993), pp. 191-208.

Laqueur, Walter, *A Terrible Secret: An Investigation into the Suppression of Information about Hitler's Final Solution* (London: Weidenfeld & Nicolson, 1980).

_____. *Fascism: A Reader's Guide*, 2nd edition (New York: Penguin, 1979).

_____. *Guerrilla: A Historical and Critical Study* (London: Weidenfeld & Nicolson, 1977).

Laska, Vera. *Nazism, Resistance and the Holocaust in World War II: A Bibliography* (Metuchen, NJ; London: Scarecrow Press, 1985).

Lepre, George, *Himmler's Bosnian Division: The Waffen SS Handschar Division, 1943-1945* (Atglen, PA: Schiffer Publishing Co. Ltd., 1997).

Lewin, Moshe, *The Making of the Soviet System: Essays in the Social History of Interwar Russia* (New York: Pantheon, 1985).

_____. *Russian Peasants and Soviet Power: A Study of Collectivisation*, translation by Irene Nove (New York: W.W. Norton & Co., 1975).

Lichtenstein, Heiner. *Himmlers gruene Helfer: Die Schutz und Ordnungspolizei im Dritten Reich* (Cologne: Bund Verlag, 1990).

Lieberman, Sanford, "Crisis Management in the USSR: The Wartime System of Administration and Control," Susan J. Linz (ed.), *The Impact of World War II on the Soviet Union.* Totowa, NJ: Rowman & Allanheld, 1985), pp. 59-76.

Longerich, Peter. *Politik der Vernichtung. Eine Gesamtdarstellung der national*sozialistischen Judenverfolgung (Munich: Piper, 1998).

Mai, Guenther, "National Socialist Factory Cell Organisation and the German Labour Front: National Socialist Labour Policy and Organisations," Conan Fischer (ed.), *The Rise of National Socialism and the Working Classes in Weimar Germany* (Oxford: Berghan, 1996), pp.117-36.

Martin, Hugh, Douglas Newton, H.M. Waddams and R.R. Williams, *Christian Counter-Attack: Europe's Churches Against Nazism* (London: Student Christian Movement Press, 1943).

Maser, Werner (ed.), *Hitler's Letters and Notes*, translated by Arnold Pomerans (London: Heinemann, 1974).

_____. *Hitler* (London: Allen Lane, 1973).

_____. *Hitler's Mein Kampf: An Analysis*, translated by R.H. Barry (London: Faber, 1970).

Matthiessen, Peter, *Partisans* (New York: Vintage Books, 1987).

McCauley, Martin, *Soviet Politics 1917-1991* (Oxford; New York: O.U.P., 1992).

_____. *Stalin and Stalinism* (London: Longman, 1983).

_____. *The Origins of the Cold War* (London; New York: Longman, 1983).

_____. *The Soviet Union Since 1917* (London; New York: Longman, 1981).

_____. (ed.), *Communist Power in Europe, 1944-1949* (London: Macmillan, 1977).

_____. *Politics in the Soviet Union* (London: New York: Penguin, 1977).

McAuley, Mary, "Political Culture and Communist Policies: One Step Forward and Two Steps Back," Archie Brown (ed.), *Political Culture and Communist Studies* (New York: M.E. Sharpe, 1985), pp. 13-39.

Merkl, Peter H., *The Making of a Stormtrooper* (New Jersey: Princeton University Press, 1980).

Messerschmidt, Manfred. "Der Minsker Prozess 1946: Gedanken zu einem sowjetischen Kriegsverbrechertribunal," in Heer & Naumann (eds.), *Vernichtungskrieg. Verbrechen der Wehrmacht, 1941 bis 1944* (Hamburg: Hamburger Edition, 1995), pp. 551-68.

_____. "Der Kampf der Wehrmacht im Osten als Traditionsproblem," in Gerd R. Ueberschaer & Wolfrum Wette (eds.), *Der deutsche Ueberfall auf die Sowjetunion. "Unternehmen Barbarossa" 1941* (Frankfurt am Main: Fischer, 1991), pp. 225-37.

_____. "Harte Suehne am Judentum. Befehlslage und Wissen in der deutschen Wehrmacht," in Joerg Wollenberg (ed.), *"Niemand war dabei und keener hats gewust". Die deutsche Oeffentlichkeit und die Judenverfolgung 1933-1945* (Munich: Piper, 1989), pp. 113-28.

_____. *Die Wehrmacht im NS-Staat. Zeit der Indoktrination* (Hamburg: R.V. Decker's, 1969).

Michel, Henri, *The Shadow War: European Resistance, 1939-1945*, translation by Richard Barry (New York, Harper & Row, 1972).

Miller, Barbara Lane and Leila J. Rupp, *Nazi Ideology Before 1933: A Documentation* (Manchester: Manchester University Press, 1978).

Milward, Alan S., *War, Economy and Society, 1939-45* (London: Allen Lane, 1977).

_____.*The German Economy at War* (London: University of London/Athlone Press, 1965).

Mitcham, Samuel W., Jr. and Gene Mueller, *Hitler's Commanders* (Lanham, MD: Scarborough House, 1992).

Mitchell, Otis C. *Hitler's Nazi State: The Years of Dictatorial Rule/1934-1945. University of Cincinnati Studies in Historical and Contemporary Europe*, vol. 1 (New York: Peter Lange, 1987).

_____. *The Years of Dictatorial Rule* (New York; London: Peter Lang, 1981).

Mommsen, Hans,(ed.), *Fascism*, 2nd edition (London; New York: Penguin, 1979).

Moskoff, William, *The Bread of Affliction: The Food Supply in the USSR during World War II* (New York: Cambridge University Press, 1990).

Mosse, George Lachmann, *Toward the Final Solution: A History of European Racism* (London: Dent, 1978).

_____. *Germans and Jews: The Right, the Left, and the Search for a "Third Force" in per-Nazi Germany* (London: Orbach & Chambers, 1971).

_____. *Nazi Culture: Intellectual, Cultural and Social Life in the Third Reich* (London: Allen, 1966).

_____. *The Crisis of German Ideology: Intellectual Origins of the Third Reich* (London; New York: Grosset & Dunlap, 1964).

Muehlberger, Detlef, *Hitler's Followers: Studies in the Sociology of the Nazi Movement* (London, New York: Routledge, 1991).

Mueller-Hildebrand, Burkhart. *Das Heer 1933-1945*, 3 vols. (Darmstadt: E.S. Mittler & Sohn, 1954, 1956, 1969).

Mueller, Ingo. *Hitler's Justice: The Courts of the Third Reich*, translated by Deborah Lucas Schneider (London: I.B. Tauris, 1991).

Mueller, Klaus-Juergen. *Das Heer und Hitler. Armee und nationalsozialistisches regime 1933-1940* (Stuttgart: Deutsche Verlag-Anstalt, 1969).

Munting, Roger, *The Economic Development of the USSR* (London: Croom Helm, 1982).

Murray, K.A.H., *History of the Second World War-Agriculture* (London: Longman, 1955).

Neumann, Robert. *Hitler: Aufstieg und Untergang des dritten Reiches: ein Dokument in Bildern* (Munich: Verlag Kurt Desch, 1961).

Nicholls, Anthony James, *Weimar and the Rise of Hitler* (London: Macmillan, 1979).

Niethammer, Lutz (ed.). *"Die Jahr weiss man nicht, wo man die heute hinsetzen soll," Faschismuserfahrungen im Ruhrgebiet* (Berlin: Dietz, 1983).

Noakes, Jeremy, *Government, Party and People in Nazi Germany* (Exeter: Books Britain, 1980).

Noakes, Jeremy and Geoffrey Pridham (eds,), *Documents of Nazism, 1919-1945* (London; New York: O.U.P., 1974).

Nolte, Ernst. "Between Myth and Revisionism? The Third Reich in the Perspective of the 1980s," in H.W. Koch (ed.), *Aspects of the Third Reich* (London: Macmillan, 1985), pp. 17-38.

_____. *Three Faces of Fascism* (London: Weidenfeld & Nicolson, 1965).

Nyomarka, Joseph, *Charisma and Factionalism in the Nazi Party* (Minneapolis: University of Minnesota Press, 1967).

Orlow, Dietrich, *The History of the Nazi Party, vol. II, 1919-1933* (London: Newton Abbot, 1971).

Overy, Richard, *War and Economy in the Third Reich* (New York; Oxford: O.U.P.,1994).

_____. *The Origins of the Second World War* (London: Longman, 1987).

_____. *The Nazi Economic Recovery, 1932-1938* (London: Macmillan, 1982).

Paul, Gerhard, *Aufstand der Bilder: Die NS-Propaganda vor 1933* (Bonn: J.H.W. Dietz, 1990).

Peukert, Detlev, *The Weimar Republic: The Crisis of Classical Modernity* (London: Penguin, 1993).

_____. Translation by Richard Deveson, *Inside Nazi Germany: Conformity, Opposition and Racism in Everyday Life* (New Haven, CT; London: Yale University Press, 1987).

Post, Walter, "Die Soldaten der sogenannten 'Taeter' in der Millionenarmee Versuch einer Quantifizierung am Beispiel der 6. Armee im Russlandfeldzug 1941," in Hans Poeppel et al (ed.), *Die Soldaten der Wehrmacht* (Munich: Herbig, 1998), pp. 500-51.

Peterson, Edward Norman, *Hjalmar Schacht* (Boston: Christopher Publishing House, 1954).

Prantl, Herbert (ed.). *Wehrmachtsverbrechen: eine deutsche Kontroverse* (Hamburg: Haupt & Campe, 1997).

Pulzer, Peter G.J. *The Rise of Political Anti-Semitism in Germany and Austria* (London: P. Halban, 1988).

Quarrie, Bruce, *Lightning Death: The Story of the Waffen SS* (London: Patrick Stephens, Ltd., 1991).

_____. *Waffen SS in Russia*, 2nd edition trade paper (New York: Harper Collins,1988).

_____. *Hitler's Teutonic Knights* (Wellingborough: Patrick Stephens, Ltd., 1986).

Rauschning, Hermann. *Hitler Speaks: A Series of Political Conversations with Adolf Hitler on His Real Aims* (London: Thornton Butterworth, 1939).

Redelis, Valdis. *Partisankrieg. Ensteheung und Bekaempfung der Partisanen und Untergrundbewegung im Mittelabschnitt der Ostfront, 1941 bis 1943* (Heidelberg: Scharnhorst Buchkameradschaft, 1958).

Remak, Joachim, *The Origins of the Second World War* (New Jersey: Prentice Hall,1976).

_____. *The Nazi Years: A Documentary Reader* (New York: Prentice Hall, 1969).

Rempel, Gerhard. *Hitler's Children: The Hitler Youth and the SS* (Chapel Hill; London: University of North Carolina Press, 1989).

Reiss, Kurt, *The Nazis Go Underground* (New York: Doubleday, 1944).

Reitlinger, Gerald. *The Final Solution: The Attempt to Exterminate the Jews of Europe, 1939-45*, 2nd edition (London: Valentine & Mitchell, 1968).

Rhodes, James M., *The Hitler Movement: The Modern Millenarian Revolution* (Stanford, CA: Hoover Institution Press, 1980).

Rings, Werner. Translation by J. Maxwell Brownjohn, *Life With the Enemy: Collaboration and Resistance in Hitler's Europe, 1939-1945* (London: Weidenfeld & Nicolson, 1982).

Ritter, Gerhard, *Sword and Sceptre: The Problem of Militarism in Germany*, 3 vols. (London: Penguin, 1973).

_____. *The German Resistance: Carl Goerdeler's Struggle Against Tyranny* (London: Croom Helm, 1958).

Robertson, Esmonde Manning (ed.), *The Origins of the Second World War* (London: Macmillan, 1971).

_____. *Hitler's Pre-War Policy and Military Plans, 1933-39* (London: Longman, 1963).

Rohde, Horst, "Politische Indoktrination in hoehren Staeben und in der Truppe untersucht am Beispiel des Kommissarbefehls," in Hans Poeppel et al (eds.), *Die Soldaten der Wehrmacht* (Munich: Herbig, 1998), pp. 124-58.

Rosenthal, Gabriele, "Vom Krieg erzaehlen, von den Verbrechen schweigen," in Heer & Naumann (eds.), *Vernichtungskrieg. Verbrechen der Wehrmacht, 1941 bis 1944* (Hamburg: Hamburger Edition, 1995), pp. 651-63.

Rossiter, Margaret, *Women in the Resistance* (New York: Praeger, 1986).

Rothfels, Hans. Translation by Lawrence Wilson, *The German Opposition to Hitler: An Assessment* (London: Oswald Wolff, 1970).

Rowbotham, Sheila, *Women, Resistance, and Revolution* (London: Penguin, 1972).

Safrian, Hans, "Komplizen des Genozids. Zum Anteil der Heeresgruppe Sued an der Verfolgung und Ermordung der Juden in der Ukraine 1941," in Walter Manoschek (ed.), *Die Wehrmacht im Rassenkrieg* (Vienna: Picus, 1996), pp. 96-115.

Schirach, Baldur von. *Die Hitler Juegend: Idee und Gestalt* (Berlin: Zeitgeschichte, 1934).

Schoenbaum, David, *Hitler's Social Revolution: Class and Status in Nazi Germany, 1933-1939* (New York: Norton, 1980).

Schramm, Percy Ernst. *Hitler, the Man and the Military Leader*, translation and introduction by Donald S. Detwiler (ed.), (London: Allen Lane, 1972).

Schulte, Theo J., "The German Soldier in Occupied Russia," in Paul Addison and Angus Calder (eds.), *Time to Kill: The Soldier's Experience of war in the West, 1939-1945* (London: Pimlico, 1997), pp. 274-83.

_____. "Die Wehrmacht und die nationalsozialistische Besatzungspolitik in der Sowjetunion," in Roland G. Foerster (ed.), *Unternehmen Barbarossa: zum historischen Ort der deutsch-sowjetischen Beziehungen von 1933 bis Herbst 1941* (Munich: Oldenbourg, 1993), pp. 163-76.

_____. *The German Army and Nazi Policies in Occupied Russia* (New York: Berg, 1989).

Schweitzer, A., *Big Business in the Third Reich* (Bloomington: University of Indiana Press, 1964).

Seaton, Albert, *The German Army, 1933-45* (London: Weidenfeld & Nicolson, 1982).

_____. *Stalin as Warlord* (London: Batsford, 1976).

_____. *The Russo-German War* (London: Barker, 1971).

Seaton, Albert, "Stalin and the Red Army General Staff in the Thirties," Adrian Preston (ed.), *General Staffs and Diplomacy before the Second World War* (London: Croom Helm, 1978).

Shirer, William L., *The Rise and Fall of the Third Reich* (New York: Simon & Schuster, 1960).

Silverman, Dan. P. *Hitler's Economy: Nazi Work Creation Programs, 1933-1936* (Cambridge, MA: Harvard University Press, 1998).

Smelser, Ronald and Rainer Zitelmann (eds.), *The Nazi Elite* (London; New York: Macmillan, 1993).

Smith, Bradley F., *Himmler: A Nazi in the Making* (Stanford: Stanford University Press, 1971).

Smith, Graham (ed.), *The Nationalities Question in the Soviet Union* (London; New York: Longman, 1990).

Smolar, Hersh, *The Minsk Ghetto: Soviet-Jewish Partisans Against the Nazis* (Washington, D.C: The U.S. Holocaust Memorial Museum Shop Memorial, 1989).

Sonntag, R.J. an J.S. Beddie (eds.), *Nazi-Soviet Relations 1939-1941: Documents from the Archives of the German Foreign Office* (Westport, CT: Greenwood Press, 1974).

Stachura, Peter D., *Unemployment and the Great Depression in Weimar Germany* (Basingstoke: Macmillan, 1986).

_____. "Traditional Elites and National Socialist Leadership," in Charles S. Maier (ed.), *The Rise of the Nazi Regime: Historical Reassessments* (Boulder, CO: Westview Press, 1986), pp. 57-73.

_____. "The NSDAP and the German Working Class, 1925-1933," Isador Walliman and Michael N. Dobkowski (eds.), *Towards the Holocaust: Fascism and Anti-Semitism in Weimar Germany* (Westport, CT: Greenwood Press, 1983).

_____. *The Shaping of the Nazi State* (London: Croom Helm, 1978).

Stackelberg, Roderick. *Hitler's Germany: Origins, Interpretations, Legacies* (London: Routledge, 1999.

Stalin, Joseph. *Economic Problems of Socialism in the USSR* (Moscow: Foreign Languages Publishing House, 1953).

Stein, George H., *The Waffen SS: Hitler's Elite Guard at War, 1939-45* (Cornell: Cornell University Press, 1984).

Steinberg, Jonathan. *All or Nothing: The Axis and the Holocaust 1941-1943* (London: Routledge, 1990)

Stern, Joseph Peter. *Hitler: The Fuehrer and the People* (Hassocks: Harvester Press, 1975).

Stone, Norman, introduction by J.H. Plumb. *Hitler* (London: Hodder & Stoughton, 1980).

Strawson, John. *Hitler as Military Commander* (London: Batsford, 1971).

Streim, Alfred. *Die Behandlung sowjetischer Kriegsgefangener im "Fall Barbarossa". Eine Dokumentation* (Heidelberg: C.F. Mueller, 1981).

Streit, Christian, "Die Behandlung der sowjetischen Kriegsgefangenen und voelkerrechtliche Probleme des Krieges gegen die Sowjetunion," in G.R. Ueberschaer & W. Wette (eds.), *Der deutsche Ueberfall auf die Sowjetunion. "Unternehmen Barbarossa" 1941* (Frankfurt am Main: Fischer, 1991), pp. 197-218.

Tec, Nechama, *Defiance: The Bielski Partisans* (New York: O.U.P., 1993).

Teske, Hermann. *Die silbernen Spiegel. Generalstabsdienst undet der Lupe* (Heidelberg: Vowinckel, 1952).

Tessin, Georg. *Verbaende und Truppen der deutschen Wehrmacht und Waffen-SS im Zweiten Weltkrieg.* 14 vols. (Osnabrueck: Biblio Verlag, 1972-1997).

Toland, John, *Adolf Hitler* (New York: Doubleday, 1976).

Trevor-Roper, Hugh R. (ed.), *Hitler's War Directives, 1939-1945* (London: Pan, 1966).

Turner, H.A. Jr., *German Big Business and the Rise of Hitler*, 2nd edition (New York: O.U.P., 1987).

_____. (ed.), *Reappraisals of Fascism*. New York: New Viewpoints, 1975.

_____. (ed.), *Nazism and the Third Reich* (New York: Quadrangle, 1972).

Vakar, Nicholas, *Belorussia: The Making of a Nation: A Case Study* (Cambridge, MA: Harvard University Press, 1956).

Viola, Lynee and Beatrice Farnsworth (eds.), *The Best Sons of the Fatherland: Workers in the Vanguard of Soviet Collectivisation* (New York: O.U.P., 1987).

Volokogonov, Dmitrii, translation by Harold Shukman, *Stalin: Triumph and Tragedy* (Rocklin, CA: Prima Publishing, 1992).

Waite, Robert G.L. (ed.). *Hitler and Nazi Germany* (New York: Holt, Rinehart and Winston, 1965).

Walliman, Isidor and Michael N. Dokowski (eds.). *Towards the Holocaust: The Social and Economic Collapse* (Westport, CT: Greenwood Press, 1983).

Ward, Chris, *Stalin's Russia* (London: Edward Arnold, 1993).

Warlimont, Walter, *Inside Hitler's Headquarters, 1939-45* (London: Weidenfeld & Nicolson, 1964).

Wasserstein, Bernard, *Britain and the Jews of Europe, 1939-1945* (New York; London: O.U.P., 1988).

Walther, Herbert, *Waffen SS* (Atglen, PA: Schiffer Publishing, Ltd., 1989).

Wegner, Bernd, *The Waffen SS: Organization, Ideology, and Function*, translation by Ronald Webster (Oxford: Basil Blackwell, 1990).

Weinberg, Gerhard L. and Rolf-Dieter Mueller. *Hitler's War in the East, 1941-1945*, vol. 5 (New York: Berghahn, 2002).

_____. *Eine Welt in Waffen. Die Geschichte des Zweiten Weltkrieges* (Stuttgart: Deutsche Verlag, 1998).

Weinberg, Gerhard L. *Germany, Hitler and World War II* (Cambridge; New York: Cambridge University Press, 1996).

_____. *A World at Arms: A Global History of World War II* (Cambridge: Cambridge University Press, 1995).

_____. *The Foreign Policy of Hitler's Germany: Diplomatic Revolution in Europe, 1933–1936*, revised paperback (Chicago: University of Chicago Press, 1983).

_____. *The Foreign Policy of Hitler's Germany: Starting World War II, 1937-1939*, vol. 2 (Chicago, IL: University of Chicago Press, 1980).

_____. "The German Generals and the Outbreak of War, 1938-1939," Adrian Preston (ed.), *General Staffs and Diplomacy Before the Second World War* (London: Croom Helm, 1978).

_____. *Germany and the Soviet Union, 1939-1941* (Leiden: E.J. Brill, 1954).

Weitz, John, introduction by Tom Wolfe. *Joachim von Ribbentrop: Hitler's Diplomat* (London: Weidenfeld & Nicolson, 1992).

Welch, David, *The Third Reich: Politics and Propaganda* (London: Routledge, 1995).

_____. *Nazi Propaganda: The Power and the Limitations* (London: Croom Helm, 1983).

Wegner, Otto, Henry Ashby Turner, Jr. (ed.). *Hitler: Memoirs of a Confidant* (New Haven, CT: Yale University Press, 1985).

Werth, Alexander, *Russia at War, 1941-1945* (New York: Avon Books; London: Barrie & Rockliffe, 1964).

Wheeler-Bennett, J.W., *Nemesis of Power: The German Army in Politics, 1918-1945* (London: Macmillan, 1961).

White, Dmitri Fedotoff, *The Growth of the Red Army* (Westport, CT: Greenwood Press, 1981).

White, Ralph, 'The Unity and Diversity of European Resistance', Stephen Hawes and Ralph White (eds.), *Resistance in Europe: 1941-1945* (London: Allen Lane, 1975), pp. 7-23.

Wilhelm, Hans-Heinrich, "Motivation und 'Kriegsbild' deutscher Generale und Offiziere im Krieg gegen die Sowjetunion," in Peter Jahn & Reinhard Ruerup (eds.), *Erobern und Vernichten. Der Krieg gegen die Sowjetunion 1941-1945. Essays* (Berlin: Argon, 1991), pp. 153-82.

Williamson, D.G. (ed.), *The Third Reich*, reprint of 1982 (Essex: Longman, 1993).

Williamson, Gordon K., *Loyalty Is My Honor* (Osceola, WI: Motorbooks International, 1995).

_____. *SS: The Bloodsoaked Soil* (Osceola, WI: Motorbooks International, 1995).

Wollenberg, Erich. *The Red Army: A Study of the Growth of Soviet Imperialism*, translated by Claud W. Sykes (Westport, CT: Hyperion Press, 1973).

Wright, Gordon, *The Rise of Modern Europe: The Ordeal of Total War, 1939-45* (New York; London: Harper & Row, 1968).

Yerger, Mark C., *Allgemeine SS: The Commands, Units and Leaders of the General SS.* Atglen, PA: Schiffer Publishing, Ltd., 1998).

_____. *Waffen SS Commanders: The Army, Corps and Divisional Leaders of a Legend: Augsberger to Kreutz* (Atglen, PA: Schiffer Publishing, Ltd., 1997).

Zeman, Z.A.B., *Nazi Propaganda*, 2nd edition (London; New York: O.U.P., 1973).

Ziemke, Earl and Magna Bauer, *Moscow to Stalingrad: Decision in the East.* United States Army Historical Series (Washington D.C., United States Army Center of Military History, 1987).

Ziemke, Earl, "Composition and Morale of the Partisan Movement," in John A. Armstrong (ed.), *Soviet Partisans in World War II* (Madison: University of Wisconsin Press, 1964), pp. 141-96.

Peer Reviewed Journals Consulted

Arnold, Klaus Jochen, "Die Eroberung und Behandlung der Stadt Kiew durch die Wehrmacht im September 1941: Zur Radikalisierung der Besatzungspolitik," *Militaergeschichtliche Mitteilungen*, vol. 58, no. 1 (1999), pp. 23-63.

Babakov, A.A., "Partisan Movements in the Great Patriotic War of the Soviet Union," *Revue Internationale d'Histoire Militarie*, vol. 44 (1979), pp. 172-80.

Bartov, Omer, "Indoctrination and Motivation in the Wehrmacht: The Importance of the Unquantifiable," *Journal of Strategic Studies*, no. 9 (1986), pp. 16-34.

Beloff, Max, "Soviet Foreign Policy, 1929-41: Some Notes," *Soviet Studies*, vol. II, no. II (October 1950), pp. 123-37.

Boldin, I. "Popular Reactions in Moscow to the German Invasion of June 22, 1941," *Soviet Union/Union Sovietique*, vol. 18, no. 1 (1991) pp. 5-18.

Borman, Arkady. "My Meetings with White Russian Generals," *The Russian Review*, vol. 27, no. 2 (April 1968), pp. 215-24.

Dallin, Alexander, "Rodianov: A Case Study in Wartime Redefection," *American Slavic and East European Review*. no. 18 (1959), pp. 25-33.

Davies, R.W. "Some Soviet Economic Controllers-III," *Soviet Studies*, vol. XII, no. 1 (July 1960), pp. 23-55.

Deutsch, H.C., "The German Resistance: Answered and Unanswered Questions," *Central European History*, vol. 14 (1981), pp. 322-31.

Deutscher, Issac, "Dogma and Reality in Stalin's Economic Problems," *Soviet Studies*, vol. IV, no. 4 (April 1953), pp. 349-63.

Eliseeva, N.E. "Plans for the Development of the Workers' and Peasants' Red Army (RKKA) on the Eve of War," David M. Glantz (ed.), *Journal of Slavic Military Studies*, vol. 8, no. 2 (June 1995), pp. 356-65.

Gallately, Robert, "The Nazi State: Machine or Morass," *History Today*, vol. 36 (January 1986) pp. 35-39.

Greenbaum, Alfred A. "Soviet Jewry during the Lenin-Stalin Period-II," *Soviet Studies*, vol. XVII, no. I (July 1965), pp. 84-92,

_____. "Soviet Jewry during the Lenin-Stalin Period-I," *Soviet Studies*, vol. XVI, no. 4 (April 1965), pp. 406-21.

von Hagen, Mark, "Soviet Soldiers and Officers on the Eve of the German Invasion: Towards a Deception of Social Psychology and Political Attitudes," *Soviet Union/Union Sovietique*, vol. 18, no. 1-3 (1991), pp. 79-101.

Hillgruber, Andreas, "Die 'Endloesung' und das deutsche Ostimperium als Kernstueck des rassenideologischen Programms des Nationalsozialismus," in *Vierteljahreshefte fuer Zeitgeschichte*, vol. 20 no. 2 (1972), pp. 133-53.

Koonz, Claudia, "Ethical Dilemmas and Nazi Eugenics: Single Issue Dissent in Religious Contexts," *Journal of Modern History*, vol. 64, no. 4 (1992) S8-S31 (supplemental).

Kuznetzov, I.I. and A.A. Maslov, "The Soviet General Officer Corps, 1943: Losses in Combat," *Journal of Slavic Military Studies*, vol. 8, no. 2 (June 1995), pp. 366-86.

Luedtke, A., "The Appeal of Exterminating 'Others:' German Workers and the Limits of Resistance," *Journal of Modern History*, vol. 64, no. 4 (December 1992) S46-S67 (supplemental).

Lumans, Valdis O., "The Military Obligation of the Volksdeutsche of Eastern Europe Towards the Third Reich," *East European Quarterly*, vol. XXIII, no. 3 (September 1989), pp. 305-25.

Nolte, Ernst, "Big Business and German Politics: A Comment," *The American Historical Review*, vol. 75, no. 1 (October 1969), pp. 71-8.

Paxton, R.O., "The German Opposition to Hitler: a Non-Germanist's View," *Central European History*, vol. 14 (1981), pp. 362-68.

Peukert, Detlev, "Young People: For or Against the Nazis?" *History Today*, vol. 35, no. 10 (October, 1985), pp. 15-22.

Simpson, Keith, "The German Experience of Rear Area Security on the Eastern Front, 1941-1945," *Journal of the Royal United Services Institute for Defence Studies*, no. 121 (1976), pp. 39-46.

Stevenson, Jill, "Middle Class Women and National Socialist 'Service'," *History*, vol. 67, no. 229 (1982), p. 8.

Stoeckli, Fritz, "Soviet and German Loss rates during the Second World War: the Price of Victory," *Journal of Soviet Military Studies*, vol. 3, no. 4 (December 1990), pp. 645-51.

Streit, Christian, "Ostkrieg, Antibolshewismus und 'Endloesung'," *Geschichte und Gesellschaft*, no. 17 (1991), pp. 242-55.

Teske, Hermann, "Ueber die deutsche Kampffuehrung gegen russische Partisanen," *Wehrwissenschatliche Rundschau*, no. 14 (1964), pp. 662-75.

_____. "Partisanen gegen die Eisenbahn," *Wehrwissenschatliche Rundschau*, no. 3 (1953), pp. 468-75.

Ward, James J., " 'Smash the Fascists...' Germany Communist Efforts to Counter the Nazis, 1930-31," *Central European History*, vol. 14 (1981), pp. 30-62.

X, (Unknown author). "The Sources of Soviet Conduct," *Foreign Affairs*, vol. 25, no. 4 (July 1947), pp. 566-82.

Yutaka, Akino, "Soviet Policy in Eastern Europe, 1943-1948: A Geopolitical Analysis," *East European Quarterly*, vol. XVI, no. 3 (September 1983), pp. 257-66.

Unpublished Papers

(Courtesy of Dr. Benjamin Shepherd)

Anderson, Truman O., "Incident at Baranikvka: German reprisals and the Soviet Partisan Movement in Ukraine, October-December 1941." (1998).

_____. "A Hungarian Vernichtungskrieg? Hungarian Troops and the Soviet Partisan War in Ukraine." (1998).

Published Primary Sources Consulted

Baade, Fritz, et al (eds.). *"Unsere Ehre haisst Treue." Kriegstagebuch des Kommandostabes RFSS. Taetigkeitsbericht des Kommandostabes RFSS. Taetigkeitsbericht der 1. und 2. SS Infanterie Brigade, der 1. SS-Kavallerie Brigade und von Sonderkommandos der SS* (Vienna: Europa Verlag, 1965).

Heer, Hannes (ed.). *"Stets zu erschiessen sind Frauen, die in der Roten Armee dienen." Gestaendnisse Deutscher Kriegsgefangener ueber ihren Einsatz an der Ostfront* (Hamburg: Hamburger Edition, 1995).

Halder, Franz. *Kriegstagebuch. Taegliche Aufzeichnungen der Chefs des Generalstabs des Heeres 1939-1942*, 3 vols. (Stuttgart: Kohlhammer, 1962-1964).

Mueller, Norbert, *Okkupation, Raub, Vernichtung. Dokumente zur Besatzungspolitik der faschistischen Wehrmacht auf sowjetischen Territorium 1941 bis 1944* (Berlin: Militaerverlag der DDR, 1980).

Mueller, Rolf-Dieter (ed.). *Die deutsche Wirtschaftspolitik in den besetzten sowjetischen Gebieten 1941-1943* (Boppard am Rhein: Harald Boldt, 1991).

Consulted Theses/Dissertations

Bessel, Richard, "The SA in the Eastern Regions of Germany, 1925-1934," Oxford University Ph.D. thesis, 1980.

Biddiscombe, Alexander P., "The Last Ditch: An Organisational History of the Nazi Werwolf Movement, 1944-45',"University of London Ph.D. thesis, 1991.

Bramwell, Anna, "The Resettlement of Ethnic Germans, 1939-41," Oxford University Ph.D. thesis, 1985.

Dobriansky, Paula J., "The Military Determinants of Soviet Foreign Policy, 1945-1988," Harvard University Ph.D. thesis, 1992.

De Zayas, Alfred M., "Mass Expulsions: Historical and Ethical Dimensions," Oxford University Ph.D. thesis, 1985.

Fattig, R.C. "Reprisal: The German Army and the Execution of Hostages during the Second World War," University of California at San Diego Ph.D. thesis, 1980.

Hasselbring, Andrew Strieter, "American Prisoners of War in the Third Reich," Temple University Ph.D. thesis, August 1991.

Hulse, Melvin Andrew, "Soviet Military Doctrine, 'Militarization' of Industry, and the First Two Five Year Plans: Developing the Military-Economic Mobilization Potential of the Soviet Union for Total War," Georgetown University Ph.D. thesis, 1991.

Interviews Conducted and Included

File located at both the University of Strathclyde, Department of History,

Glasgow, Scotland; Temple University, Department of History, Center for the

Study of Force and Diplomacy, Philadelphia, Pennsylvania.

Mario Antonucci, May 1990 (telephonic), April 1991.

Hans Baur, January 1984 through December 1989.

Leon Degrelle, March 1984, April 1993 (telephonic) and personal visit in April 1984.

Hans-Dietrich Hossfelder, January-February 1985, March 1994 (telephonic).

Adolf Galland, March 1984 through January 1996.

Gregor Koronov, January 1985, November 1993.

Otto Kumm, with Jeffrey L. Ethell from 1980-82; by Colin D. Heaton from February 1984, January 1985.

Karl Wolff, December 1983, January 1984.

Dietrich Hrabak, various interviews from 1984-1993.

ENDNOTES

1 Colin D. Heaton, *German Anti-Partisan Warfare in Europe, 1939-1945* (Atglen, PA, 2001), pp. 18-22.

2 *Nationalsozialistische Deutscher Arbeiter Partei*, or "National Socialist German Workers' Party," hence the acronym '*Nazi*'. For clarity German units and special designations are italicized as opposed to Soviet designations.

3 Alexander Dallin, *Odessa, 1941-1945: A Case Study of Soviet Territory under Foreign Rule*, introduction by Larry L. Watts (Iasi, Portland, Oxford, 1998).

4 Benjamin Shepherd, "German Army Security Units in Russia, 1941-1943: A Case Study," University of Birmingham PhD thesis, Institute for German Studies (2000).

5 The following by Stephen Ambrose; *Beyond the Beachhead: The 29th Infantry Division in Normandy*, 2nd edition (New York, 1999); *Citizen Soldiers: The US Army from the Normandy Beaches to the Bulge to the Surrender of Germany, June 7, 1944 to May 7, 1945* (New York, 1998); *Band of Brothers: E Company, 506th Regiment, 101st Airborne from Normandy to Hitler's Eagle's Nest* (New York, 1993). These are prime examples of interviews converted into secondary historical texts.

6 Bryan Mark Rigg, *Hitler's Jewish Soldiers: The Untold Story of Nazi Racial Laws and Men of Jewish Descent in the German Military* (Lawrence, KS, 2002).

7 James Bradley and Ron Powers, *Flags of Our Fathers* (New York: Bantam Doubleday Dell, 2000).

8 Johannes Steinhoff, Peter Pechel, Dennis Showalter and Helmut D. Schmidt, *Voices from the Third Reich: An Oral History* (New York, 1994).

9[1] German military oath as instituted on 2 August 1934, cited in Hans Bucheim, Martin Broszat, translation by Dorrian Long and Marian Jackson, *Anatomy of the SS State*, 2nd edition (London, New York, 1970), p. 130.

10 Steinhoff, Pechel, et al, *Voices from the Third Reich*, p. xxix.

11 See Adolf Hitler record at *Militaerarchiv* Koblenz, Germany, *Nachlasse* (hereafter referenced as N for all files) N-1128.

12 Adolf Hitler, *Mein Kampf* (New York, 1969), p. 596.

13 Hugh Trevor-Roper, *Hitler's Table Talk, 1941-1944: His Private Conversations* (New York: 2000), p. 3.

14 Jonathan Steinberg, "Third Reich Reflected: German Civil Administration in the Occupied Soviet Union, 1091-4," *The English Historical Review*, vol. CX (June 1995), p. 648.

15 Ian Kershaw, " 'Working Towards the Fuehrer': Reflections on the nature of the Hitler Dictatorship," *Contemporary European History*, vol. 2, no. 2 (1993), p. 105.

16 Conan Fischer, *The Rise of the Nazi's* (Manchester; New York, 1995), p. 128.

17 Richard Lokowski, "Zwischen Professionalismus und Nazismus: Die Wehrmacht des Dritten Reiches vor dem Ueberfall auf die UdSSR," in Bernd Wegner, et al, *Zwei Wege nach Moskau: Vom Hitler-Stalin Pakt zum Unternehmen Barbarossa* (Munich; Zurich, 1991), pp. 149-66.

18 Steinhoff, Pechel, et al, *Voices from the Third Reich*, p. xix.

19 Horst Ueberhorst, *Elite fuer die Diktatur: Die Nationalpolitischen Erziehungstalten 1933-1945-Ein Dokumentarbericht* (Duesseldorf, 1969), pp. 180-7.

20 Steinhoff, Pechel, et al, *Voices from the Third Reich.* p. 33. On Kumm see also *Geheime Tagesberichte-Die Geheimen Tagesberichte der Deutschen Wehrmachtfuehrung im Zweiten Weltkrieg, Band 7, 1. Juni 1943-31 August 1943* (Osnabrueck, 1988), p. 362.

21 Benjamin Shepherd, "German Army Security Units in Russia, 1941-1943: A Case Study," Unpublished thesis, University of Birmingham (June 2000), p. 24.

22 Adolf Hitler, *Mein Kampf* (New York, 1939), pp. 390, 392, 406, 441-50.

23 Trevor-Roper, *Hitler's Table Talk*, p. 7.

24 William Carr, *Arms, Autarky and Aggression* (London, 1979), p. 20.

25 Mark Roseman, *The Wannsee Conference and the Final Solution: A Reconsideration* (New York, 2002), p. 6. Also Christopher R. Browning, *Fateful Months: Essays on the Emergence of the Final Solution* (New York, 1985); also by Browning, *The Path to Genocide: Essays on Launching the Final Solution* (Cambridge, 1992); Saul Friedlaender, *Nazi Germany and the Jews: The Years of Persecution, 1933-1939* (London, 1997); Ulrich Herbert, *Best: Biographische Studien ueber Radikalismus, Weltanschauung und Vernunft, 1903-1989* (Bonn, 1996); Peter Longerich, *Politik der Vernichtung: Eine Gesamtdarstellung der nationalsozialismus Judenverfolgung* (Munich, 1998).

26 Bucheim, et al, *Anatomy of the SS State*, p. 128.

27 Eberhard Jaeckel, *Hitler's World View: A Blue Print for Power* (Cambridge, MA, 1981), p. 16, citing Harold J. Laske, *Reflections on the Revolution of our Time* (London, 1940), pp. 108-10.

28 Jaeckel, *Hitler's World View*, citing Alan Bullock, *Hitler: A Study in Tyranny*, 2nd edition (London, 1962), p. 735.

29 Ibid. p. 19.

30 Shepherd, p. 24. See also Mommsen, "National Socialism: Continuity and Change," in Walter Laquer (ed.), *Fascism: A Reader's Guide. Analyses, Interpretations, Bibliography* (Berkeley, LA, 1976), pp. 179-84; also Mommsen, "The Realisation of the Unthinkable: the 'Final Solution' in the Third Reich," in Gerhard Hirschfeld (ed.), *The Policies of Genocide: Jews and Soviet Prisoners of War in Nazi Germany* (London, 1986), p. 115.

31 Richard Rhodes, *Masters of Death: The SS Einsatzgruppen and the Invention of the Holocaust* (New York: 2002), p. 83.

32 See examples in Timothy P. Mulligen, *The Politics of Illusion and Empire: German Occupation Policy in the Soviet Union, 1942-1943* (New York, 1988), pp. 137-46. See also Martin Van Creveld, *Fighting Power: German and US Army Performance 1939-1945* (Westport, CT, 1982), p. 164.

33 Mulligen, *Politics*, p. 124.

34 US National Archives microfilm section, Roll T-501, section 15, file 24693, frame 3, hereafter cited as T-501/15/24693/3, p. 7, "Besprechungspunkte fuer Divisions-Kommandeur-Besprechung," dated 12 June 1942. All NA prefixes refer to the US National archive. All BA-MA prefixes refer to joint listings at *Bundesarchiv* Koblenz and *Militaerarchiv* Freiburg respectively. All BA-MA records are hard copies or originals and many are found at both locations. All PRO prefixes refer to the Public Record Office in Kew Gardens, Surrey, United Kingdom, whilst PRO WO refers to PRO "War Office" documents at the same location, which are all hard copy files. For a list of Gerd von Schenckendorff's directives, see NA T-315/1668/16748/12, *221 Sicherheits Division, Abteilung Ia* (hereafter *221 SD, Abt. Ia*), dated 4.11.41, p. 2, 3, 49.

35 Steinberg, "Third Reich," p. 644.

36 See K. Vonk, "The Transportation System," *Annals of the American Academy of Social and Political Science*, vol. 245 (1946), pp. 70-8. See also Major General Hans Baur interview by Colin D. Heaton, located at Temple University Department History, Center for the Study of Force and Diplomacy. All "interviews" unless otherwise noted are in this collection at both locations.

37 Jackson Spielvogel, *Hitler and Nazi Germany: A History*, vol. 3 (New Jersey, 1996), p. 221.

38 See Louis P. Lochner (ed.), *The Goebbels Diaries 1942-1943* (New York, 1948), pp. 95-6.

39 Roseman, p. 9. See also John Lukacs, *The Hitler of History* (New York, 1997), p. 182.

40 Roseman, p. 25. See also Alan S. Rosenbaum, (ed.), *Is the Holocaust Unique? Perspectives on Comparative Genocide* (Boulder, 2001), p. 21; also Ian Hancock, "Responses to the Porrajmos: The Romani Holocaust," in Alan S. Rosenbaum (ed.), *Holocaust*, pp. 69-90. See also Michael Burleigh and Wolfgang Wippermann, *The Racial State: Germany 1933-1945* (Cambridge, 1991) on their perspectives in the unique qualities of the Jewish Holocaust and racial research, pp. 45, 48-9, 51-6; on racial policy pp. 57-73. See also Steven Beller, "'Your Mark is Your Disgrace': Liberalism and the Holocaust," *Contemporary European History*, vol. 4, no. 2 (1995), pp. 209-21.

41 William Manchester, *The Arms of Krupp* (New York; London, 1969), p. 533. See also Detlev Peukert, "The Genesis of the 'Final Solution' from the Spirit of Science," in David Crew (ed.), *Nazism and German Society: 1933-1945* (London; New York, 1994), pp. 274-96.

42 Burleigh and Wippermann, *The Racial State*, pp. 73, 103. On the euthanasia policy, see Vera Laska, *Women in the Resistance and Holocaust: Voices of Eyewitnesses-Contributions to Women's Studies No. 37* (Westport, CT, 1983), p. 14; on Gypsies p. 253; on Ukrainians and Russian laborers pp. 260-3. On religious intolerance and the Catholics, see G.O. Kent, "Pope Pius and Germany: Some Aspects of German-Vatican

Relations, 1933-1943," *American History Review*, no. 70 (October 1964), pp. 59-68; also J.S. Conway, *The Nazi Persecution of the Churches, 1933-1945* (London, 1968), pp. xiii, vi; see also Karl Dietrich Bracher, *The German Dictatorship: The Origins, Structure and Consequences of National Socialism* (London, 1970), pp. 461, 470, 480. See also Rhodes, p. 7.

43 Beller, "Your Mark," pp. 212-3.

44 Overy, *Why the Allies Won* (London, 1995), p. 66; Joachim Fest, *The Face of the Third Reich*, translation by Michael Bullock (London, 1970), pp. 111, 172; also William M. Carr, *Hitler: A Study in Personality and Politics* (London, 1978), pp. 70-81; also Peter Padfield, *Himmler: Reichsfuehrer-SS* (New York; London, 1990 in total. See Himmler record at *Militaerarchiv* N-1126. See also references in Rhodes, first at pp. 3, 266, then the index for further references.

45 Ibid. p. 69.

46 Roseman, p. 10

47 Burleigh and Wippermann, *The Racial State*, p. 44.

48 Ibid. Also "Hitler's Testament," *Der Prozess gegen die Hauptkriegsverbrecher von dem Internationalen Militaergeschichtshof*, Nuremberg, 14 November-1 October 1946, vol. 41 (Nuremberg, 1947-49), p. 552.

49 Overy, *Why the Allies Won*, p. 42; Mommsen, *From Weimar to Auschwitz* (Princeton, 1991), p. 234; Richard Breitman, *Official Secrets: What the Nazis Planned-What the British and Americans Knew* (London, 1998), p. 163. See also Adolf Hitler, *Mein Kampf* (New York, 1939), pp. 398-419.

50 Overy, *Why the Allies Won*, p. 81; Manchester, p. 695; Mommsen, *From Weimar to Auschwitz*, p. 224.

51 Mommsen, *From Weimar to Auschwitz*, p. 235.

52 J.J. Ward, "Smash the Fascists?" p. 62. See also James Lucas, *Kommando: German Special Forces in World War II* (London, 1985), pp. 9-10.

53 See Foerster, "Hitlers Wendung," in Wegner, et al, *Zwei Wege*, p. 119.

54 Mommsen, *From Weimar to Auschwitz*, p. 225. See also Juergen Foerster, "Hitlers Wendung nach Osten. Die deutsche Kriegspolitik 1940-1941," in Wegner, et al, *Zwei Wege*, pp. 113-32.

55 Foerster, "Die Sicherung des 'Lebensraumes'," in Horst Boog, et al, *Der Angriff auf die Sowjetunion*, 2nd edition (Frankfurt-am-Main, 1991), p. 1240. Also on the joint military understanding see Foerster, "Hitlers Wendung," in Wegner, et al, *Zwei Wege*, p. 127; also Andreas Hillgruber, "Das Russland-Bild fuehrenden deutschen Militaers vor Beginn des Angriff auf die Sowjetunion," in Wegner, et al, *Zwei Wege*, p. 169. See also Richard Lokowski, "Zwischen Professionalismus und Nazismus. Die Wehrmacht des Dritten Reiches vor dem Ueberfall auf die UdSSR," in Wegner, et al, *Zwei Wege*, pp. 157-62.

56 Dan Diner, "Zwische Aporie und Apologie Ueber Grenzen der Historisierbarkeit des Nationalsozialismus," *Ist der Nationalsozialismus Geschicht?* Frankfurt am Main, 1987), pp. 62-73. Also Burleigh and Wippermann, *The Racial State*, pp. 19, 36-7.

57 See Rolf-Dieter Mueller, "Von der Wirtschaftsallianz zum kolonialen Ausbeutungskrieg," in Horst Boog, et al, *Der Angriff*, pp. 141-245; also R-D Mueller, "Das Scheitern der Wirtschaftlichen 'Blitzkriegstrategie'," in ibid. pp. 936-1029,

1168-1202; Christian Gerlach, *Krieg, Ernaehrung, Voelkermord. Forschungen zur deutschen Vernichtungspolitik im Zweiten Weltkrieg* (Hamburg, 1998), pp. 13-30.

58 Richard Z. Chesnoff, *Pack of Thieves: How Hitler and Europe Plundered the Jews and Committed the Greatest Theft in History* (New York, 1999).

59 Breitman, *Official Secrets*, p. 24.

60 Ibid. p. 213.

61 Ibid. pp. 15-6. See also Alan S. Rosenbaum, *Holocaust*, p. 13. See also Rhodes, p. 48.

62 See references in Ian Kershaw, *Hitler, 1889-1936 "Hubris"* (London, 1998), p. 24; T. Taylor (ed.), *Hitler's Secret Book* (New York, 1961), p. 22; John W. Hiden and John E. Farquharson (eds.), *Explaining Hitler's Germany: Historians and the Third Reich* (London, 1983), pp. 10-151. See also references to Wilhelm Marr, Eugen Duehring and Paul de Lagarde in Roseman, p.11. See also Klaus Latzel, *Deutsche Soldaten-nationalsozialistischer Krieg? Kriegserlebnis-Kriegserfahrung 1939-1945* (Munich, 2000), p. 14. See also Spielvogel, *Hitler and Nazi Germany*, vol. 3, p. 42.

63 Roseman, p. 17. See also Krausnick, Broszat, et al, *Anatomy of the SS State*, pp. 32, 49, 59.

64 Goldhagen, *Hitler's Willing Executioners: Ordinary Germans and the Holocaust*, 1st paperback edition (London, 1997).

65 See Wilfried Strik-Strikfeldt, translation by David Footman, *Against Stalin and Hitler: Memoir of the Russian Liberation movement, 1941-1945* (New York; London, 1970), pp. 42-3, 60, 94, 109-10, 166. See also Alexander Dallin and Ralph Mavrogordato, *German Rule in Russia, 1941-1945: A Case Study in Occupational Politics*, 2nd edition (Boulder, CO, 1981) in total.

66 Spielvogel, *Hitler and Nazi Germany*, vol. 3, pp. 161-4. See also Josef Goebbels, *Die Tagebuecher von Josef Goebbels: Im Auftrage des Instituts fuer Zeitgeschichte und mit Unterstuetzung des Staatlichen Archivdienstes Russlands, Band 9* (London; New York; Paris, 1995-98), entry dated 5/4/40, p. 36.

67 Breitman, *Official Secrets*, p. 49.

68 Strikfeldt, p. 96. This refers to the Soviet POWs being converted to *NSDAP* ideology and recruited in the anti-Communist effort.

69 BA-MA, RH 26-221/70, 5.11.41, Anlage 34, p. 6, as cited in Shepherd, p. 65.

70 Ibid. p. 19. See Himmler record at N-1126.

71 Ian Kershaw, *The Nazi Dictatorship: Problems and Perspectives of Interpretation*, 3rd edition (New York, 1993), p. 73.

72 See record at N-1110.

73 Christopher A. Browning, *Nazi Policy, Jewish Workers, German Killers* (New York, 2000), p. 15.

74 Hans Mommsen, *From Weimar to Auschwitz*, p. 172.

75 Wulf Kansteiner, "The Rise and Fall of Metaphor: German Historians and the Uniqueness of the Holocaust," in Alan S. Rosenbaum, *Holocaust*, p. 223

76 See Roseman, pp. 39-40; Jeremy Noakes and Geoffrey Pridham, *Nazism, 1919-1945: A Documentary Reader, vol. 3: Foreign Policy, War and Racial Extermination* (Devon, 1991). See also Spielvogel, *Hitler and Nazi Germany*, vol. 3, pp. 275-6, 282.

77 Shepherd, p. 1. See also Theo Schulte, *The German Army and Nazi Policies in Occupied Russia* (Oxford, 1989), pp. 2-7.

78 On their controversial value see Klaus Latzel, "Tourismus und Gewalt: Kriegswahrnehmungen in Feldpostbriefen," in Hannes Heer and Klaus Naumann (eds.), *Vernichtungskrieg. Verbrechen der Wehrmacht, 1941 bis 1944* (Hamburg, 1995), pp. 447-59; also Klaus Latzel, "Vom Kriegserlebnis zur Kriegserfahrung. Theoretische und Methodische Ueberlangen zur erfahrungsgeschichtlichen Untersuchung von Feldpostbriefen," in *Militaergeschichtliche Mitteilungen* Vol. 56 (1997), pp. 1-30. Klaus Latzel, *Deutsche Soldaten*, p. 24. See also NA T-315/1680/29380/12, *221 SD, Abt. Ib 'Anlagen'*, 22.6-31.12.42.

79 Shepherd, p. 82; Christian Gerlach, "Die deutsche Wirtschafts und Vernichtungspolitik im Weissrussland 1941-1944," unpublished thesis, Technical University of Berlin, 1997, p. 557.

80 Truman O. Anderson, "Conduct of Reprisals by the German Army of Occupation in the Southern USSR, 1941-1943." Unpublished thesis, University of Chicago (1994), pp. 21-8.

81 Ibid. See information in Army Group South Rear Area's 1943 *Kriegstagebuch* did not survive the war, p. 25. See also Latzel, *Deutsche Soldaten*, pp. 27-31.

82 Omer Bartov, *The Eastern Front, 1941-45. German Troops and the Barbarisation of Warfare* (Basingstoke, 1985); see also Bartov, *Hitler's Army. Soldiers, Nazis, and War in the Third Reich* (New York, 1992). See NA T-315/1678, file 29380/1, *221. Sicherheit-Division Ia*, 28.7.-21.8.42; also T-315/29186/1. *203. Sicherheit-Division Ia*, 12.6, 13.7., 8.8.42; T-315/2247/41762/1. *707 Inf.Div. Ic*, 1.1.31; and T-315/1681/35408/1 *221. Sicherheit-Division Ia, Monatsberichte*, Juli-August 1942.

83 Ibid. p. 153; see also Latzel, *Deutsche Soldaten*, p. 18.

84 French L. MacLean, *The Field Men: The SS Officers Who Led the Einsatzkommandos-the Nazi Mobile Killing Units* (Atglen, PA, 1999), p. 139.

85 Ibid. Table 4, p. 132.

86 Ibid.

87 Bartov, *The Eastern Front*, pp. 7-39, 68-105; *Hitler's Army*, pp. 12-28. See also Ian Kershaw, *Popular Opinion and Political Dissent in the Third Reich: Bavaria 1933-1945* (Oxford, 1983), pp. 373-85; also Kershaw, "Alltaegliches und Ausseralltaegliches: ihre Bedeutung fuer die Volksmeinung 1933-1939," in Detlev Peukert and Juergen Ruerup (eds.), *Die Reihen fast geschlossen. Beitraege zur Geschichte unterm Nationalsozialismus* (Wueppertal, 1981), pp. 273. See also Wolfrum Wette, "Rassenfeind. Antisemitismus und Antislawismus in der Wehrmachtpropaganda," in Walter Manoschek (ed.), *Die Wehrmacht in Rassenkrieg* (Vienna, 1996), pp. 58-72.

88 Zygmunt Bauman, *Modernity and the Holocaust* (Ithaca, 1989), p. 153.

89 Heaton, *German Anti-Partisan Warfare*, p. 121.

90 Bartov, *Hitler's Army*, p. 94 (en 149); Heaton, *German Anti-Partisan*, p. 175.

91 Bartov, *Hitler's Army*, pp. 129-30 (en 59). See also Christian Streit, *Keine Kameraden: Die Wehrmacht und die sowjetische Kriegsgefangener im 'Fall Barbarossa'. Eine Documentation* (Stuttgart, 1978), p. 115. This book uses both the 1978 and 1981 editions as cited in Heaton, *German Anti-Partisan*, p. 128.

92 Bartov, *The Eastern Front*, pp. 40-67. See also Roseman, p. 24; Heaton, *German Anti-Partisan*, p. 126.

93 Breitman, *Official Secrets*, p. 32.

94 See Heaton, *German Anti-Partisan*, p. 126.

95 See Latzel, *Deutsche Soldaten*, p. 59.

96 NA T-315/1672/16748/19, *Voraus-Abteilung IR 350*, 14.10.41, p. 2, as cited in Shepherd, p. 87;.

97 See both authors in the following collection; Michael Geyer, "'Es muss daher mit schnellen und drakonisch Massnahmen durchgegriffen werden': Civitella in val di Chiana am 29. Juni 1944" in total; also Mark Mazower, "Militaerische Gewalt und nationalsozialistische Werte: Die Wehrmacht im Griechenland 1941 bis 1944," in Heer and Naumann (eds.), *Vernichtungskrieg*, pp. 208-38.

98 Geyer in *Vernichtungskrieg*, pp. 213-24.

99 Schulte, *The German Army*, pp. 28-42; also Schulte, "The German Soldier in Occupied Russia," in Paul Addison and Angus Calder (eds.), *Time to Kill* (London, 1997), pp. 53-68; Shepherd, pp. 26-7.

100 Ibid. pp. 28-36, 74-7, 273-6, 284-96.

101 NA T-315/1673/16748/23, *221 SD, Abt. Ic*, 18.8.41, as cited in Shepherd, p. 126.

102 Otto Kumm interview of 1988. See full interview at University of Strathclyde Department of History and Temple University, Center for the Study of Force and Diplomacy. See also Heaton, *German Anti-Partisan*, pp. 157-8. See also post-war interrogation record at microfilm NA-M-1019/80.

103 T-315/1685/36509/13, *221. SD Ia,*, 6.4.43, p. 2.

104 T-315/1681/35408/1, *221. SD Ia* 12.7.42.

105 T-315/1685/36509/13 *221. SD Ia*; also file 36509/12, *Sicherungs-Regiment 36 Ia*, 9.2.43.

106 Peter G. Tsouras, *Fighting in Hell: The German Ordeal on the Eastern Front* (London, 1995), p. 155. Also Heaton, *German Anti-Partisan*, p. 147.

107 Anderson, "Conduct of Reprisals," p. 34.

108 Browning, *Nazi Policy*, p. 5.

109 Martin Broszat, et al (eds.), Alltag und Wiederstand-Bayern im Nationalsozialismus (Zurich, 1987); Lutz Niethammer (ed.), *"Die Jahre weiss man nicht, wo man die heute hinsetzen soll." Faschismuserfahrungen im Ruhrgebiet* (Berlin, 1983); Detlev Peukert, *Inside Nazi Germany. Conformity, Opposition and Racism in Everyday Life* (London, 1993); Ian Kershaw, *The Hitler Myth. Image and Reality in the Third Reich* (Oxford, 1989). Christopher R. Browning, *Ordinary Men: Reserve Police Battalion 101 and the Final Solution in Poland* (New York, 1992). See also Browning, *Nazi Policy, Jewish Workers, German Killers* (Cambridge, 2000).

110 Overy, *Russia's War* (London, 1997), p. 133. See also Heaton, *German Anti-Partisan Warfare*, p. 163.

111 Roseman, p. 42.

112 Gerlach, "Wirtschafts und Vernichtungspolitik," pp. 902-3.

113 NA T-315/1687/36509/24, *221 SD, Abt. Ia*, 6.7.43. *Monatsbericht fuer die Zeit vom 1. bis 30. Juni 1943*, pp. 3-4, as cited in Shepherd, p. 202;

114 Norman Rich, *Hitler's War Aims: Ideology, The Nazi State, and the Course of Expansion*. Vol. 1 of 2 (London 1973), p. xi.

115 Sigrid Wegner-Korfes, "Botschafter Friedrich Werner Graf von der Schulenberg und die Vorbereitung von 'Barbarossa'," in Wegner, et al, *Zwei Wege*, p. 192.

116 Manfred Messerschmidt, *Die Wehrmacht in NS Staat. Zeit der Indoktrination* (Hamburg, 1969).

117 Klaus-Juergen Mueller, *Das Heer und Hitler. Armee und nationalsozialistisches Regime 1933-1940* (Stuttgart, 1969).

118 Streit, *Keine Kameraden,* 2nd edition (Heidelberg, 1981), pp. 83-127.

119 See also Hillgruber, "Das Russland," in Wegner, et al, *Zwei Wege,* pp. 178-9.

120 Roseman, p. 44; also Philippe Burrin, *Hitler and the Jews: The Genesis of the Holocaust* (London, 1994). p. 62. For more on the various *Einsatzgruppen* see MacLean, *The Field Men* in total. For an in depth analysis of the death squads, see Yitzhak Arad, Krakowski and Shmuel (eds.), *The Einsatzgruppen Reports* (New York, 1989) in total.

121 NA T-175/234. der Chef der Sipo etc., 25.10.41. EM Nr. 124, p. 2; also report dated 14.11.41. EM Nr. 133, pp. 24-5.

122 MacLean, *The Field Men,* Table 19, p. 146. See also Longerich, *Politik,* pp. 293-418; Goldhagen, pp. 181-280; Tim C. Richter, "Die Wehrmacht und der Partisanenkrieg in den Besetzten Gebieten der Sowjetunion," in Rolf-Dieter Mueller and Hans-Erich Volkmann, *Die Wehrmacht: Mythos und Realitaet* (Munich, 1999), p. 841.

123 Streit, "Die Behandlung der sowjetischen Kriegsgefangenen und voelkerrechtliche probleme des Krieges gegen die Sowjetunion," in Gerd R. Ueberschar and Wolfram Wette (eds.), *Der deutsche Ueberfall auf die Sowjetunion. 'Unternehmen Barbarossa' 1941* (Frankfurt am Main, 1991), pp. 197-218.

124 See Wolfram Wette, "Wir hatten geglaubt," in Hans-Heinrich Wilhelm, *Rassenpolitik und Kriegsfuehrung. Sicherheitspolizei und Wehrmacht in Polen und der Sowjetunion* (Passau, 1991), pp. 84-5. See also Roseman, pp. 40-1. See also Latzel's figures in *Deutsche Soldaten,* p. 39.

125 H.W. Koch, "Hitler's 'Programme' and the Genesis of Operation Barbarossa," *The Historical Journal,* vol. 26, no. 4 (1983), pp. 891-920; also Koch, "Hitler and the Origins of the Second World War-Second Thoughts on the Status of Some Documents," *The Historical Journal,* vol.11, no. 1 (1968), pp. 125-43.

126 See Latzel, *Deutsche Soldaten,* p. 15.

127 See Hans-Adolf Jacobsen, "Kommissarbefehl und Massenexekution sowjetischer Kriegsgefangener," in Hans Buchheim (ed.), *Anatomie des SS-Staates,* vol. 2 (Munich, 1967), pp. 135-232. On Goering's edict regarding this matter see Roseman, p. 45.

128 See Shepherd, p. 45; Hannes Heer, "Die Logik des Vernichtungskrieges. Wehrmacht und Partisankampf," in *Mittelweg 36,* vol. 1 no. 12 (1994), pp. 105, 107; also NA T-315/1666/16748/7, 2.9.41, *Kriegstagebuch* (hereafter referred to as *KTB*), 221st Sicherheit Division, Abteilung Ia (intelligence), 6.5-13.12.41. See Gerlach, "Wirtschafts und Vernichtungspolitik," p. 893.

129 See Rundstedt's capture and interrogation record at PRO WO 208/3504 and 208/4416.

130 See record at N-22.

131 *Ritter* means "knight" or "Sir" in British parlance. Leeb was knighted by Kaiser Wilhelm I in 1917.

132 Tsouras, p. 32; Heaton, *German Anti-Partisan,* p. 163. See Leeb record at N-145.

133 Gerlach, "Wirtschafts und Vernichtungspolitik," p. 893.

134 NA T-315/1680/29380/9, *221 SD, Abt. Ic,* 12.9.42.

135 *Graf* means "Baron" or "Count."

136 See Halder capture and Interrogation record at PRO WO 208/3504 and 208/4413 with photograph. See his personnel record at *Militaerarchiv* N-220; also Manchester, pp. 29, 539.

137 Thoma and Cruewell openly disobeyed Hitler's Commando Order to execute British soldiers while under Rommel's command in North Africa. Rommel also disobeyed the order. See von Thoma capture and interrogation records at PRO WO 208/3433.

138 For more on Bittrich and his background and wartime career, see Michael Reynolds, *Sons of the Reich: The History of II SS Panzer Corps in Normandy, Arnhem, The Ardennes and on the Eastern Front* (Havertown, PA, 2002). Refer to the index at p. 346. Also Mark C. Yerger,, *Knights of Steel: The Structure, Development and Personalities of the 2. SS-Panzer Regiment* (Yerger, self-published, 1994) in total.

139 Karl Wolff interview of 1983-4. See Wolff record at *Militaerarchiv* N-1465. See Wolff's interrogation record at NA-M-1019/80.

140 Wolff interview. See also Heaton, *German Anti-Partisan*, pp. 206-7. Much of Wolff's post-war activities with *Organization Gehlen* are still classified under Central Intelligence Agency and National Security Agency agreements. Also on Wolff see Rhodes, p. 151.

141 On Mueller's meeting with SS Lieutenant General Reinhard Heydrich regarding Silesian Jews, see Browning, *Nazi Policy*, pp. 5-6; also Roseman, p. 20.

142 See Sven Steenberg, *Vlasov*, trans. by Abe Farbstein (New York, 1970), p. 143. Steenberg collected this information from his interview with Guenther d'Alquen, which was corroborated by Lieutenant General Hans Baur and Karl Wolff during their respective interviews. See also Heaton, *German Anti-Partisan*, p. 214. See also Spielvogel, *Hitler and Nazi Germany*, vol. 3, p. 282.

143 Wolff interview.

144 Helmut Krausnick and Hans-Heinrich Wilhelm, *Die Truppe des Weltanschauungskrieges. Die Einsatzgruppen der Sicherheitspolizei und des SD 1938-1942* (2 Vols.) (Stuttgart, 1981)

145 Ibid. On Army acceptance of these methods see Roseman, p. 41.

146 Krausnick, *Hitlers Einsatzgruppen. Die Truppe des Weltanschauungskrieges 1938-1942* (Frankfurt am Main, 1985) paperback edition.

147 Peter Jahn, "Russenfurcht und Antibolshewismus: Zur Entstehung und Wirkung von Feindbildern," in Peter Jahn and Reinhard Ruerup (eds.), *Erobern und Vernichten. Der Krieg gegen die Sowjetunion 1941-1945. Essays* (Berlin, 1991), pp. 51-3; see also Burleigh and Wippermann, *The Racial State*, pp. 23-8.

148 Jahn, "Russenfurcht," pp. 51-3. See also Bernhard R. Kroener, "Die Personellen Ressourcen des Dritten Reiches im Spannungsfeld zwischen Wehrmacht, Buerokratie und Kriegswirtschaft 1939-1942," in *Das Deutsche Reich und der Zweite Weltkrieg, Band 5/1. Organisation und Mobilisierung des deutschen Machtbereichs 1939-1942* (Stuttgart, 1988), pp. 271-5. See also Martin Broszat, "Soziale Motivation und Fuehrer-Bindung im Nationalsozialismus," in *Vierteljahreshefte fuer Zeitgeschichte, 18* (1970) in total.

149 MacLean, *The Field Men*, p. 133.

150 Ibid.

151 Ibid. It is interesting to note that German SS Divisions were designated "*Waffen SS*" while non-German volunteer (*Freiwilligen*) units were designated "*der SS*" (of the SS).

152 Ibid. p. 134.

153 Ibid. For a complete list of all of the senior officers, their careers, ranks, decorations, religion, education, place and date of birth, SS number, NSDAP number, units assigned, post-war punishment (if any) and military service in total as listed alphabetically along with the locations of these files in the US National Archives see pp. 36-130. For a complete list of SS officers records see NA-A3343, *Records of SS Officers from the Berlin Documentation Center, Series SSO: Officer Personnel Records*.

154 Broszat, "Soziale Motivation," p. 401.

155 This is supported in the opinion of Kumm. See Steinhoff, Pechel, et al, *Voices from the Third Reich*, pp. xxix, 32-3.

156 Shepherd, p. 3. See also Krausnick and Wilhelm, *Die Truppe*, pp. 103-4.

157 Latzel, *Deutsche Soldaten*, p. 17.

158 Wilhelm, *Rassenpolitik*, pp. 147-8. See also Roseman, p. 42. See also Latzel, *Deutsche Soldaten*, p. 49.

159 Andreas Hillgruber, "Die 'Endloesung' und das deutsche Ostimperium als Kernstueck des rassenidiologischen Programms des Nationalsozialismus," in *Vierteljahreshefte fuer Zeitgeschichte*, 20, 2 (1972), pp. 141. See also Christopher R. Browning, "Wehrmacht Reprisal Policy and the Mass Murder of Jews in Serbia," in *Militaergeschichtliche Mitteilungen*, 33, 1 (1983), pp. 311-49. On German perceptions of irregulars see also Anderson, "Conduct of Reprisals," pp. 302-3; also Anderson, "Incident at Baranivka: German Reprisals and the Soviet Partisan Movement in the Ukraine, October-December 1941," unpublished paper (1998), courtesy of Benjamin Shepherd.

160 Richard M. Fattig, "Reprisal: The German Army and the Execution of Hostages during the Second World War." Unpublished thesis, University of California at San Diego (1980), pp. 48-68. See also Michael Howard, *The Franco-Prussian War: The German Invasion of France 1870-1871* (London, 1961), pp. 249-56. See also Geoffrey Best, *Humanity in Warfare* (London, 1980), pp. 193-7; also Manfred Messerschmidt, "Der Kampf der Wehrmacht im Osten als Traditionsproblem," in Gerd R. Ueberschar and Wolfram Wette (eds.), "'Unternehmen Barbarossa' 1941," pp. 231-2

161 Rolf-Dieter Mueller, "Das Scheitern der wirtschaftlichen: 'Blitzkriegstrategie'," in Horst Boog, et al, *Der Angriff auf die Sowjetunion*, 2nd edition paperback (Frankfurt, 1991), pp. 936-1029. See also Latzel, *Deutsche Soldaten*, p. 55. See also Hans Umbreit, "Strukturen Deutscher Besatzungspolitik in der Anfangsphase des deutsch-sowjetischen Krieges," in Wegner, et al, *Zwei Wege*, p. 237.

162 R-D Mueller, "Die Rekruitierung sowjetischer Zwangsarbeiter fuer die deutsche Kriegswirtschaft," in Ulrich Herbert (ed.), *Europa und der "Reichseinsatz"* (Essen, 1991), pp. 234-50. See also R-D Mueller, "Menschenjagd: Die Rekruitierung von Zwangsarbeitern in der besetzten Sowjetunion," in Heer and Naumann (eds.), *Vernichtungskrieg*, pp. 92-103. Also Ulrich Herbert, *Hitler's Foreign Workers* (Cambridge, 1997), pp. 167-71. For general works that refer to this topic see also H.C. Deutsch, *The Conspiracy Against Hitler in the Twilight War* (Minneapolis, 1968); Wolfgang Foerster,

Generaloberst Ludwig Beck (Munich, 1953); Michael R.D. Foot, *Resistance: European Resistance to Nazism, 1940-45*, 2ⁿᵈ edition (London, 1977); Fraenkel and Manvel, *The Canaris Conspiracy: The Secret Resistance to Hitler in the German Army* (New York, 1969); also by Heinrich Fraenkel and Roger Manvel, *Der 20 Juli* (West Berlin, 1964); Robert J. O'Neill, *The German Army and the Nazi Party, 1933-1939* (London, 1966); T. Prittie, *Germans Against Hitler* (London, 1964); Gerhard Ritter, *The German Resistance: Carl Goerdeler's Struggle Against Tyranny* (Glasgow, 1958); H. Rothfels, *The German Opposition to Hitler* (London, 1961); Fabien von Schlabrendorff, *The Secret War Against Hitler* (London, 1966); On specific references see also Hans-Joachim Reichhardt, H. Graml and Hans Mommsen, *The German Resistance to Hitler* (London, 1970), p. 146; Carr, *Arms, Autarky and Aggression: A Study in German Foreign Policy, 1933-1939* (London, 1972), p. 172; Hans-Adolf Jacobson (ed.), *July 20, 1944: The German Opposition to Hitler as Viewed by Foreign Historians, an Anthology* (Bonn, 1969), p. 23; Klaus Hildebrand, *The Foreign Policy of the Third Reich* (London; Los Angeles, 1973), p. 75.

163 Michael Geyer, *Aufruestung oder Sicherheit: Die Reichswehr in der Krise der Machtpolitik 1924-1936* (Wiesbaden, 1980), pp. 30-3.

164 Bartov, *Hitler's Army*, p. 93.

165 Messerschmidt, *Die Wehrmacht*, pp. 38 ff. See also Streit, *Keine Kameraden*, pp. 56-9.

166 Burleigh and Wippermann, *The Racial State*, pp. 23-8. See also Latzel, *Deutsche Soldaten*, p. 73.

167 Streit, *Keine Kameraden*, p. 58.

168 See examples in the works of Walter Manoschek, *"Serbien ist Judenfrei": Militaerische Besatzungspolitik und Judenvernichtung in Serbien 1941/42*, 2ⁿᵈ edition (Munich, 1995); " 'Gehts mit Juden erschiessen?' Die Vernichtung der Juden in Serbien," in Heer and Naumann (eds.), *Vernichtungskrieg*, pp. 39-56; also "Die Vernichtung der Juden in Serbien," in Ulrich Herbert (ed.), *Nationalsozialistische Vernichtungspolitik 1939-1945. Neue Forschungen und Kontroverse* (Frankfurt, 1998), pp. 209-34.

169 See references to J.H. Posthumus, "The Structure of the Occupation Government," *The Annals of the American Academy of Social and Political Science*, vol. 245 (May 1946), pp. 1-2.

170 Hans-Ulrich Wehler, "The Goldhagen Controversy: Agonizing Problems, Scholarly Failure and the Political Dimension," in *German History*, vol. 15, no. 1, pp. 80-91; Dieter Pohl, "Die Holocaust-Forschung und Goldhagens Thesen," in *Vierteljahreshefte fuer Zeitgeschichte*, vol. 45 (1997), pp. 1-48.

171 Meir Michaelis, "Fascism, Totalitarianism and the Holocaust: Reflections on Current Interpretations of National Socialist Anti-Semitism," *European History Quarterly*, vol. 19, no. 1 (January 1989), pp. 85-6.

172 Anderson, "A Hungarian Vernichtungskrieg? Hungarian Troops and the Soviet Partisan War in Ukraine," unpublished paper, 1998. Courtesy of Benjamin Shepherd. See also Heaton, *German Anti-Partisan*, p. 134; see also N-39/317, 456; also record of General of the Cavalry Ernst Koestring at N -123/1-2, *Militaerarchiv* Freiburg, Germany. See also NA T-315/1686, file 36509/19 recording the actions of the 221ˢᵗ *Sicherheit* (Security) *Division* operating in Army Group Center, dated 2.7.43. These are listed hereafter as T-315/1686/36509/19 with the date following, such as 2.7.43.

173 Browning, *Nazi Policy*, p. 5.

174 See Browning, *Ordinary Men* in total.

175 Shepherd, p. 5.

176 Alfred Streim, *Die Behandlung sowjetischer Kriegsgefangener im "Fall Barbarossa."* *Eine Dokumentation* (Heidelberg, 1981).

177 Ernst Nolte, "Between Myth and Revisionism? The Third Reich in the Perspective of the 1980s," in H.W. Koch (ed.), *Aspects of the Third Reich* (London, 1985), pp. 17-38. See also Alan S. Rosenbaum, *Holocaust*, p. 5; Michael Berenbaum and A. Peck (eds.), *The Holocaust and History* (Bloomington; Washington, DC, 1998), pp. 16, 22. See also Saul Friedlaender, *Memory, History, and the Extermination of the Jews of Europe* (Bloomington, IN, 1993), p. 34; also Wolfgang J. Mommsen, "Neither Denial nor Forgetfulness Will Free Us from the Past," in James Knowlton and Truett Cates, *Forever in the Shadow of Hitler?* (Atlantic Highlands, NJ, 1993), pp. 202-15.

178 Joachim Hoffman, "Die Kriegsfuehrung aus der Sicht der Sowjetunion," in Horst Boog, et al, *Der Angriffe auf die Sowjetunion* (Frankfurt am Main, 1991), pp. 848-964.

179 Joerg Friedrich, *Das Gesetz des Krieges. Das deutsche Heer in Russland 1941 bis 1945. Der Prozess gegen das Oberkommando der Wehrmacht* (Munich, 1993), pp. 247-673.

180 Juergen Foerster, "Die Unternehmen 'Barbarossa' als Eroberungs und Vernichtungskrieg," in Boog, et al, *Der Angriff*, pp. 498-538; also by Foerster, "Die Sicherung," pp. 1227-87; also by Foerster, "Das nationalsozialistische Herrschaftssystem und der Krieg gegen die Sowjetunion", in Reinhard Ruerup (ed.), *Der Krieg gegen die Sowjetunion 1941-1945: eine Dokumentation* (Berlin, 1991), pp. 28-45.

181 See Shepherd, p. 6; Foerster, "Die Sicherung," pp. 1232-7; "Das nationalsozialistische Herrschaftssystem," pp. 41-3; "The Relation between Operation Barbarossa as an Ideological War of Extermination and the Final Solution;" in David Cesarani (ed.), *The Final Solution: Origins and Implementation* (London, 1994), pp. 85-102.

182 See Latzel, *Deutsche Soldaten*, p. 50.

183 Foerster, "Die Sicherung," pp. 1232-7, 1246-50; "Das nationalsozialistische Herrschaftssystem," pp. 41-3; "The Relation," pp. 90-7; "Wehrmacht, Krieg und Holocaust," in Mueller and Volkmann (eds.), *Die Wehrmacht*, pp. 948-63.

184 Overy, *Russia's War*, p. 135.

185 See in total Ulrich Herbert, "Neue Antworten und Fragen zur Geschichte und Holocaust," in *Neue Forschungen*, p. 28.

186 Omer Bartov, *Hitler's Army*, p. 150 (en 120) citing H.F. Richardson, *Sieg Heil! War Letters of Tank Gunner Karl Fuchs* (London, 1987), p. 69.

187 Ibid. p. 153.

188 See Latzel, *Deutsche Soldaten*, p. 54.

189 Heaton, *German Anti-Partisan Warfare*, p. 220; also Hitler's opinion on this subject as related to Major General Gunther Rall in Heaton, "*Luftwaffe* Ace Gunther Rall Remembers," *World War II*, vol. 9, no. 6 (March 1995), p. 39.

190 Hans Hossfelder interview, 1985, located at the University of Strathclyde Department of History and Temple University Center for the Study of Force and Diplomacy. See also Heaton, *German Anti-Partisan*, p. 109.

191 Klaus-Jochen Arnold, "Die Eroberung und Behandlung der Stadt Kiew durch die Wehrmacht im September 1941: Zur Radikalisierung der Besatzungspolitik," in *Militaergeschichtliche Mitteilungen*, vol. 58 no. 1 (1999), pp. 23-63.

192 Rigg, pp. 1-5.

193 Hans Mommsen, *From Weimar to Auschwitz*, p. 162.

194 Ibid. pp. 32, 40, 206-7, 362-3. See also Roseman, *Wannsee*, pp. 84, 102, 116-9, 135-6, 140, 142-3, 145-6, 156. See also Browning, *Ordinary Men*, p. 178.

195 Rigg, pp. 29-39, 139-40, 177-8, 193, 201, 231, 257-9, 288.

196 See Naumann, "Wenn ein Tabu bricht. Die Wehrmachtausstellung in der Bundesrepublik," in *Mittelweg, Vol. 36* (February-March 1996), pp. 11-24. See also Shepherd, pp. 10-11.

197 Heer, "Die Logik des Vernichtungskrieges. Wehrmacht und Partisanenkampf," in Heer and Klaus Naumann (eds.), *Vernichtungskrieg*, pp. 104-38.

198 Ibid.

199 Richard Overy, *Russia's War* p. 135.

200 Roseman, *Wannsee*, pp. 39, 41. See also Eberhard Jaeckel, "On the Purpose of the Wannsee Conference," *Perspectives on the Holocaust: Essays in Honor of Raul Hilberg*, James S. Pacy and Alan P. Wertheimer (eds.), Boulder, CO, 1995), p. 39. See also Rhodes, p. 230.

201 Guy Sajer, *Forgotten Soldier*, 2nd edition (Baltimore, 1988), pp. 296-303.

202 Karl Wolf (1900-1984) record located at *Bundesarchiv*, N-1465. Interviews of December 1983-January 1984. Wolff's admission is supported by the details in Roseman, *Wannsee*, p. 5.

203 Browning, *Ordinary Men* in total.

204 Gerlach, "Wirtschafts und Vernichtungspolitik;" also by Gerlach, *Krieg, Ernaehrung, Voelkermord. Forschungen zur deutschen Vernichtungspolitik im Zweiten Weltkrieg* (Hamburg, 1998).

205 Rolf-Dieter Mueller, "Die Wehrmacht-Historische Last und Verantwortung. Die Historiographie im Spannungsfeld von Wissenschaft und Vergangenheitsbewaeligung," in Ueberschar and Volkmann (eds.), *Die Wehrmacht*, pp. 3-35.

206 See the following in total: Browning, *Path to Genocide*; Cesarani (ed.), *Final Solution*; Goetz Aly, "*Endloesung*" *Voelkerverschiebung und der Mord an den europaeischen Juden* (Frankfurt am Main, 1996); Ralf Ogorreck, *Die Einsatzgruppen und die "Genesis der Endloesung"* (Berlin, 1996); Hans-Heinrich Wilhelm, *Die Einsatzgruppe A der Sicherheitspolizei und des SD 1941/42* (Frankfurt am Main, 1996); Longerich, *Politik*; Peter Klein (ed.), *Die Einsatzgruppen in der besetzten Sowjetunion 1941/42. Die Taetigkeits und Lageberichte des SD* (Berlin, 1997); Christian Gerlach, *Kalkulierte Morde. Die deutsche Wirtschafts und Vernichtungspolitik in Weissrussland 1941 bis 1944* (Hamburg, 1999). See also overviews by Kershaw, *The Nazi Dictatorship*, pp. 80-107; Raul Hilberg, *The Destruction of the European Jews*, 3 vols. (New York, 1985), especially vol. 1, pp. 274-367.

207 From Himmler speech to the SS leadership of "*Leibstandarte*" on 7 September 1940, as cited in Reitlinger, *The SS*, p. 367.

208 Rhodes, p. 69.

209 Ibid, pp. 133-5, on Canaris, p. 212.

210 Ibid. p. 254.

211 George Ginsburgs, "Laws of War and War Crimes on the Russian Front during World War II: The Soviet View," *Soviet Studies*, vol. XI, no. 3 (January 1960), p. 254.

212 Shepherd, p. 153; Na T-315/1585/29186/1, *203 SD, Abt. Ia*, 11.6., 26.6, 28.8., 12.9., 14.9., 28.9.42. *KTB* 1.4-31.12.42; also T-315/1678/29380/1, *221 SD, Abt. Ia*, 28.8., 5.9., 7.9., 25.9., 27.10.42. *KTB* 18.6-31.12.42.

213 Shepherd, p. 106; Gerlach, "Wirtschafts und Vernichtungspolitik," p. 563.

214 Juergen Foerster, "The Relation between Operation Barbarossa as an ideological War of Extermination and the Final Solution," in David Cesarani (ed.), *The Final Solution: Origins and Implementation* (London, 1994), p. 94; also Foerster, "Zum Russland-Bilde des Militaers 1941-1945," in Hans-Erich Volkmann (ed.), *Das Russland im dritten Reich* (Cologne, 1994), p. 153. See also Breitman, "Himmler's Police Auxiliaries," p. 2.

215 Wette and Ueberschar, *Ueberfall*, pp. 251-4, 258-60.

216 Ibid. See also Shepherd, p. 51 (en 8). See also Rhodes, p. 52 on use of multiple soldiers in executions, and pp. 152, 154, 163-4, 168 on Bach-Zelweski's challenge to Himmler regarding morale and mental cases among soldiers and their abuse of alcohol.

217 Wette and Ueberschar (eds.), *Ueberfall*, pp. 251-4; also Streit, *Keine Kameraden*, pp. 33-50; Foerster, "Unternehmen 'Barbarossa'," pp. 506-25.

218 Rhodes, pp. 186-7.

219 Foerster, "Unternehmen 'Barbarossa'," p. 525. For a complete compilation of the various Geneva and The Hague Conventions in their entirety, see "The Avalon Project at the Yale Law School," *Yale University Law School* website at www.AvalonProject. com, www.thehagueconventions.com or see also the particular section at www. GenevaConventions.com. See also Breitman, "Himmler's Police Auxiliaries," p. 3.

220 See Matthew Cooper, *The Phantom War: The German Struggle Against the Soviet Partisans1941-1944* (London: MacDonald & Jane's, 1979), p. 48; Breitman, "Himmler's Police Auxiliaries," p. 4. Interestingly the USSR abandoned hostage taking as a military method in 1919. See Ginsburgs, "Laws," p. 271.

221 Shepherd, p. 217; NA T-315/1685/36509/13, *221 SD, Abt. Ia*, 29.4.43; idem., *SR 45*, 29.4.43.

222 Ibid. p. 218; NA T0315/1684/36509/8. *Grenadier Regiment (GR) 930 Abt. Ia*, 8.4.43.

223 Shepherd, p. 219; NA T-315/1684/36509/9, *SR 930, Abt. Ia*, 23.6.43.

224 Cooper, p. 48; also Shepherd, p. 52 (en 10). See also Rhodes, p. 50.

225 Shepherd, p. 107: Gerlach, "Wirtschafts und Vernichtungspolitik," p. 892.

226 Overy, *Why the Allies Won*, p. 23.

227 Shepherd, p. 62; Anderson, *Conduct and Reprisals*, p. 254; Hilberg, "Wehrmacht und Judenvernichtung," p. 34.

228 Ibid. Ibid. Ibid.

229 Lucas, *Das Reich*, p. 97.

230 Ibid. p. 98.

231 Ibid. pp. 100-1.

232 Shepherd, p. 131; also NA T-315/1677/22639/6, *221 SD, Abt. Ic*, 16.6.42, *Uebergabeverhandlung*, p. 1.

233 Anderson, "Incident," p. 52.

234 See NA T-3151677/22639/6, *221 SD Abt. Ic*, 18.6.42, *KTB* 22.3-17.6.42, which provides figures of civilians killed in the same area. Also T-315/1676/22639/1, *221 SD Abt. Ic*, 18.6.42, 28.3, 8.4, 27.4, 12.5, 30.5, 1.6, 4.6, 8.6.42. *KTB* 20.3-17.6.42. Also T-315/1676/22639/1, *221 SD Abt. Ia*, 24.5.42. *KTB* 20.3-17.6.42 on the handing over of 100 refugees and a cow to the *SD* for "treatment'."

235 Shepherd, p. 30; also Schulte, *The German Army*, p. 290.

236 Bartov, *Hitler's Army*, p. 161 (en 180) citing *Deutsche Soldaten shen die Sowjetunion* (Berlin, 1941), pp. 44-5. This collection was published under the direction of the Propaganda Ministry under the personal attention of Josef Goebbels. See also Breitman, "Himmler's Police Auxiliaries," p. 3.

237 See Wiemann record at BA-MA per. 6 6900.

238 Shepherd, p. 137; NA T-315/1679/29380/5, *45 SR*, 23.6. 42, p. 2. On the amended order following the ruthless nature of this mission see T-315/1679/29380/5, *Reserve Police Battalion 91*, 20.7.42, *Einsatz Befehl* Nr. 28.

239 See Vera Laska, *Women in the Resistance and the Holocaust: Voices of Eyewitnesses. Contributions to Women's Studies No. 37* (Westport, CT: The Free Press, 1983), p. 99; NA M-1270/24/0827.

240 SS Brigadier General.

241 Burleigh and Wippermann, *The Racial State*, pp. 100-1, citing Ernest Klee, Willi Dressen, Volker Riess (eds.), *Schoene Zeiten. Judenmord aus der Sicht der Taeter und Gaffer* (Frankfurt am Main, 1988), pp. 84-5. See also references to Ukrainian and Lithuanian volunteers in *The Racial State*, p. 272

242 Ibid. pp. 100-1.

243 Ibid. p. 102.

244 Steinhoff, et al, *Voices from the Third Reich*, p. 8.

245 See Schlieben capture and interrogation record at PRO WO 208/3504 and 3433.

246 Breitman, *Official Secrets*, p. 82.

247 Mommsen, *From Weimar to Auschwitz*, pp. 182-4.

248 Overy, *Why the Allies Won*, p. 302. See also Breitman, "Himmler's Police Auxiliaries" in total.

249 Wilhelm Keitel, translation by David Irving, *In The Service of the Reich: The Memoirs of Field Marshal Keitel, Chief of the German High Command, 1938-1945*, introduction and epilogue by Walter Gorlitz, 3rd reprint of 1966 edition (New York, 1979), pp. 135-6.

250 Reitlinger, *The SS*, p. 306.

251 Ibid. pp. 372-3.

252 Steinberg, "Third Reich," p. 632.

253 Ibid. p. 634.

254 Shepherd, p. 149; NA T-315/1586/29186/3, *203 SD, Abt. VII*, 2.8.42, p. 4.

255 Mommsen, *From Weimar to Auschwitz*, p. 181; Breitman, *Official Secrets*, p. 77.

256 Albert Kesselring, forward by Kenneth Macksey, *The Memoirs of Field Marshal Kesselring* (London, Novato, CA: Presidio Press, 1988), p. 226.

257 Ginsburgs, "Laws," p. 272; on Hague, p. 273.

258 Ibid.

259 Koronov interview.

260 Ibid. p. 273.

261 Ibid.

262 Ibid. p. 274.

263 Ibid. pp. 276-7.

264 Ibid. p. 276.

265 Fitzroy Maclean, *Josip Broz Tito: A Pictorial Biography* (London, 1980), p. 72.

266 Rich, *Hitler's War Aims*, p. 65.

267 Mommsen, *From Weimar to Auschwitz*, p. 225.

268 Shepherd, p. 149; also DeWitt and Moll, "The Bryansk Area," in John A. Armstrong (ed), *Soviet Partisans in World War II* (Madison: University of Wisconsin Press, 1964), pp. 466-7.

269 "The Avalon Project."

270 Ibid. See also Shepherd, p. 20; also Ginsburgs, "Laws," in total, especially p. 258 on guerrilla warfare and hostages.

271 Overy, *Why the Allies Won*, p. 302.

272 "The Avalon Project."

273 Ibid.

274 See Robert Barr Smith, "Nuremberg: Final Chapter for the Thousand Year Reich," *World War II*, vol. 10, no. 4 (November 1995), p. 38; also by R.B. Smith, "Final Verdict at Nuremberg," *World War II*, vol. 11, no. 4 (November 1996), pp. 38-44, 83, 88.

275 "The Avalon Project," Maria Trombly, "Geneva Conventions" (2000), p. 2.

276 On the Nuremberg Trials see also "The Avalon Project." See also *Wilmington Star News* (UPI), "Ex-Nazi Officer Gets 5 Years," 25 July 1997, Sec. A-1, p. 2, Wilmington, North Carolina. Article on SS Captain Erich Priebke and the Ardeatine Cave massacre near Rome, Italy in 1944; also *Wilmington Star News* (UPI), "Ex-Vichy Official to Stand Trial," 27 January 1997, Sec. A-1, p. 2.

277 "The Avalon Project."

278 Michael Walzer, *Just and Unjust Wars: A Moral Argument with Historical Illustrations* (New York, 1977), p. 21.

279 All treaties and conferences may be found at The Avalon Project at the Yale Law School.

280 Hitler also violated the law with his *Kommandobefehl* of 18 October 1942, ordering the execution of British commandos captured. See Heaton, *German Anti-Partisan*, p. 227; Walzer, p. 38.

281 Christian Streit, "Partisans, Resistance and Prisoners of War," *Soviet Union-Union Sovietique*, vol. 18, nos. 1-3 (1991), pp. 260-76.

282 Burleigh and Wippermann, *The Racial State*, p. 302; this fact is covered throughout in Streit, "Partisans, Resistance," pp. 260-76.

283 US NA M-1270/24/0508. This microfilm collection is located at College Park, Maryland.

284 Ibid.

285 Ibid. On Bormann, see William Manchester, *The Arms of Krupp*, pp. 24, 428, 430, 440, 506-8, 515, 664, 794. See also comments by Major General Hans Baur during

his interviews, located at University of Strathclyde and Temple University. See also Hugh Trevor-Roper, *The Last Days of Hitler*, 4th edition (London, 1972), p. 181.

286 Heaton, *German Anti-Partisan*, p. 134; Laska, p. 13; Overy, *Russia's War*, pp. 140-1; also Breitman, *Official Secrets*, p. 66. See reference in Goebbels record at *Militaerarchiv* N-1118. See also Rhodes, pp. 170-9 on Babi Yar in detail.

287 See Keitel record at N-54.

288 Heaton, *German Anti-Partisan*, p. 24; Broszat and Krausnick, *The Anatomy of the SS State* (Cambridge, 1968), pp. 32, 49, 59; Bartov, *Hitler's Army*, p. 83. See also Noakes and Pridham, *Nazism, 191-1945*, p. 1048; Kershaw, *The Nazi Dictatorship*, p. 195. See also Breitman, "Himmler's Police Auxiliaries" in total.

289 See Heaton, *German Anti-Partisan*, p. 124; see Schoerner records at *Militaerarchiv* N-60; also Brian Lindsey, "Personality," *World War II*, vol. 14, no. 2 (July 1999), pp. 68-76. Lindsey states Schoerner's death as 6 July 1973, however the *Nachlasse* states this was 2 June 1973.

290 Heaton, *German Anti-Partisan*, p. 133; Robert Barr Smith, "Nuremberg: Final Chapter for the Thousand Year Reich," *World War II*, vol. 10, no. 4 (November 1995), p. 38; also Robert Barr Smith, "Final Verdict at Nuremberg," *World War II*, vol. 11, no. 4 (November 1996), pp. 38-44, 83, 88.

291 "The Avalon Project."

292 Heaton, *German Anti-Partisan*, p. 133; Overy, *Russia's War*, pp. 84-5.

293 "The Avalon Project."

294 NA T-315/1685/36509/11. SR 36 Ia, 26.12.42. *Betr.: "Unternehmen Ankar,"* p. 1; also Shepherd, p. 173.

295 Ibid. Ibid.

296 Overy, *Russia's War*, p. 149.

297 Antonucci interview, University of Strathclyde and Temple University. See also Heaton, *German Anti-Partisan*, p. 94.

298 Browning, *Ordinary Men*, p. 10.

299 The rank was *Oberfuehrer*, which was between a full colonel and brigadier general in the Allied rank structure. *Oberfueher's* were accorded the same privileges as generals.

300 Heaton, *German Anti-Partisan*, p. 210; Degrelle interview at Strathclyde and Temple Universities. *See* also "Belgian Volunteer in the Waffen SS," *Military History*, Vol. 23 , No. 8, ISSN-0889-7328 (Nov. 2006). Weider Publishing Group, Leesburg, VA, pp. 46-53. This is the edited version. The full length located at the university archives.

301 Heaton, *German Anti-Partisan*, p. 125; Bartov, *Hitler's Army*, p. 91; also *Bundesarchiv-Militaerarchiv* (hereafter referenced as BA-MA) /RH26-12/245 dated 17/11/41, 20/11/41, 11/12/41.

302 See Lucas, *Kommando*, pp. 45, 132. Wearing an enemy uniform is not in itself a capital offence, as long as the weapons are carried openly and the soldier reveals his own uniform underneath before engaging the enemy. The same applies to naval warfare while flying foreign colors.

303 "The Avalon Project."

304 Ibid.

305 Ibid.

306 Ibid.

307 Ibid.

308 Ibid.

309 Walzer, p. 182.

310 Overy, *Russia's War*, p. 151.

311 Heaton, *German Anti-Partisan*, p. 18.

312 Ibid. pp. 18-9.

313 "The Avalon Project."

314 Ibid.

315 Ibid.

316 Strikfeldt, p. 30.

317 See this evaluation in Andrew Strieter Hasselbring, "American Prisoners of War in the Third Reich," unpublished Temple University PhD thesis (1991).

318 Richard Overy, *Why the Allies Won*, p. 311.

319 See Ginsburgs, "Laws," p. 268.

320 "The Avalon Project."

321 Ibid.

322 Ibid. See the website for the list of signatory nations.

323 Ibid.

324 Ibid.

325 Rhodes, p. 16.

326 Steinberg, "Third Reich," p. 635.

327 Ginsburgs, "Laws," p. 254.

328 Ibid. pp. 254-5.

329 Ibid. p. 256.

330 Steinberg, "Third Reich," Article 2 of 1929 was rewritten and revised as Article 12 in the Convention of 1949.

331 Ibid.

332 Ibid.

333 Ibid.

334 Ibid.

335 Ibid. These provisions are also covered under the Geneva Convention of 22 August 1864 and ratified subsequent to 1929, 1949.

336 Ibid.

337 Ibid.

338 Ibid.

339 For a modern adaptation on Ireland and Britain, see Raymond Gilmour, *Dead Ground-Infiltrating the IRA* (New York, 1998). See also Heaton, *German Anti-Partisan*, p. 19.

340 "The Avalon Project."

341 Ibid.

342 Ibid.

343 Bartov, *Hitler's Army*, p. 85; Heaton, *German Anti-Partisan*, p. 124.

344 Ibid. p. 91 (en 135); Ibid. p. 127;

345 Ibid. (fn 104); Ibid. p. 125; also BA-MA/RH26-12-246 dated 31/1/42.

346 Hossfelder interview; see Heaton, *German Anti-Partisan*, p. 127.

347 "The Avalon Project."

348 Yitzhak Arad, Krakowski and Shmuel (eds.), *The Einsatzgruppen Reports* (New York, 1989), p. 89; Heaton, *German Anti-Partisan*, p. 372.

349 "The Avalon Project."

350 Heaton, *German Anti-Partisan*, p. 80; Mazower, *Inside Hitler's Greece*, p. 153.

351 Wilfred P. Deac, "City Streets Contested," *World War II*, vol. 9, no. 3 (September 1994), p. 38. See also Bruce Quarrie, *Hitler's Samurai: The Waffen SS in Action* (Wellingborough: Patrick Stephens, 1984), p. 150; Gordon K. Williamson, *The SS-Hitler's Instrument of Terror: The Full Story from Street Fighters to the Waffen SS* (Osceola, WI: Motorbooks International, 1994), pp. 134, 191.

352 Ginsburgs, "Laws," pp. 264, 267.

353 Ibid. pp. 264-5.

354 See Student capture and interrogation record at PRO WO 208/3504 and 208/4417 (copy) dated 28 May 1945.

355 See Heilmann capture and interrogation record at PRO WO 208/3504. See also Mazower, *Inside Hitler's Greece*, p. 173; also, NA BA-MA RH28-5/4b, "Vergeltungsmassnahmen," dated 31 May 1941.

356 Ibid. Ibid. Ibid.

357 Time-Life Inc., *Conquest of the Balkans* (Alexandria, VA, 1990), p. 160 with still photograph images taken from the actual film footage. See also Kelly Bell, "Costly Capture of Crete," *World War II*, vol. 14, no. 1 (May 1999), pp. 50-6. The village of Alikianos was paid a similar visit. See Mazower, p. 173.

358 Ibid. Ibid. Ibid.

359 See *Wilmington Star News* (UPI), "Ex-Nazi Officer Gets 5 Years," 25 July 1997, section 1A, p. 2.

360 On Kesselring and his involvement with volunteers, see Strikfeldt, p. 181.

361 *Wilmington Star News*, 25 July 1997, sec. 1a, p. 2.

362 MacLean, *The Field Men* in total.

363 Ibid. Table 17, p. 142. For the list of those killed in action see Table 15, p. 141; for a list of all general officers of the *Einsatzgruppen* see Table 16, pp. 141-2. For a breakdown of the numbers of officers in each *Einsatzgruppe*, see Table 14, pp. 140-1. See also Rhodes; on Blobel pp. 3, 12, 59-60, 130, 163fn, 171-4, 219, 274fn, 275, 279; see index for other relevant references.

364 Shepherd, p. 83; also Cooper, *Phantom War*, p. 56.

365 Ibid. Ibid.

366 Kesselring, *Memoirs*, p. 227.

367 Ginsburgs, "Laws," p. 278.

368 Trevor-Roper, *Hitler's Table Talk*, p. 7.

369 Ibid, p. 4.

370 David Welch, "Manufacturing a Consensus: Nazi propaganda and the Building of a 'National Community' (Volksgemeinschaft)," *Contemporary European History*, vol. 2, no. 1 (1993), pp. 1-15.

371 Hugh Trevor-Roper, *The Last Days of Hitler*, 4th edition (London, 1972), p. 57.

372 Rhodes, p. 4.

373 Foerster, "Die Sicherung," p. 1233.

374 Ibid. pp. 1234-5; also Shepherd, p. 45.

375 Shepherd, p. 45; also Gerlach, "Wirtschafts und Vernichtungspolitik," p. 801. See also Dallin, et al, "Partisan Psychological Warfare and Popular Attitudes," in John A. Armstrong (ed.), *Soviet Partisans*, p. 322; Schulte, *The German Army*, p. 123.

376 NA T-501/1677/22639/6, *221 SD, Abt. Ic*, 24.3.42, as cited in Shepherd, p. 123.

377 See Richard Breitman, "Himmler's Police Auxiliaries in the Occupied Soviet Territories," located at the Simon Wiesenthal Center, www.motlc.wiesenthal.com/resources/books/annual7/chap02.html online, p. 1 of 21.

378 See the following on Hitler's various partisan directives: Matthew Cooper, *The Phantom War: The German Struggle against the Soviet Partisans, 1941-1944* (London, 1979), pp. 79-81; Mulligen, *Politics*, pp. 137-46; Bernd Wegner, "Der Krieg gegen die Sowjetunion 1942/43," in Horst Boog, et al, *Das Deutsche Reich und der Zweite Weltkrieg Band 6: Der Global Krieg. Die Ausweitung zum Weltkrieg und der Wechsel der Initiativ 1941-1943* (Stuttgart, 1990), pp. 918-23. See also Ortwin Buchbender, *Das toenende Erz, Deutsche Propaganda gegen die Rote Armee im Zweiten Weltkrieg* (Stuttgart, 1978), pp. 281. See also on recruitment and dwindling numbers of foreign youths, Horst Ueberhorst, *Elite fuer die Diktatur*, pp. 163-5.

379 NA T-175/234. *Der Chef der Sipo*, etc. 8.10.41. EM Nr. 107, p. 5; ibid. 22.10.41. EM Nr. 121, p. 7; ibid. 14.11.41. EM Nr. 133, p. 8. See also reference in Shepherd, p. 181.

380 Adolf Hitler, *Mein Kampf*, 1st edition translation (1925), p. 579, as cited by Jaeckel, *Hitler's World View*, p. 79.

381 Mulligen, *Politics*, p. 144; Shepherd, p. 111.

382 NA T-315/1684/36509/9, *221 SD, Abt. Ia*, 4.7.43, cited in Shepherd, p. 206. See also Rhodes, p. 6 on numbers of destroyed towns and villages.

383 Ibid. p. 164.

384 Ibid; also NA T-315/1680/29380/9, *221 SD, Abt. Ic*, 3.12.42.

385 Reitlinger, *The SS*, pp. 305-6.

386 NA T-315/1677/22639/2, *221 SD Abt. Ic*, 8.4.42; NA T-77/1147/WiID/856. *WiKo Klinzy*. '*Kuerzer ueberlick ueber die Taetigkeit der Gruppe Ia in der Zeit vom 1.4. bis 30.6.43*', pp. 3-4, cited in Shepherd, pp. 123, 206. See also NA T-315/1683/36509/5, *221 SD, Abt. Ia*, 25.6.43. *Betr.: Aktivierung der Bandenbekaempfung*.

387 Bucheim, *Anatomy of the SS State*, p. 167. On the creation of the SD see pp. 166-87. On the '*Reichsicherhauptamt*' see also Bucheim, "Further Development of the Regional and Local Organisation of the *Sicherheitspolizei* and the *SD*," in *Anatomy of the SS State*, pp. 172-87.

388 NA T-315/1680/29380. *221 SD, Abt. Ic*, 19.7.42, p. 2, cited in Shepherd, p. 170. See also Rhodes on Romanian atrocities, p. 241.

389 Breitman, *Official Secrets*, p. 51.

390 Ibid. pp. 85-6.

391 As an example see NA T-315/1680/221 SD, Abt. Ic, 31.12.42, *Taetigkeitsbericht*, 18.6-31.12.42, p. 11.

392 Mommsen, *From Weimar to Auschwitz*, pp. 237-8.

393 Heer, "Die Logik," pp. 111-15.

394 Yehoshua Buchler, "Kommandostab Reichsfuehrer-SS: Himmler's Personal Murder Brigades in 1941," *Holocaust and Genocide*, vol. 1 (1986), pp. 15-7.

395 NA T-315/1687/36509/24, *221 SD, Abt. Ic*, 4.7.43, cited in Shepherd, p. 207.

396 BA-MA, RH 26-221-10, 8.7.41, cited in Shepherd, p. 56

397 Bucheim, *Anatomy of the SS State*, p. 172.

398 Courtesy of French L. MacLean and Schiffer Publishing, Ltd. Maps located in Maclean, *The Field Men*, pp. 228-31 respectively.

399 See MacLean, *The Field Men*, p. 33. For a list of all *Sonderkommando* and *Einsatzkommando* units, dispositions and leadership see pp. 21-30.

400 See also Bucheim, *Anatomy of the SS State*, p. 177.

401 NA T-315/1687/36509/24, *221 SD, Abt. Ic*, 19.11.43. *Taetigkeitsbericht des Ic vom 1.1. bis 31.8.43, "Anlage 34: Flugblatt Uebersetzung aus den Russischen: 'Kameraden der Gruppe Fjodorow',"* cited in Shepherd, p. 208.

402 NA T-315/1672/16748/18, no date. *Geschaeftsverteilung fuer Feldkommandantur 528 (V) fuer den Einsatz im Osten.*

403 Shepherd, p. 89; also BA-MA RH-26-286/3, *286 SD Abt. Ia*, 7.11.41, *Betr. Partisanentaetigkeit*, p. 1.

404 Shepherd, p. 57. See also BA-MA, RH 26-221/70, dated 1.10.41; also NA –T-315/1673/16748/23, 30.10.41.

405 Bartov, *Hitler's Army*, p. 126.

406 On the use of propaganda and coercion to recruit and convert, see Mulligen, *Politics*, pp. 93-106, 123-46. On the recruitment of 40,000 Spanish volunteers see *The Goebbels Diaries, Band 9*, entry dated 30 June 1941, p. 413.

407 Reitlinger, *The SS*, p. 382.

408 See Inquart capture and interrogation file at PRO WO 208/4503 and his military record at *Militaerarchiv* N-1180.

409 Breitman, *Official Secrets*, pp. 52-3, 79-80, 83-5. See also Richard Overy, "Hitler's War and the German Economy: A Reinterpretation," *Economic History Review*, vol. 35 (1982), pp. 272-92. See also Strikfeldt, p. 64. See also Mommsen, *From Weimar to Auschwitz*, pp. 191, 194; Edward L. Homze, *Foreign Labor in Nazi Germany* (Princeton, 1967) in total; also Tim Mason, "The Workers' Opposition in Nazi Germany," *History Workshop Journal*, issue 11 (Spring 1981), pp. 120-37; also by Mason, "Labor in the Third Reich, 1933-1939," *Past and Present*, no. 33 (1966), pp. 112-41. Also on Daluege, see Rhodes, p. 17. See also Rhodes, pp. 39, 43; on Bach-Zelewski, p. 47 and index for other references.

410 Special leader was a rank equivalent to a Warrant Officer, someone highly specialized in his or her field.

411 Strikfeldt, pp. 42, 78, 83, 86-7, 94, 96-7, 100, 105, 107-8, 113-4, 116, 120-1, 124, 127, 130, 134-5, 140, 178-9, 190, 209; also Manchester, pp. 264-6; Mommsen, *From Weimar to Auschwitz*, p. 212; Overy, *Why the Allies Won*, p. 307.

412 On Ley see Rich, *Hitler's War Aims*, p. 61; Mommsen, *From Weimar to Auschwitz*, p. 157; Lucas, *Kommando*, p. 222.

413 Strikfeldt, p. 160. See also Richard Overy, "Hitler's War and the German Economy: A Reinterpretation," *Economic History Review*, vol. 35 (1982), pp. 272-92. See also Strikfeldt, p. 64. See also Mommsen, *From Weimar to Auschwitz*, pp. 191, 194;

Edward L. Homze, *Foreign Labor in Nazi Germany* (Princeton, 1967) in total; also Tim Mason, "The Workers' Opposition in Nazi Germany," *History Workshop Journal*, issue 11 (Spring 1981), pp. 120-37; also by Mason, "Labor in the Third Reich, 1933-1939," *Past and Present*, no. 33 (1966), pp. 112-41. Manchester, pp. 428, 459; Overy, *Why the Allies Won*, pp. 204-5.

414 Rich, *Hitler's War Aims*, p. 71; Strikfeldt, p. 160; Gerlach, "Wirtschafts und Vernichtungspolitik," p. 917.

415 Foerster, "Herrschaftssystem," p. 42.

416 NA T-77/1147/WiID/856. *WiKo Klinzy. "Kuerzer Ueberlick ueber die Taetigkeit der Gruppe Ia in der Zeit vom 1.4. bis 30.6.43,"* p. 1, cited in Shepherd, p. 205.

417 See Shepherd, p. 82; also Gerlach, "Wirtschafts und Vernichtungspolitik," p. 557.

418. NA T-315/1586/29186/3, 203 SD, *Abt. VII. Lagebericht, April 1943*, pp. 12-3, cited in Shepherd, pp. 195-6. See also Neil Gregor, "Big Business and the 'Blitzkriegswirtschaft': Daimler-Benz AG and the Mobilisation of the German War Economy, 1939-42," *Contemporary European History*, vol. 6, no. 2 (1997), pp. 193-208.

419 Strikfeldt, pp. 42, 78, 87.

420 NA T-315/1687/36509/24, 221 SD, *Abt. Ic*, 30.4.43, p. 1, cited in Shepherd, p. 189.

421 Ibid. p. 189; comments of a Corporal Paul Meynecken who was held prisoner by partisans and escaped. See NA T-315/1687/36509/24, 221 SD, *Abt. Ic*, 8.6.43. *Betr.: Vernehmung des Ogfr. Paul Meynecken von der Propaganda-Staffel Gomel, der aus Banditengefangenschaft befreit wurde.*

422 NA T-175/235, *Der Chef der Sipo*, etc. 3.4.42. EM Nr. 189, p. 17. See also Mulligen, *Politics*, pp. 93-105.

423 See NA T-315/1680/29380/9, 221 SD, *Abt. Ic*, 2.1.43, pp. 1-2; also Dallin, et al, "Psychological Warfare," pp. 227-41; Kenneth Slepyan, "The People's Avengers: Soviet Partisans, Stalinist Society and the Politics of Resistance, 1941-1944," unpublished thesis, University of Michigan (1994), pp. 281-8.

424 Shepherd, p. 104; also Dallin, "Psychological Warfare," p. 271.

425 Shepherd, p. 105; Mulligen, *Politics*, pp. 95-6.

426 NA T-175/235, 24.7.42, p. 2.

427 Overy, *Why the Allies Won*, pp. 282-3.

428 On the Muslims in the USSR, see Yaacov Ro'I, "The Task of Creating the New Soviet Man: 'Atheistic Propaganda' in the Soviet Muslim Areas," *Soviet Studies*, vol. XXXVI, no. 1 (January 1984), pp. 26-44.

429 Trevor-Roper, *Hitler's Table Talk*, p. 3.

430 Overy, *Russia's War*, p. 162. See also David Kowalewski, "Protest for Religious Rights in the USSR: Characteristics and Consequences," *The Russian Review*, vol. 39, no. 4 (October 1980), pp. 426-41.

431 Strikfeldt, pp. 30-1.

432 Ibid.

433 See NA M-1270/24/0430.

434 NA M-1270/24/0430; M-1270/24/083 regarding p. 51 of the secret report CI-FIR/123.

435 NA T-315/1680/29380/9, 221 SD, Abt. Ic, 2.1.43, p. 2; T-175/236. *Der Chef der Sipo*, 23.12.42. MadbO Nr. 35, p. 8.

436. NA T-315/1680/29380/9, *221 SD, Abt. Ic,* 3.11.42. *Betr.: Monatsbericht fuer die Zeit vom 1.10.-31.10.42,* p. 2, cited in Shepherd, p. 169

437 NA T-315/1586/29186/3, *203 SD, Abt VII,* 25.4.43, p. 3, cited in Shepherd, p. 145.

438 Strikfeldt, pp. 83, 85, 90, 96-7, 108-10, 112, 130, 137-8, 140, 143-4, 193, 202, 211.

439 NA T-175/235. *Der Chef der Sipo, etc.,* 29.5.42. MadbO Nr. 3, p. 7; also T-175/236, 23.10.42, MadbO Nr. 26, p. 8.

440 T-315/1687/36509/24, *221 SD Ic,* 1/7/43, p. 1; also T-315/1683/36509/5, *221 SD Ia,* 7.6.43, p. 1.

441 NA T-315/1687/36509/24, *Propaganda Abteilung* (hereafter *Prop. Abt.*) W Staffel Gomel, 20.1.43. *Betr.: Monatsbericht vom 20.12.42-20.1.43, 221 SD, Abt. Ic.* 1.1.43. *Betr.: Hoergemeinschaft in den Besetzten Ost-Gebieten,* p. 1, cited in Shepherd, p. 164.

442 Ibid. pp. 193-4; Ibid.

443 Ibid. p. 146; Ibid.

444 Ibid. p. 110.

445 Shepherd, p. 122; Also Weinberg, "Yelnya-Dorogobuzh," p. 26.

446 Ibid. p. 110; Ibid. pp. 395-6.

447 For an example into how casual POWs were treated in theory, see *The Josef Goebbels Diaries, Band 9,* entry dated 3 July 1941, pp. 422-4. See also Rhodes, p. 110.

448 Norbert Mueller (ed.), *Deutsche Besatzungspolitik in der UdSSR 1941-1944. Dokumente (Cologne, 1980),* pp. 134-5. See also Gerlach, "Wirtschafts und Vernichtungspolitik," pp. 914-24.

449 Strikfeldt, pp. 78-9, 83, 100, 134-5, 178; also Wolff interview.

450 See Lucas, *Das Reich,* pp. 179-80.

451 NA T-315/1687/36509/24, *221 SD, Abt. Ic,* 31.5.43. *Betr.: Politische Ueberwachung der Bevoelkerung,* p. 2, cited in Shepherd, p. 199.

452 Steenberg in total; NA T-315/1687/36509/24, *221 SD, Abt. Ic,* 20.6.43. *Betr.: Wirkung der Propaganda des Generals Wlassow;* T-315/1586/29186, *203 SD, Abt. VII,* 26.3.43. *Betr.: Lagebericht fuer Maerz 1943,* p. 7. See also the Soviet report that Vlasov was dead in *The Goebbels Diaries, Band 13,* entry dated 29/8/44, p. 352. See other entries regarding Vlasov at *Band 15,* pp. 216, 267, 269, 391-2, 486.

453 Steenberg, pp. 5-6, 14, 22, 229-30; Strikfeldt, pp. 94, 116, 246.

454 See Robert H. Johnston, "The Great Patriotic War and the Russian Exiles in France," *The Russian Review,* vol. 35, no. 3 (July 1976), p. 303. See also Maurice Friedberg, "The USSR and Its Émigrés," *The Russian Review,* vol. 27, no. 2 (April 1968), pp. 131-48.

455 See Lieutenant Colonel Leonid Damianov Ivanovich Maximciuc interview; also Strikfeldt, pp. 55-6, 91-2, 124, 143, 146-7.

456 See T-315/1687/36509/27, *221 SD Ib,* 29.6.43, cited in Shepherd, pp. 122-4. For a pro-Soviet viewpoint see J.K. Zawodny, "Soviet Partisans," *Soviet Studies,* vol. XVII, no. 3 (January 1966), p. 375.

457 NA T-315/1585/29380/9, *221 SD, Abt. Ic,* 5.8.42. *Betr.: Monatsbericht fuer die Zeit von 1-31 Juli 1942,* pp. 131, 157.

458 See BA-MA RH 26-221/74, *221 SD, Abt Ic. Taetigkeitsbericht,* 18.6.-21.12.42, p. 13, cited in Shepherd, p. 146.

459 NA T-315/1680/29380/9, *221 SD, Abt Ic,* 4.12.42.

460 Ibid. pp. 3, 281.

461 NA T-315/1687/36509/24, 221 SD, *Abt. Ic*, 28.7.43, cited in Shepherd, p. 203.

462 NA T-315/1870/15954/4, *Tagebuch eines Partisanen*, 10.9.41.

463 NA T-315/1680/29380/9, 221 SD, *Abt. Ic, Taetigkeitsbericht*, 18.6.42, p. 12.

464 See Zawodny, "Soviet Partisans," p. 375.

465 NA T-315/1870/15954/4, 12.10.41, cited in Shepherd, p. 69.

466 Shepherd, p. 110; Mulligen, *Politics*, p. 140; Wegner, "Krieg," p. 921.

467 NA T-315/1687/36509/24, 221 SD, *Abt. Ic*, 19.11.43, cited in Shepherd, p. 203.

468 See Richard H. Bradford, review of Johann Ewald, "Treatise on Partisan Warfare," *The Journal of Military History*, vol. 57, no. 1 (January 1993), pp. 141-2; also Jeffrey Brooks, "Official Xenophobia and Popular Cosmopolitanism in Early Soviet Russia," *American Historical Review*, vol. 97, no. 5 (December 1992), pp. 1431-48. See also Buchler, "*Kommandostab*," pp. 11-25; also William Carr, "A Final Solution: Nazi Policy Towards the Jews," *History Today*, vol. 35, no. 11 (November 1985), pp. 665-9.

469 See Shepherd, p. 105; also N. Mueller (ed.), *Deutsche Besatzungspolitik*, p. 120.

470 Shepherd, p. 104; Wegner, "Krieg," p. 920.

471 On Daimler-Benz, see Gregor, "Big Business" in total, especially p. 197 on production quotas and problems with foreign labor.

472 On I.G. Farben see Breitman, *Official Secrets*, p. 114.

473 Rich, *Hitler's War Aims*, p. 532.

474 Ibid. p. 72.

475 Gerlach, *Kalkulierte Morde* (Hamburg, 1999), pp. 996-9.

476 Mommsen, *From Weimar to Auschwitz*, p. 249.

477 See translation and forward by David Footman in Strikfeldt, p. 223. See also Russell H.S. Stolfi, "10th Panzer's Lightning Eastern Front Offensive," *World War II*, vol. 12, no. 3 (September 1997), pp. 34-40.

478 See Strikfeldt, p. 223.

479 NA T-315/1585/29186/2, 203 SD Abt. Ia, 6.10.42, cited in Shepherd, p. 127.

480 See Foerster, "Die Sicherung," p. 1256; Shepherd, p. 127.

481 Mommsen, *From Weimar to Auschwitz*, p. 178.

482 Overy, *Why the Allies Won*, pp. 21-2.

483 Ibid. p. 281.

484 See Lucas, *Kommando: German Special Forces of World War II* (London, 1985), pp. 22-3; Mommsen, *From Weimer to Auschwitz*, p. 176.

485 Breitman, *Official Secrets*, pp. 41-2.

486 Mommsen, *From Weimar to Auschwitz*, p. 252.

487 Ibid. p. 121.

488 Ibid. p. 259; also Strikfeldt, p. 51.

489 Lucas, *Das Reich*, p. 186.

490 NA T-315/1676/22639/2, 221 SD Abt. Ia, 6.5.42, 'Anlage 201', pp. 1-2.

491 Mommsen, *From Weimar to Auschwitz*, p. 161.

492 Ibid. p. 156.

493 See Schweppenburg record at Militaerarchiv N-254. On his counterinsurgency operations see N-254/51.

494 Strikfeldt, p. 47.

495 See List record at *Militaerarchiv* N-33 and capture/interrogation record at PRO WO 208/4415 with photograph. See also Strikfeldt, pp. 62, 238-9, 241.

496 *The Goebbels Diaries, Band 11*, entry dated 30/1/44, p. 200.

497 Shepherd, p. 213.

498 NA T-315/1684/36509/9. *Kommandeur SR 183, 13.7.43. Betr.: Verpflegung*, cited in ibid.

499 Ibid. p. 214; ibid. Also Anthony Kellett, *Combat Motivation* (Boston: Kluwer Boston, 1982), p. 246.

500 Overy, *Russia's War*, p. 117.

501 See Kershaw, *The Nazi Dictatorship*, pp. 146-7 (en 113) citing Mommsen, "Kriegsfahrungen," *Ueber Leen und Krieg*, U. Borsdorf and M. Jamin (eds.) (Hamburg, 1989).

502 Rich, *Hitler's War Aims*, p. 4.

503 James Lucas, *Das Reich: The Military Role of the 2nd SS Division* (London, 1991), p. 128. See also Bucheim, *Anatomy of the SS State* on military cooperation, p. 178.

504 Heaton, *German Anti-Partisan*, p. 121.

505 See NA T-315/1673/16748/23, 18.8.41, *Betr.: Lagebericht an 221 SD Abt. VII*, p. 3.

506 Overy, *Why the Allies Won*, p. 40.

507 Ibid. p. 130.

508 See K. Jean Cottam, "Soviet Women in Combat in World War II: Rear Services, Resistance Behind Enemy Lines, and Military Political Workers," *International Journal of Women's Studies*, vol. 5, no. 4 (1982), pp. 363-78.

509 See Ulrich Herbert, "Labor and Extermination: Economic Interest and primacy of Weltanschauung in National Socialism," *Past and Present* no. 138 (February 1993), pp. 144-95; also Tim Mason, "Labor in the Third Reich, 1933-1939," *Past and Present*, no. 33 (1966), pp. 112-41; also Rich, p. 15. See also NA T-315/1672/16748/18, *Feldkommandantur 551*, 8.9.41, "Merkblatt fuer die Buergermeister," p. 2.

510 See T-315/1687/36509/24, *221 SD Ic*, 4.3.43, p. 2

511 Rich, p. 4.

512 See T-315/1687/36509/24, *221 SD Ia*, 2.2.43, 30.1.43, 1.3.43. See also Steinberg, "Third Reich," p. 645.

513 Hans Mommsen, *From Weimar to Auschwitz* (Princeton, 1991), p. 180.

514 Jaeckel, *Hitler's World View* (New York, 1981), p. 62.

515 On official policies and meetings se the Public Records Office (hereafter referenced as PRO) Foreign Office (hereafter referenced as FO) 371/25240/1 ff. (W2812/38/48); PRO FO 371/25253/140 (W8686/8686/48). PRO FO 371/25252/198 (W10429/8261/48) PRO FO 371/25248/369 ff. (W8972/7848/48); PRO FO 371/25248/365 (W8972/7848/48); PRO FO 371/25248/366-367 (W8972/7848/48); PRO FO 371/25254/487 (W12667/12667/48).

516 J.H. Posthumus, pp. 1-2; Heaton, *German Anti-Partisan*, p. 28.

517 Michael R.D. Foot, *SOE in France: An Account of the Work of British Special Operations Executive in France, 1940-1944*. Reprint of 1966 edition (Baltimore, MD: University Publications of America, 1984), p. xxi. See also Heaton, *German Anti-Partisan*, p. 78.

518 Rich, *Hitler's War Aims*, p. 63. See Darre capture and interrogation records at PRO WO 208/4449; also Conan Fischer, *The Rise of the Nazis* (Manchester, New York,

1995), p. 51. See also NA T-77/1100/Wi/ID/370, *Wirtschaftsinspektion Mitte Stab/Abt. I/Id*, 1.5.43; also Stab I/Ic 17.5.43.

519 See Gehlen capture and interrogation file at NA M-1270/24/0395. See also Trevor-Roper, The *Last Days of Hitler*, p. 92; Strikfeldt, pp. 15, 25, 61, 65-9, 77-8, 92, 95, 97-8, 115, 124, 136, 138, 140, 142-7, 166, 170, 175, 188, 196, 201, 209, 221-3, 225, 237.

520 Strikfeldt, p. 30.

521 Heaton, *German Anti-Partisan*, p. 78, citing Mark Mazower, *Inside Hitler's Greece: The Experience of Occupation, 1941-44* (New Haven, CT, 1993), pp. 20-2.

522 Gerlach, "Wirtschafts und Vernichtungspolitik," pp. 805-13.

523 Heaton, *German Anti-Partisan*, p. 78; Mazower, *Hitler's Greece*, pp. 20-2

524 Steenberg, *Vlasov*, p. 34; Heaton, *German Anti-Partisan*, p. 370. Rosenberg (1893-1946) was hanged at Nuremberg. See also Alfred Rosenberg, *Future Roads for German Policy* (Berlin, 1932). See also Mulligen, *Politics*, pp. 123-46; Hans Umbreit, "Das unbewaeltigte Problem. Der Partisankrieg im Ruecken der Ostfront," in Juergen Foerster (ed.), *Stalingrad: Erignis-Wirkung-Symbol* (Zurich, 1992), pp. 138-42.

525 NA T-315/1678/29380/2. *RHGeb. Mitte, Abt. Ia*, 5.7.42.

526 Gerlach, "Wirtschafts und Vernichtungspolitik," p. 45.

527 BA-MA, RH 26-221/12, *221 SD Abt. Ia*, 18.7.41. *Anlage 381*. See Pflugbeil record at BA-MA RH7/714 Pers. 6. See also NA T-315/1676/22639/2, *221 SD Ia*, 14.4.42.

528 NA T-315/1681/35408/1, *221 SD, Abt. Ia. Betr.: 'Unternehmen Dreieck'*. See also Shepherd, p. 147.

529 Ibid, pp. 70-1. Ibid, p. 148.

530 NA T-315/1672/16748/18, *Feldkommandantur 551*, 8.9.41, p. 2.

531 BA-MA RH 26-403/2 *403 SD, Abt. Ic. Monatsbericht* Oktober 1941, p. 4.

532. NA T-315/1672/16748/18, *350 IR Abt. Ia*, 19.8.41; also Foerster, "Wehrmacht, Krieg und Holocaust," p. 955 (fn 36), cited in Shepherd, p. 74

533 Shepherd, p. 73; Foerster, "Die Sicherung," pp. 1250-1.

534 NA T-315/1667/16748/10, *221 SD Abt. Ia*, 6.9.41. *Divisionsbefehl fuer die am 6.9.41 erfolgende Uebernahme des erweiterten Divisions Bereiches.*

535 Strikfeldt, p. 32.

536 Breitman, *Official Secrets*, pp. 111-2.

537 NA T-315/1585/29186, *203 SD, Abt. Ia*, 1.7.42. *KTB* 18.6-31.12.42, cited in Shepherd, p. 148.

538 Heaton, *German Anti-Partisan*, p. 201; Major General Adolf Galland interview of 1995, also confirmed by Major General Johannes Steinhoff during his interview, 1993. Galland is located at Strathclyde and Temple Universities. See Galland edited interview by Colin D. Heaton, *World War II*, vol. 11, no. 5 (January 1997), pp. 46-52. See edited Steinhoff interview also by Heaton, *World War II*, vol. 13, no. 1 (May 1998), pp. 28-34, 74. On foreign volunteers see David Littlejohn, *Patriotic Traitors: A History of Collaboration in German Occupied Europe, 1940-45* (London, 1972) and Valdis O. Lumins, *Himmler's Auxiliaries* (Chapel Hill, 1991) in total. See also Meir Michaelis, "Fascism," p. 91.

539 Trevor-Roper, *Hitler's Table Talk*, p. 404, citing a meeting on 5 April 1942.

540 See Laska, *Women*, p. 51; A.H. Sollum, "Nowhere yet Everywhere," in Franklin Mark Osanka (ed.), *Modern Guerrilla Warfare: Fighting Communist Movements* (New York, 1962), pp. 15-24. See also David L.G. Stewart, *The White Armies of Russia: A Chronicle of*

Counter-Revolution and Allied Intervention, reprint of 1933 edition (New York, 1970), pp. 279, 299, 324-5, 352, 382-3, 387, 393-5; also John Erickson and Carol Gerrard (eds.), "Soviet Women at War," *World War 2 and the Soviet People: Selected Papers from the Fourth World Congress for Soviet and East European Studies* (London, 1993), pp. 50-76; also by Erickson and Gerrard, "Bitter Victory," *World War 2,* pp. 1-27. See also Nicholas Galay and B.H. Liddell-Hart (eds.), "The Partisan Forces," *The Red Army* (New York, 1956), pp. 153-76; Zvi Bar-On, "On the Position of the Jewish Partisan in the Soviet Partisan Movement," *First International Conference on the History of the Resistance Movements* (New York, 1960), pp. 65-70; G.A. Kumanyev, "On the Soviet People's Partisan Movement in the Hitlerite Invader's Rear, 1941-1944," *Revue Internationale d'Histoire Militaire,* no. 47 (1980), pp. 180-8; Brooks McClure, "Russia's Hidden Army," *Modern Guerrilla Warfare,* pp. 80-98; also Cooper, *The Phantom War,* in total.

541 Slepyan, "Avengers," pp. 25-50.

542 Shepherd, p. 108; N. Mueller (ed.), *Deutsche Besatzungspolitik,* pp. 139-40.

543 Ibid. Ibid.

544 Ibid. Ibid. On this directive and its varying compliances during anti-partisan operations *Zugspitz, Ankara I* and *Ankara II* see also NA T-315/1684/36509/9, *Sicherheits Regiment* (hereafter *SR*) 45, 31.5.43.

545 Shepherd, p. 108; Mulligen, *Politics,* pp. 140-1.

546 BA-MA RH 26, *221 SD, Abt. Ic,* 4.6.42, cited in Shepherd, p. 125.

547 For a complete distinction between the two groups, see Heaton, *German Anti-Partisan,* pp. 18-9.

548 Mommsen, *From Weimar to Auschwitz,* p. 8.

549 William Manchester, *The Arms of Krupp, 1587-1968* (London, 1969), p. 482.

550 See also on Hitler's thoughts on recruiting for the SS in Gerald Reitlinger, *The SS: Alibi of a Nation* (New York, 1957), pp. 190, 196.

551 Ibid. p. 200. This concerns the creation of the 14th SS *Panzergrenadier Division "Galizische".* On General Helmuth von Pannwitz and his 50,000 volunteer Cossacks see p. 201.

552 NA T-315/1673/16748/23, p. 2. See also reference in Shepherd, p. 71.

553 Heaton, *German Anti-Partisan,* p. 199; Wolff interview .

554 NA T-501/15/24693/3, *RHGeb. Mitte Abt. Ia,* 31.5.42, p. 1.

555 Shepherd, p. 124; Schulte, *The German Army,* p. 259.

556 Browning, *Ordinary Men,* pp. 83-4. Reitlinger, *The SS,* pp. 202-4, 205-6,

557 See Seeckt record at *Militaerarchiv* N-247; also Manchester, pp. 388, 423. See Reinhardt record at N-86. See Lettow-Vorbeck record at N-103, and his obituary at PRO WO 208/4415 with photograph; also Barry Taylor, "Personality," *Military History,* vol. 8, no. 2 (August 1991), pp. 8, 12-6; Christopher Lew, "Undercover," *World War II,* vol. 11, no. 2 (July 1996), pp. 8, 20; James Lucas, *Kommando* p. 24; also Frank A. Contey, "British Debacle in East Africa," *Military History,* vol. 13, no. 5 (December 1996), pp. 58-65, 86-7.

558 Shepherd, p. 28; Weinberg, "The Yelnya-Dorogobuzh Area of Smolensk Oblast," in Armstrong (ed.), *Soviet Partisans of World War II* (Madison, 1964), p. 434.

559 BA-MA, RH 26-221/34, *221 SD, Abt. Ic*, p. 3. On deserters and civilians working for German departments and agencies, see NA T-315/1677/22639/6, *221 SD, Abt. Ic*, 16.6.42.

560 See Heaton, *German Anti-Partisan*, p. 36; Steenberg, p. 36.

561 Ibid. p. 36; Ibid. pp. 37, 57, 78; Overy, *Russia's War*, p. 130. See also Mulligen, *Politics*, pp. 163-81; Mueller and Gerd R. Ueberschar, *Hitler's War in the East 1941-1945: A Critical Assessment* (Oxford, 1997), pp. 333-4.

562 Heaton, *German Anti-Partisan*, p. 114; Isaac Deutscher, *"Stalin": Political Leaders of the Twentieth Century* (New York, 1979), p. 432; Overy, *Russia's War*, p. 150.

563 Heaton, *German Anti-Partisan*, p. 208.

564 Forward by David Footman in Strikfeldt, p. 14.

565 David Footman note in Strikfeldt, p. 45.

566 Heaton, *German Anti-Partisan*, p. 142.

567 Ibid. p. 164.

568 See Heinrich August Winkler, "German Society, Hitler and the Illusion of Restoration, 1930-33," *Journal of Contemporary History*, vol. 11, no. 4 (October 1976), pp. 1-16. See also James Kleinwald, "No Relief for Stubborn Volunteers," *World War II*, vol. 7, no. 1 (May 1992), pp. 30-6.

569 Heaton, *German Anti-Partisan*, p. 167; Overy, *Russia's War*, p. 134.

570 See Laska, p. 272; Steenberg, p. 170; Heaton, *German Anti-Partisan*, p. 61; Wilfred P. Deac, "Undercover," *World War II*, vol. 13, no. 3 (September 1994), pp. 32-44, 66; Time-Life Books, *The Apparatus of Death* (Alexandria, VA, 1991), pp. 136, 138.

571 Strikfeldt, p. 110.

572 Jay Bergman, "The Idea of Individual Liberation in Bolshevik Visions of the New Soviet Man," *European History Quarterly*, vol. 27, no. 1 (January 1997), p. 81. See also Zev Katz, "Party Political Education in Soviet Russia, 1918-1935," *Soviet Studies*, vol. VII, no. 3 (January 1956), pp. 237-47; E. Koutaissoff, "Soviet Education and the New Man," *Soviet Studies*, vol. V, no. 2 (October 1953), pp. 103-57.

573 Katz, "Party Political Education," pp. 237-44; Koutaissoff, "Soviet Education," pp. 104, 109, 112-5. See also William Moskoff, "Soviet Higher Education Policy during World War II," *Soviet Studies*, vol. XXXXVIII, no. 3 (July 1986, pp. 406-15.

574 See Heaton, *German Anti-Partisan*, p. 140; Steenberg, pp. 103, 122, 151-2, 168, 171, 177, 179, 196, 212-3; *Militaerarchiv* Freiburg, *Nachlasse* 123 section 11, 17 (hereafter referenced as N-123/11,17), personal file of General Ernst Koestring. Most of these 'divisions' would be paper strength only; most never growing above regimental or brigade strength.

575 See Bruce Quarrie, *Hitler's Samurai: The Waffen SS in Action* (Wellingborough, 1984), pp. 33, 139.

576 See capture record of General of Paratroops Hermann Bernhard Ramcke at PRO WO 208/3433 and 208/3504.

577 Lucas, *Kommando*, pp. 25, 43-4.

578 Strikfeldt, p. 100.

579 *Oberkommando der Wehrmacht*, the High Command of the Armed Forces.

580 *Oberkommando des Heeres*, the High Command of the Army.

581 Wolff interview; Heaton, *German Anti-Partisan*, p. 164.

582 On the most effective *Einsatzgruppen*, see Breitman, *Official Secrets*, pp. 44, 47, 73. On *Einsatzgruppe A* under SS Brigadier General Dr. Franz Walter Stahlecker, see p. 44; on *Einsatzgruppe B* under SS Major General Arthur Nebe, p. 47; on *Einsatzgruppe C* under SS Brigadier General Dr. Otto Rasch, p. 73. These men commanded the units in the early days, and command would change as the war progressed. See also French L. MacLean, *The Field Men*, pp. 141-2 for all; on Rasch, p. 98; Stahlecker, p. 115; Nebe, p. 92. Also on Stahlecker see Rhodes, p. 11 and index locations.

583 Kumm interview. Ibid. p. 167.

584 Heaton, *German Anti-Partisan*, p. 173; Steenberg, p. 42.

585 Heaton, *German Anti-Partisan*, p. 169.

586 Ibid.

587 Wolff interview.

588 Ibid.

589 Ibid. See also Rhodes, p. 9.

590 Heaton, *German Anti-Partisan*, p. 174; Steenberg, p. 138. Also regarding d'Alquen see *The Goebbels Diaries, Band 13*, entry dated 17/9/44, p. 502

591 Jaeckel, *Hitler's World View*, p. 75.

592 Breitman, *Official Secrets*, p. 34.

593 This was the Battle of Kursk-Orel.

594 Kumm interview; Heaton, *German Anti-Partisan*, p. 181.

595 Ibid. Ibid.

596 Shepherd, p. 22; also Cooper, pp. 145-6.

597 Heaton, *German Anti-Partisan*, p. 198; Steenberg, p. 225. These figures seemed accurate to Karl Wolff, as he was the first source to mention them. See also Rich, *Hitler's War Aims*, p. 36.

598 Mark P. Gingerich, "*Waffen* SS Recruitment in the Germanic Lands, 1940-41," *The Historian*, vol. 59, no. 4 (Summer 1997), pp. 818-30.

599 Albert Speer, *Inside the Third Reich* (New York, 1976). See record at *Bundesarchiv Koblenz*, N-1340.

600 See Stewart, *The White Armies of Russia*, p. 279.

601 See David Bullock, "Reds versus Whites," *Military History*, vol. 9, no. 2 (June 1992), pp. 42-9; also Robert Szymczack, "Bolshevik Wave Breaks at Warsaw," *Military History*, vol. 11, no. 6 (February 1995), pp. 54-61, 90; also David Welch, "Propaganda and Indoctrination in the Third Reich: Success or Failure?" *European History Quarterly*, vol. 17, no. 4 (1987), pp. 403-22; reference in Overy, *Why the Allies Won*, p. 63; David Scott Foglesong, "America's Secret War against Bolshevism: United States Intervention in the Russian Civil War, 1917-1920," unpublished University of California at Berkeley PhD thesis (1991). See also Paul Avrich, "Russian Anarchists and the Civil War," *The Russian Review*, vol. 27, no. 3 (July 1968), pp. 296-306.

602 See Steenberg, pp. 8-9; Albert L. Weeks, "Personality," *World War II*, vol. 12, no. 4 (November 1997), pp. 8-10, 78. See also Stephen Cohen, "Stalin's Terror as Social History," *Russian Review*, vol. 45, no. 4 (October 1986), pp. 375-84; Robert Conquest, "What is Terror," *Slavic Review*, vol. 45, no. 2 (Summer 1986), pp. 235-7; also by Conquest, *The Great Terror: A Reassessment* (New York), Ch. 16 in total; and *The Harvest of Sorrow: Collectivisation and Terror* (New York, 1986), p. 303; see also the following in

total on Stalin's pogroms: Josef Stalin, *The Great Patriotic War of the Soviet Unions* (New York, 1945); Leon Trotsky, *Stalin* (London, 1947); Martin McCauley, *Politics in the Soviet Union* (New York, 1977); Alan B. Ulam, *Stalin: The Man and His Era*, 2nd ed. (New York, 1973); R.A. Medvedev, *Let History Judge* (New York, 1972); Roger Reese, "The Impact of the Great Purge on the Red Army: Wrestling with the Hard Numbers," *Soviet and Post Soviet Review*, vol. 19, nos. 1-3 (1992), pp. 71-90 respectively. See also Olga Nariewics, "Soviet Administration and the Grain Crisis of 1927-28," *Soviet Studies*, vol. 20, no. 2 (1968), pp. 235-41; also by Nariewics, "Stalin, War, Communism and Collectivisation," *Soviet Studies*, vol. 18, no. 1 (1966), pp. 20-37; also Lynn Viola, "The Peasant Nightmare: Visions of the Apocalypse in the Soviet Countryside," *Journal of Modern History*, vol. 62, no. 4 (December 1990), pp. 747-70. See also Laska, *Women*, p. 272. See also Daniel L. Bower, "Collectivised Agriculture in Smolensk: The Party, the Peasantry, and the Crisis of 1932," *The Russian Review*, vol. 36, no. 2 (April 1977), pp. 151-66. Also Martha Brill Olcott, "The Collectivisation Drive in Kazakhstan," *The Russian Review*, vol. 41, no. 2 (April 1981), pp. 122-42. See also Jane P. Shapiro, "Soviet Historiography and the Moscow Trials: After Thirty Years," *The Russian Review*, vol. 27, no. 1 (January 1968), pp. 68-77; also Arkady Borman, "My Meetings with White Russian Generals," *The Russian Review*, vol. 27, no. 2 (April 1968), pp. 215-24. See also L. Kochan, "The Russian Road to Rapallo," *Soviet Studies*, vol. II, no 2 (October 1950), pp. 109-22; M. Beloff, "Soviet Foreign Policy, 1929-41: Some Notes," *Soviet Studies*, vol. II, no. 2 (October 1950), pp. 123-37; also Isaac Deutscher, "Dogma and Reality in Stalin's 'Economic Problems'," *Soviet Studies*, vol. IV, no. 4 (April 1953), pp. 349-63. See also Dana G. Dalrymple, "The Soviet Famine of 1932-1934," *Soviet Studies*, vol. XV, no. 3) January 1964), pp. 250-84. See also Kestutis Girnius, "The Collectivisation of Lithuanian Agriculture, 1944-1950," *Soviet Studies*, vol. XL, no. 3 (July 1988), pp. 460-78. Michael Ellman, "A Note on the Number of 1933 Famine Victims," *Soviet Studies*, vol. 43, no. 2 (1991), pp. 375-9. See also Edwin Bacon, "Glasnost and the Gulag: New Information on Soviet Forced Labor around World War II," *Soviet Studies*, vol. 44, no. 6 (1992), pp. 1069-86. See also Ian Kershaw, "Working Towards the Fuehrer," p. 107.

603 See Amnon Sella, "Red Army Doctrine and Training on the Eve of the Second World War," *Soviet Studies*, vol. XXVII, no. 2 (April 1975), pp. 245, 251; also Norman Davies, "The Soviet Command and the Battle of Warsaw," *Soviet Studies*, vol. XXIII, no. 4 (April 1972), p. 573. See also D.W. Spring, "The Soviet Decision for War Against Finland, 30 November 1939," *Soviet Studies*, vol. XXXVIII, no. 2 (April 1986), p. 214. See also James M. McCann, "Beyond the Bug: Soviet Historiography of the Soviet-Polish War of 1920," *Soviet Studies*, vol. XXXVI, no. 4 (October 1982), p. 483; also Timo Vihavainen, "The Soviet Decision for War Against Finland, November 1939: A Comment," *Soviet Studies*, vol. XXXIX, no. 2 (April 1987), pp. 314-7; see also Roger Reese, "A Note on the Consequence of the Expansion of the Red Army on the Eve of World War II," *Soviet Studies*, vol. XLI, no. 1 (January 1989), pp. 135-40; specifically on his analysis of the purge see p. 138.

604 Dalrymple, "The Soviet Famine," p. 264.

605 Ibid. p. 269.

606 Ibid. p. 275.

607 Ibid. p. 279.

608 See George Liber, "Urban Growth and Ethnic Change in the Ukrainian SSR, 1923-1933," *Soviet Studies*, vol. XLI, no. 4 (October 1989), pp. 574-91. See also Robert W. Thurston, "Social Dimensions of Stalinist Rule: Humour and Terror in the USSR, 1935-1941," *Journal of Social History*, vol. 24 (1991), pp. 542-62; also Thurston, "Fear and Belief in the USSR's Great Terror," *Slavic Review*, vol. 45, no. 2 (1986), pp. 213-34. Also George Thayer, *Guerrilla* (New York, 1963), p. 65

609 Originally known as the "Cheka" in 1917 and later designated the OGPU in 1922, then NKVD in 1934. Later it was reorganized as the MGB and in 1954 designated KGB (Komitet Gosudarstvennoi Bezopasnosti).

610 An important documentary on the Soviet treatment of its citizens and the gulags is "The Death Train," October Films Production, British Broadcasting Company (1998). See also John Erickson, "The Soviet Union at War (1941-1945): An Essay on Sources and Studies," *Soviet Studies*, vol. XIV, no. 3 (January 1963), pp. 249-74. See p. 253 on the Great Purge. Also by Erickson, "The Soviet Response to the Surprise Attack: Three Directives, 22 June 1941," *Soviet Studies*, vol. XXIII, no. 4 (April 1972), p. 524.

611 Overy, *Why the Allies Won*, pp. 184-5.

612 Ibid. p. 291.

613 Bonwetsch, Bernd, "Sovietische Partisanen 1941-1945. Legende und Wirklichkeit des allgemeinen Volkskrieges,'" in Gerhard Schulz (ed), *Partisanen und Volkskrieg. Zur Revolutionierung des Krieges 20. Jahrhundert* (Goettingen: Vandenhoek & Rupprecht, 1985), p. 110.

614 Shepherd, p. 24; Dallin, "Psychological Warfare," pp. 320-37; Weinberg, "Yelnya-Dorogobuzh," in Ibid. pp. 430-7.

615 Wolff interview. Heaton, *German Anti-Partisan*, p. 106.

616 Heaton, *German Anti-Partisan*, p. 61 citing Overy, *Russia's War*, p. 145. See also Ortwin Buchbender, *Das Toenende Erz*, pp. 272-84; also Witalij Wilenchik, "Die Partisanenbewegung in Weissrussland 1941-1944," *Sonderdruck aus: Forschungen zur osteuropaeischen Geschichte*, vol. 34 (1984), pp. 195-201.

617 Ibid, p. 36. Ibid, pp. 163-4.

618 See Breitman, *Official Secrets*, pp. 32, 36, 40, 61-2. See Zelewski capture and interrogation file at PRO WO 208/4419 and his SS file at the Berlin Documentation Centre (henceforth BDC) A-3343, located also on NA SSO-023. On Wolff and his association with Kurt Daluege see BDC A-3342 and NA SSO-134. See also PRO N-11630/96/55; PRO C-2919/12/18; PRO FO 371/55/392.

619 Wolff interview.

620 See Doerr record at *Militaerarchiv N-29*.

621 Kumm interview.

622 NA T-315/1681/35408/2. *221 SD, Abt. Ia*, as cited in Shepherd, p. 151.

623 Ibid. p. 204; NA T-315/1683/36509/5, *221 SD, Abt. Ia*, 7.6.43.

624 Shepherd, p. 204.

625 Ibid.; NA T-315/1684/36509/9. *III/SR 930 Stab*, 10.8.43.

626 Mommsen, *From Weimer to Auschwitz*, p. 250. On Kube see Breitman, *Official Secrets*, p. 85.

627 See examples in Mommsen, "Nationalsozialismus," *Sowjetsystemund demokratische Gesellschaft*, vol. 4 (Freiburg, 1971), pp. 695-713. See also reports on the general mood at NA T-315/1586/29186/2. *203 SD, Abt. VII*, 28.11.42, pp. 1-2.

628 Cooper, pp. 137-46, citing SS Brigadier General Herf. See also Timothy P. Mulligen, "Reckoning the Costs of the People's War: The German Experience in the Central USSR," *Russian History*, vol. 9, no. 45 (1982), pp. 45-7. Mulligen cites the partisan dead as 300,000. See also BA-MA 26-201/11, *201. Sicherungs-Division*, 1a, 27.1, 12.3, 3.4.43.

629 Rich, *Hitler's War Aims*, p. 77.

630 Wolff interview.

631 Overy, *Russia's War*, pp. 150-1.

632 Wolff interview. See also NA T-501/27 file 31491/6, "*Der Kommandierende General der Sichertruppen und Befehlshaber im Heersgebiet Mitte (RHGeb. Mitte), 1a, Monatsberichte, Juni-Dezember 1942*" in total; Alfred Toppe, et al, *German Military Government* (United States Army Europe Historical Division, 1948, Manuscript No. P-033; Schulte, in Addison and Calder, pp. 53-68. See also German records on sabotage at T-315/1682/36509/1, 4; T-315/1683/36509/5, *221 SD Ia, Monatsberichte*, April-Mai 1943; also BA-MA RH 26-221/53, report of 1st Lieutenant Andre on the railways attacks in the Gomel-Dowsk-Tscherikoff region, 8.4.43; also T-315/1684/36509/9, *Sicherungs-Regiment 45*, 31.5.43. See also Erich Hesse, *Der Sowjetrussische Partisankrieg 1941-1944 im Spiegel Deutscher Kampfanweissungen und Befehle*, 2nd edition (Goettingen, 1993), pp. 249-55; Gary Gordon, *Soviet Partisan Warfare 1941-44: The German Perspective*, unpublished thesis, University of Iowa (1972), pp. 80-120. See also NA T-315.2247/41762/1, *707 ID, Abt. Ic*, 1.1.43. "*Zahlenmaessige Feindlage.*" *Verlust und Beuteuebersicht, 1 Juli bis 31 Dezember 1942.*

633 NA T-315/1683/36509/5, *221 SD, Abt. Ia*, 6.5.43. *Monatsbericht fuer die Zeit vom 1. bis 30.4.43*, p. 1, cited in Shepherd, p. 186

634 From "*Der Partisan, sine Organisation und seine Bekaempfung,*" NA T-501/2/14684/3, *RHGeb. Mitte Abt. Ia*, 12.10.41, p. 14.

635 See examples in Foerster, "Die Sicherung," pp. 1246-50; also on Reichenau see Rhodes, p. 59

636 Gerlach, "Wirtschafts und Vernichtungspolitik," p. 832.

637 Shepherd, p. 185.

638 NA T-315/1687/36509/24, *221 SD, Abt. Ic*, 2.6.43. *Betr.: Beitrag zu Monatsbericht 221. SD Ia fuer die Zeit vom 1. bis 31. Mai 1943*, p. 1.

639 See NA T-315/1673/16748, *Feldpostamt 221 SD* 12.8.41; also Schulte, *The German Army*, pp. 46-8, 73-85, 117-49, 258-71; Shepherd, p. 154.

640 NA T-175/235, *Der Chef der Sipo*, etc., 19.6.42. MadbO Nr. 8, p. 8.

641 NA-T-1870/15954/4, *Tagebuch eines Partisanen.*

642 NA T-315/1684/36509/9, *45 SR*, 31.5.43; ibid, *Der Kommand der Feldkommandantur 528 (V) Abt. Ia*, 11.5.43, cited in Shepherd, p. 187.

643 Dallin, "Partisan Psychological Warfare and Popular Attitudes," in Armstrong (ed), *Soviet Partisans*, pp. 218-9. See also Shepherd, p. 63.

644 Foerster, "Die Sicherung," pp. 1253-4.

645 Shepherd, p. 22; Dallin, et al, "Psychological Warfare," pp. 216-27; Schulte, *The German Army*, pp. 42-52, 69-85, 117-49, 253-67.

646 See NA T-77/1147/WiID/857, *Wiko 210 'Klinzy', Gruppe Landwirtschaft*, 11.7.43, p. 1; also T-77/1099/WiID/368, *Wiln. Mitte Stab/Abt. I/Id*, 4.2.43, p. 5.

647 On the specialized Hungarian anti-partisan units of the Hungarian VIII Corps see T-315/1686/36509/19, 2.7.43.

648 Rhodes, p. 5.

649 NA T-1683/36509/5, *221 SD, Abt. Ia*, 6.7.43. *Monatsbericht fuer die Zeit vom 1. bis 30. Juni 1943*, pp. 3-4, cited in Shepherd, p. 201.

650 RH 26-221/38a, *221 SD, Abt. Ia*, 25.6.42. "*Anlage 53*".

651 NA T-315/1681/35408/1. *RHGeb. Mitte, Chef des Generalstabs*, 29.9.42, pp. 1-2. Also NA T-315/1586/29186/3. *Feldkommandantur 550 Kr. Verwaltungsgruppe, Starje Dorogi*, 24.7.42. *Betr.: Lage und Taetigkeitsbericht fuer die Zeit vom 24.6. bis 24.7.42*, as cited in Shepherd, p. 175.

652 Foerster, "Die Sicherung," pp. 1234-5.

653 For more reports see NA T-315/1683/36509/5, *221 SD, Abt. Ia*, 3.7.43. *Betr.: Unternehmen der 102. le. ung. Div.*

654 T-315/1686/36509/19, *221 SD Ia*, 2.7.43.

655 T-315/1684/36509/9, *RHGeb. Mitte Ia*, 16.7.43.

656 See T-315/1586/29186/3, *203 SD Abteilung VII*, 29. 10.42, pp. 6, 8; also on this microfilm see *Feldkommandantur 550, Kriegsverwaltungsgruppe* Staryje Dorogi, 24.7.42; *Feldkommandantur 581 Verwaltungsgruppe*, 19.8.42, p. 5. See also T-315/1687/36509/24, 7.3.43, p. 1.

657 T-315/1684/36509/8, *Feldkommandantur 528 (V) Ia*, 11.5.43; also file 36509/9, *Meldung*, 11.6.43; T-315/1683/36509/5, *221 SD Ia*, 6.7.43, pp. 4-6. See also T-315/1687/36509/24, *221 SD Ic*, 1.8.43, p. 2. Also RH 26-221/53, *2/Sonder Battalion* (hereafter *SB*) *791*, 25.1.43, "*Anlage 84*"; *SB 791*, 25.1.43. NA T-315.1682/36509/4.

658 RH 26-221/79, *221 SD, Abt. Ia. Taetigkeitsbericht*, 17.6.42-15.3.42, p. 1, cited in Shepherd, p. 175. Also Gerald Reitlinger, *The House Built on Sand: The Conflicts of German Policy in Russia* (London, 1961), p. 110.

659 On Hungarian fighting qualities see Cooper, *The Phantom War*, p. 145. On atrocities in general due to frustration see Cooper, p. 1; Schulte, *The German Army*, pp. 127, 266-7. See also T-315/1686/36509/19, *III/Sicherheits-Regiment 45 Verbindungs-Offizier*, 11/7/43.

660 See *The Goebbels Diaries, Band 15*, entry dated 1/2/45, p. 35.

661 Shepherd, p. 166.

662 Ibid. p. 189; also NA T-315/1687/36509/24, *221 SD, Abt. Ic*, 20.2.43. *Betr.: Italienische 8. Armee im Bereich der Division; Gruppe Geheime Feldpolizei 729*, 23.2.43. *Betr.: Zerstzende Verhalten italienischer Soldaten Bericht.*

663 Easter Rabbit, or Bunny.

664 Shepherd, p. 215 and Table at p. 103 on units and figures; NA T-315/1685/36509/13, *221 SD, Abt. Ia*, 2.5.43, p. 2.

665 See NA T-501/2/14684/3, *RHGeb. Mitte Abt. Ia*, 12.10.41, "*Der Partisan, seine Organisation und seine Bekaempfung*," p. 14, as cited in Shepherd, p. 46.

666 See Gerlach, "Wirtschafts und Vernichtungspolitik," p. 801.

667 Ibid. p. 806.

668 See Mulligen, "Reckoning," p. 32. See also Gerlach, "Wirtschafts und Vernichtungspolitik," pp. 826-31.

669 Ibid. p. 557. Shepherd, p. 49.

670 See Hannes Heer, "Killing Fields: Die Wehrmacht und der Holocaust," in *Vernichtungskrieg. Verbrechen der Wehrmacht*, pp. 69-73; Hilberg, "Wehrmacht und Judenvernichtung," in Manoschek (ed.), *Die Wehrmacht im Rassenkrieg*, p. 34; Gerlach, "Wirtschaft und Vernichtungspolitik," pp. 562-79; Foerster, "Wehrmacht, Krieg und Holocaust," in R-D Mueller and H-E Volkmann (eds.), *Die Wehrmacht*, pp. 958-9.

671 See Gerlach, "Wirtschafts und Vernichtungspolitik," pp. 833-4. On Soviet partisan ruthlessness as a justification for German actions see Joachim Hoffmann, "Die Kriegsfuehrung aus der Sicht der Sowjetunion," in Horst Boog et al, *Der Angriff*, pp. 889-95.

672 Shepherd, p. 23.

673 Ibid. p. 19. For more detailed reading on this topic see Rolf-Dieter Mueller and Gerd R. Ueberschar (eds.), *Hitler's War in the East 1941-1945* (Oxford, 1997) in total; also Truman O. Anderson, "Incident at Baranivka: German Reprisals and the Soviet Partisan Movement in Ukraine, October-December 1941," *Journal of Modern History*, vol. 71, no. 3 (1999), pp. 585-623. See also Mulligen, *Politics*, pp. 137-46; John A. Armstrong and Kurt DeWitt, "Organization and Control of the Partisan Movement," in Armstrong (ed.), *Soviet Partisans in World War II* (Madison, 1964), pp. 84-93; Gerhard Weinberg, "Yelnya-Dorogobuzh," pp. 411-22; Kurt DeWitt and Wilhelm Moll, "The Bryansk Area," in Armstrong (ed), *Soviet Partisans*, pp. 461-2. Bonwetsch, "Sowjet Partisanen," p. 98; Earl Ziemke, "Composition and Morale of the Soviet Partisan Movement," in Armstrong (ed), *Soviet Partisans*, p. 151; Hesse, *Partisankrieg*, p. 205.

674 See Shepherd, p. 102; Armstrong and DeWitt, "Organization," pp. 98-103; Wilenchik, *Partisanenbewegung*, pp. 262-84; Slepyan, "Avengers," pp. 119-127.

675 See Ziemke, "Composition," p. 151; also Bonwetsch, "Sowjetische Partisanen," p. 98; Leonid Grenkevich, *The Soviet Partisan Movement 1941-1944* (London, 1999), pp. 227-9; also Wilenchik, "Die Partisanenbewegung," p. 209; also Hoffmann, "Die Kriegsfuehrung," p. 893.

676 Ziemke, "Composition," pp. 151-3; also Zawodny, "Soviet Partisans," p. 369.

677 BA-MA 26-201/11. *201. Sicherungs-Division* 1a, 27.1., 12.3., 3.4.43.

678 Mulligen, "Reckoning," pp. 45-7. See example in T-315/1687/36509/24, *221 SD* Ic, 26.5.43.

679 Robert L. O'Connell, *Of Arms and Men: A History of War, Weapons and Aggression* (New York, 1989), p. 286, quoted from S.L. Meyer (ed.), *The Russian War Machine 1917-1945* (London, 1977), pp. 44, 195. See also Tsouras, p. 33 regarding the first person account of Colonel General Eberhard Rauss regarding partisan women. See also Heaton, *German Anti-Partisan*, p.225.

680 T-315/1687/36509/24, *Prop/Abt. W. Staffel Gomel*, 21.7.43

681 Ralph Mavrogordato and Earl Ziemke, "The Polotzk Lowland," in Armstrong (ed.), *Soviet Partisans*, pp. 532-4, where Ziemke estimates the partisan strength to be 30,000 in 1941 and 200,000 by the summer of 1943; Erich Hesse, *Der Sowjetische Partisanenkrieg, 1941-1944*, 2nd edition (Goettingen, 1993), Ch. 8 in total; Bonwetsch, "Sowjetische Partisanen," pp. 100-1; Christian Gerlach, *Kalkulierte Morde*, pp. 862-3;

682 NA T-315/1685/36509/13, *221 SD, Abt. Ia*, 2.5.43, p. 5, cited in Shepherd, p. 215.

683 For the specific distinctions between partisans, guerrillas, terrorists and freedom fighters according to international law and this author's analysis with historical references and examples, see Heaton, *German Anti-Partisan*, pp. 18-21. These distinctions between the various groups are currently being introduced into training courses offered by the US Department of Defense and taught at the various military institutions, where this author has taught for the United States Marine Corps and US Naval Officer's Degree Completion Program at Camp Lejeune, North Carolina in 1999.

684 See Overy, *Why the Allies Won*, p. 26 (en 12), citing Reitemeir, *Geschichte der preussischen Staaten vor und nach ihrer Vereinigung in eine Monarchie* (Frankfurt an der Oder, 1801-05), p. 33.

685 J.J. Ward, "Smash the Fascists? The German Communist Efforts to Counter the Nazis, 1930-1931," *Central European History*, vol. 14 (1981), p. 61; also Ulrich von Hassell, *The von Hassell Diaries, 1938-44: The Story of the Forces Against Hitler Inside Germany* (New York, 1947), p. 333; also Mommsen, *From Weimar to Auschwitz*, pp. 195, 198, 205.

686 See Quarrie, *Hitler's Samurai*, pp. 30-2, 34, 39, 45, 47, 81, 97, 105-6, 118, 139; also Tsouras, pp. 145-67 citing Eberhard Rauss.

687 District.

688 T-77/1147/WiID/857, *WiKo 210 "Klinzy," Gruppe Landwirtschaft*, 11.7.43, p. 1.

689 NA T-315/1685/36509/12, *221 SD, Abt. Ia*, 12.2.43. *Betr.: "Unternehmen Klette I,"* p. 2.

690 Village headmen.

691 See T-315/1693/36509/5, *221. SD Ia*, 6.5.43, p. 1; T-315/1685/36509/13 *221. SD Ia*, 2.5.42 and 36509/12 *36 SR Ia*, 9.2.43.

692 NA T-315/1684/36509/8, *SB 242*, 10.5.43. *Betr.: Bandenlage im Bereich des Sich Batl 242*, p. 2, cited in Shepherd, p. 213

693 Ibid. p. 213; NA T-315/1684/36509/9. *SB 242*, 30.5.43. *Betr.: Lage im Bereich des Sich Btl 242*.

694 Overy, *Russia's War*, p. 140; Quarrie, *Hitler's Samurai*, p. 150; Gordon K. Williamson, *The SS: Hitler's Instrument of Terror: The Full Story from Street Fighters to the Waffen SS* (Osceola, WI, 1994), pp. 134, 191; Manchester, p. 693.

695 Rhodes, p. 140.

696 See Hans Umbreit, "Das unbewaeltigte Problem. Der Partisanenkrieg im Ruecken der Ostfront," in Juergen Foerster (ed.), *Stalingrad: Ereignis-Wirkung-Symbol* (Zurich, 1992), pp. 142-6; also Tim Richter, "Die Wehrmacht und der Partisanenkrieg in den besetzten gebieten der Sowjetunion," in Rolf-Dieter Mueller and Hans-Erich Volkmann (eds.), *Die Wehrmacht*, pp. 855-7.

697 Overy, *Russia's War*, p. 145.

698 Tsouras, p. 285. See also Bonwetsch, "Partisanen," p. 110.

699 Lucas, *Kommando*, p. 9.

700 For a more in depth look at Dirlewanger and his unit, see French L. MacLean, *The Cruel Hunters: SS-Sonderkommando Dirlewanger-Hitler's Most Notorious Anti-Partisan Unit* (Atglen, PA, 1998). On the officers assigned to *Kommando Dirlewanger*, see MacLean, *The Cruel Hunters*, Appendix 5, p. 163. See also Rhodes, p. 91 and index for other references.

701 Steenberg, p. 170; British intelligence report on Dirlewanger at PRO WO 208/4419. See also Deac, "Personality," *World War II*, pp. 32-44; Time-Life Books, Inc., *The Apparatus of Death* (Alexandria, VA, 1991), pp. 136, 138-43; Steenberg, Vlasov, p. 170 On Kaminsky and his fate see Wolff interview.

702 See, *The German Army*, pp. 42-52, 69-85, 117-49, 253-76; also Cooper, *The Phantom War*, pp. 89-93, 143-61.

703 Browning, *Ordinary Men*, pp. 56, 67-70.

704 Breitman, *Official Secrets*, pp. 5-6.

705 Bartov, *Hitler's Army*, pp. 98-105. On an example of such an event, see p. 97 on a Lance Corporal Franz Aigner; also NA BA-MA.RH27-18/74, dated 30/12/41.

706. NA T-315/1681/35408/2, *221 SD*, *Abt. Ia*, 30.10.42, cited in Shepherd, p. 167

707 Department of the Army Pamphlet no. 20-291, *Effects of Climate on Combat in European Russia*, Washington, DC (October 1951); No. 20-292, *Warfare in the Far North* (October 1951); No. 20-23, *Combat in Russian Forests and Swamps* (July 1951); no. 20-230, *Russian Combat Methods in World War Two* (November 1950); Toppe, et al, *German Military Government* (1948) in total. See also Wilbur D. Jones and Franz A.P. Frisch, "A Panzer Soldier's Story," *World War II*, vol. 10, no. 3 (September 1995), p. 50.

708 Mommsen, *From Weimar to Auschwitz*, p. 259.

709 Breitman, *Official Secrets*, pp. 48-9.

710 Overy, *Why the Allies Won*, p. 304.

711 See reference to the use of aircraft and combined arms in anti-partisan operations in the division records of the *213 SD* at NA T-315/1667/16748/10, *RHGeb. Mitte Abt. Ia*, 15.9.41, especially p. 2; also *221 SD Abt. Ia*, 18.9.41,

712 Ibid.

713 See Lucas, *Das Reich: The Military Role of the 2nd SS Division* (London, 1991), p. 12. See also Quarrie, *Hitler's Samurai*, p. 32; Brian L. Davis, *Waffen SS*, 2nd edition (New York, 1986), pp. 13-4; also Time-Life, *The SS* (Alexandria, 1989), pp. 135, 145-6.

714 Tsouras, p. 121.

715 Heaton, *German Anti-Partisan*, pp. 121-2; Kumm interview.

716 Heaton, *German Anti-Partisan*, p. 160. Koronov interview.

717 T-315/1687/36509/24, 27.6.43, p. 1.

718 Heaton, *German Anti-Partisan*, p. 143.

719 Ibid. See also Gerlach, "Wirtschafts und Vernichtungspolitik," pp. 818-9.

720 See Breitman, *Official Secrets*, p. 37; Daluege capture and interrogation record at PRO WO 208/4448.

721 See Condoleezza Rice, "The Making of Soviet Strategy," Peter Paret (ed.), *Makers of Modern Strategy from Machiavelli to the Nuclear Age* (Princeton, 1986), pp. 648-76.

722 Heaton, *German Anti-Partisan*, p. 157. Degrelle interview at Strathclyde and Temple. For Josef Goebbels' perspective on Degrelle, see *The Goebbels Diaries, Band 11*, entries dated 19/2/44, 22/2/44, and 23/2/44, pp. 316-27.

723 The same tactic would be used by the Viet Cong against American forces during the Vietnam War.

724 Heaton, *German Anti-Partisan*, p. 148 citing Tsouras, p. 285. These are the comments of Colonel General Hans von Greiffenberg.

725 This was in the Ukraine near Kiev. See Heaton, *German Anti-Partisan*, p. 141. See also interview with Kumm.

726 Ibid. pp. 141-2.

727 Ibid. p. 150; Kumm interview.

728 Shepherd, pp. 150-2.

729 T-315/1683/36509/5, 25.6.43.

730 T-315/1687/36509/24, *Prop/Abt. W, Staffel* Gomel, 21.7.43; *221 SD Ic*, 28.7.43.

731 Heaton, *German Anti-Partisan*, p. 148; Tsouras, p. 120.

732 Heaton, *German Anti-Partisan*, p. 146.

733 Ibid. p. 146.

734 See NA T-501/27/31391/6, Juni-Dezember 1942; also Toppe, et al, *German Military Government* in total.

735 Heaton, *German Anti-Partisan*, p. 147.

736 Ibid.

737 Ibid.

738 Headed by Fritz Todt and upon his death Albert Speer replaced him. See Speer record at N-1340. On Speer and slave labor for military use see Manchester, pp. 553-4, 546, 561. On Speer as Armaments Minister see pp. 526-7; on his Nuremberg trial see pp. 556, 695, 698; on his imprisonment in Spandau, pp. 875, 944. See also Speer, *Inside the Third Reich*, 4th edition (New York, 1975) in total.

739 Heaton, *German Anti-Partisan*, p. 147. Hrabak interview of 1993, located at Temple University, Department of History, Center for the Study of Force and Diplomacy, and is pending publication with Primedia Publications.

740 For a detailed schematic on how this process was formulated, see Heaton, *German Anti-Partisan*, pp. 148-52.

741 Ibid. pp. 157-8; Kumm interview.

742 See Heaton, *German Anti-Partisan*, pp. 184-201.

743 See Ulrich Herbert, "Labor and Extermination," p. 167; Alan Milward, *War, Economy, and Society: 1939-1945* (London, 1977), p. 225; Heaton, *German Anti-Partisan*, p. 396.

744 Heaton, *German Anti-Partisan*, p. 221.

745 Ibid. p. 129; Kumm interview at Strathclyde and Temple Universities.

746 NA T-315/1685/36509/12, 221. *Sicherheit-Division, Abt. Ia, 7.1.43, Betr.: "Unternehemen Ankara I,"* p. 3. See also NA T-315/1678/29380/1, *221 SD, Abt. Ia, 7.12.42. KTB,* 18.6.-31.12.42; NA T-315/1682/36509/1, *221 SD, Abt. Ia,* 21.1.43. *KTB,* 1.1.-1.6.43.

747 NA T-315/1685/36509/12, *221 SD, Abt. Ia, 7.1.43,* p. 3. See also NA T-501/26/31242/2, *Kraefteuebersicht,* 15.10.42; also T-501/27/31491/4. *RHGeb. Mitte Ic bandentaetigkeit, August-November 1942* (maps); NA T-315/1678/29380/1, *221 SD, Abt. Ia,* 22.12.42, *KTB* 18.6-31.12.42. Also T-315/1685/36509/11, *36 Sicherheits Regiment, Abt. Ia,* (here-after *36 SR*) 26.12.42, *Betr.: "Unternehmen Ankara"; Gefechtsbericht fuer die Zeit vom* 19-24.12.42, p. 1. On *"Ankara II"* see T-315/1682/36509/1, *221 SD, Abt. Ia,* 19.1.43, *KTB* 1.1.-1.6.43; NA T-315/1685/36509/11, *221 SD Abt. Ia,* 16.1.43, p. 1; NA T-315/1685/36509/12, *36 SR, Abt. Ia,* 25.1.43. *Betr.: "Unternehmen Ankara I" Gefechtsbericht,* 17. -21.1.43. On *"Klette"* see NA T-315/1682/36509/4, *221 SD, Abt. Ia,* 12.2.43. *Betr.: "Unternehmen Klette II" Gefechtsberichte;* ibid. 9.2.43. *Betr.: Regimentsbefehl fuer die Sicherung des bei 'Ankara' und "Klette II" befriededeten Raumes;* for *Operation "Zugspitz,"* see NA T-315/1686/36509/17, *Grenadier Regiment 930* (hereafter *930 Gren-Rgt*), *Abt. Ia,*

18.1.43. *Betr.: "Unternehmen Zugspitz"*; Ibid., 8.2.43. *Bericht ueber Verlauf und Ergebnis des "Unternehmens Zugspitz"*; *Gren.-Rgt. 930, Abt Ib, 9.2.43. Betr.: Erfassung beim "Unternehmen Zugspitz"*. On *Operation "Osterhase"* see NA T-315/1685/ 36509/13, 221 SD, Abt. Ia, 2.5.43. *Betr. Bericht ueber "Unternehmen Osterhase"*. On *Operation "Nachbarhilfe"* see NA T-3151686/ 36509/15, Korueck 559, Abt. Ia, 13.5.43. *Operationsbefehl fuer das "Unternehmen Nachbarhilfe"*. Also NA T-315/1686/36509/16, *Kampfgruppe Nord (221 SD) 25.5.43. Befehl fuer 26.5.43; Abschussmeldung, 27.5.43.* On *Operation "Junikaefer"*, NA T-315/1686/36509/18, 45 SR, Abt. Ia, 2.6.43. *Betr. "Unternehmen Junikaefer"; Erfassungsstab "Junikaefer,"* 7.6.43. *Betr.: Ib 394/ 43; 221 SD, Abt. Ia, 11.6.43. Betr.: Gefechtsbericht ueber das "Unternehmen Junikaefer."* On *Operatio "'Sommerfest"* see NA T-315/1687/36509/27, *930 SR Abt. Ib, 10.7.43. Erfahrungsbericht ueber Erfassung und Evakuierung beim "Unternehmen Sommerfest."* See also Mavrogordato and Ziemke, pp. 517-21, 534-7; Hesse, *Partisankrieg*, pp. 320-1.

748 T-315/1687/36509/24, 221 SD Ic, 4.7.43, p. 2

749 Heaton, *German Anti-Partisan*, pp. 156-7. See also Degrelle interview.

750 See Degrelle interview at Strathclyde and Temple. See also Heaton, *German Anti-Partisan*, p. 157.

751 Armstrong, "Organization," pp. 89-93; Hesse, *Partisankrieg*, Ch. 8 in total; Bonwetsch, "Partisanen," pp. 100-1; Weinberg, "Yelnya-Dorogobuzh," pp. 411-22; DeWitt and Moll, "Bryansk," pp. 461-2; Mavrogordato and Ziemke, "Polotzk Lowland," pp. 532-4.

752 Strikfeldt, p. 59. Rhodes, pp. 105-6, 109.

753 Heaton, *German Anti-Partisan*, p. 25 citing Overy, *Russia's War*, p. 150.

754 On Felix Steiner's training program see Lucas, *Das Reich*, pp. 22-3.

Index